Israel, Covenant, Law

Israel, Covenant, Law

A Third Perspective on Paul

KIM PAPAIOANNOU

Foreword by Ioannis Giantzaklides

WIPF & STOCK · Eugene, Oregon

ISRAEL, COVENANT, LAW
A Third Perspective on Paul

Copyright © 2017 Kim Papaioannou. All rights reserved. Except for brief quotations in critical publications or reviews, no part of this book may be reproduced in any manner without prior written permission from the publisher. Write: Permissions, Wipf and Stock Publishers, 199 W. 8th Ave., Suite 3, Eugene, OR 97401.

Wipf & Stock
An Imprint of Wipf and Stock Publishers
199 W. 8th Ave., Suite 3
Eugene, OR 97401

www.wipfandstock.com

PAPERBACK ISBN: 978-1-5326-3728-5
HARDCOVER ISBN: 978-1-5326-3730-8
EBOOK ISBN: 978-1-5326-3729-2

Manufactured in the U.S.A.   10/13/17

Contents

Foreword by Ioannis Giantzaklides | vii
Introduction | xi

1 Reformation Perspectives and New Perspectives:
   The Current Impasse | 1

2 Paul and Israel: Towards an Understanding
   of Early Christian Self-Identity | 22

3 Paul and the Covenant: The Ritual Dimension of Covenant | 43

4 Paul and the Law: The Ritual Dimension of Law
   Part I—Establishing a Historical Context | 71

5 Paul and the Law: The Ritual Dimension of Law
   Part II—Paul's Attacks on the Law | 102

Synopsis and Synthesis | 140

Bibliography | 145
Scripture Index | 155

Foreword

Nobody can doubt Paul's impact on Christianity. He was instrumental in spreading the gospel from Palestine to the ends of the known world. He was tireless, fearless, and persistent in his missionary journeys. His contribution was not limited to the first century AD. His letters to the early churches form a large part of the New Testament canon and his theology as emerging from these letters has been formative to Christianity in all its stages. In the 1st century, he helped transform the Christian church from being a Jewish sect concentrating on the Jewish population in Palestine and the diaspora to being a worldwide multi-ethnic movement. In the 16th century, Paul's words from Rom 1:17 inspired Luther to begin the Reformation. Today his Letters are being read to churches throughout the world and countless sermons are being preached on Paul's theology on a weekly basis.

As a theologian and philosopher, Paul has received praise for his wisdom and learning both from his contemporaries (Acts 26:24) and from later theologians. Heikki Räisänen lists in his introduction of *Paul and the Law*, "a catena of eulogies" from theologians representing different schools of thought. Some of the accolades include "patron" of "Christian philosophy," "prince of thinkers," "thinker and theologian par excellence of Christianity," and "giant" of the "philosophy of religions."[1] While all these praises sound justified in light of Paul's contribution, equally loud sound Paul's critics. As early as the 3rd century, Porphyry claimed that "Paul displays the ignorant person's habit of constantly contradicting himself and that he is feverish in mind."[2] We should not be quick to dismiss Porphyry's view as simply a biased opinion of an early

---

1. Räisänen, *Paul and the Law*, 1–2.
2. Found in ibid., 2.

Foreword

critic of Christianity. Two centuries earlier, Peter had already noted how difficult Paul's writings were (2 Pet 3:15–16). And though nearly two millennia have passed since Paul wrote his Epistles, even modern scholars have found it difficult to understand Paul. Their conclusions are often contradictory, and it seems virtually impossible to find agreement as to what Paul's message really was.

Paul's attitude towards the law is the primary focus of this book. It is precisely on this subject that most debates concerning Paul's theology arise. Some have noted that Paul's teachings on the law if taken literally lead to absurd and contradicting conclusions. Albert Schweitzer claimed that Paul believed the law to have been given to humans by evil angels and obedience to the law was therefore obedience to these evil powers![3] And yet Paul makes claims about the law that certainly do not harmonize with negative views on the law.

Many scholars have tried to harmonize Paul and make him appear consistent but to no avail. Some have tried to argue for a development of thought from Galatians to 1 Corinthians to Romans. They propose that Paul is a "libertine" in Galatians; a "legalist" in 1 Corinthians; and in Romans, he provides a "mature synthesis." But the time span between Galatians and Romans does not allow for such a spectacular development in Paul's theology. Others choose to attribute large parts of Galatians and Romans to later interpolations. But these suggestions are not grounded on external evidence of later invasions upon Paul's text. They are based on an effort to harmonize the apparent contradictions of the text.

Still others choose to maintain that Paul used a dialectical approach in which Paul's ideas should not be taken literally; rather they are "a theological interpretive device which shows where man stands without the gospel."[4] All these attempts to reconcile Paul's views underline the fact that his theology appears muddled, confusing, and contradictory to the modern reader.

This book attempts to propose a new way to look at Paul. It does not take one set of texts and highlight them at the expense of others. It does not take, say, apparently antinomian texts, and put them over and above texts that take a high view of the law; nor does it take the opposite approach. Rather, Papaioannou carefully and meticulously studies several Pauline texts that appear to be against the law and concludes that they

---

3. Schweitzer, *Die Mystik des Apostels Paulus*, 71ff.
4. Räisänen, *Paul and the Law*, 5.

are against specific parts of the law (Torah): namely, the sacrifices and other ceremonial aspects. Papaioannou proposes that the issue Paul was addressing was not people trying to be saved by keeping moral aspects of the law, but people clinging to the temple cultus. As he correctly points out, forgiveness and atonement in the Jewish religion were obtained through sacrifices and the services of the temple. But since according to New Testament theology, the sacrifice and priestly ministry of Jesus supersedes the sacrifices and ministry of the earthly temple, it would be logical to expect that Paul would be attacking the retention or even return of some Christians to these kinds of methods of attaining salvation.

Interesting and congruent to the above is Papaioannou's contribution on Paul's discussion of circumcision. Why was Paul worried if Gentile believers underwent circumcision? What was behind the significance of an outward action that as a matter of fact was not all that outward or visible? We know from history that non-circumcised males were not allowed to enter the temple and offer sacrifices. Could it be that some believers of Jewish background were urging new Christian converts of a Gentile background to undergo circumcision precisely so that they would be able to participate in the temple services? Papaioannou suggests exactly that and backs his suggestion with considerable evidence from Jewish sources. If Papaioannou's argument holds true, it is easy to understand why Paul was so strongly against such attempts.

These are not the only notable contributions of this book. One of the most interesting discussions pertains to Paul's views on Israel and the covenant. Papaioannou convincingly argues against a major cornerstone of contemporary Israel studies, that of a physical Israel, and demonstrates that for Paul, Israel was never a racial concept but a spiritual entity. He demonstrates that even in the Old Testament, Israel was not comprised only of people from Israelite origin but also of foreigners who had accepted to join God's people. This notion together with a careful exegesis of Rom 11:26 helps clarify one of Paul's difficult and widely misunderstood texts.

For me, the overall value of this book is that it presents a "sane" Paul. Not a person who contradicts himself in the span of few verses or a theologian who "develops" his theology from antinomianism to legalism to a bit of both within the span of less than ten years. Papaioannou's proposal portrays a consistent Paul who battled against Judaizing Christians who urged Gentile believers to adopt ceremonial temple practices to obtain

Foreword

salvation. Papaioannou's exegesis of some passages may sound strange, as it did to me the first time I read drafts of this book. I paid, however, close attention to his reasoning and his argument and I was convinced—as I hope you will after reading this book.

Ioannis Giantzaklidis
Turku, Finland
July 24, 2017

Introduction

This book is the result of a theological journey of discovery that begins nearly 10 years ago. It is late 2008, or perhaps early 2009, I can't remember. I am a young professor of NT at the AIIAS Seminary in the Philippines. I am sitting in my office when there is a knock on my door. In comes my good friend Michael, a PhD student, who is about to start working on his dissertation. He is the first student I will be supervising on my own.

After the initial pleasantries, he informs me that he wants to write his dissertation on Col 2:16–17. I feel rather apprehensive about the suggestion and tell him that a lot has been written on that text already. "Michael, do you have something new to say, or will you repeat things that have already been said?" "I think I have something new to say," he responds and explains that he believes that when Paul speaks about food, feast, new moon, and Sabbaths, he is not addressing these as such but sacrifices. I look at him somewhat bewildered. I have not heard anything like this before. I take out my Greek NT, open it to Col 2:16–17, and hand it over to him. "Michael, where do you see sacrifices?"

With his always pleasant and smiling manner, Michael begins to explain his viewpoint. There are linguistic connections to Heb 10; the food and drink mentioned are probably the food offerings prescribed in the OT; and there is an OT background of the triplet, feast, new moon, and Sabbath in the OT that is connected to sacrifices. Some of the arguments he outlines that day, you can read about in Chapter 5 of this study. I begin to see some sense in his argument but I am far from convinced. "Listen Michael, what you have just outlined is interesting. I don't know if you are right or wrong, but I will be happy to help you present your case as best as possible."

Fast forward perhaps two years or more. Michael has completed his dissertation successfully and has returned to his native South Africa to begin a distinguished career of academic ministry. I am sitting in my office looking, I don't remember why, at Col 2:16–17 in the Greek text. I happen to be half Greek by birth, and modern Greek is my native language. I was born and grew up in Greece. So I am reading looking at the Nestle-Aland text and suddenly two words jump out of the page, ἐν μέρει, dative of μέρος. It is a phrase that I know very well because though in modern Greek the dative case has more or less disappeared, it is retained in some expressions maintained from times past when the dative was still in regular use. ἐν μέρει is one such example and we use the expression in everyday speech. It always means, in part. "I agree with you ἐν μέρει," means, "I agree with you partly." Some things I agree, some things I don't. "You are right ἐν μέρει," means, "You are partly right." In some part you are right, in some other wrong.

But in the English translation of Col 2:16–17, ἐν μέρει is translated as "with regard" (NIV), "in respect" (KJV), "in questions of" (ESV), and "regarding" (NKJV). There is a big difference in meaning when you say, "let no one judge with regards to something" than when you say "let no one judge you in a part of something." In the first instance you have the whole of that something in view. In the second instance, you have only one part of that something in view. Suddenly, Michael's argument makes perfect sense. Paul was not interested in the feasts, new moon, and Sabbaths as such, but in one part of these.

It is weird because I had been working with Michael on his dissertation for so long, I had looked at the text so many times but amazingly had not picked up on that little detail. You see, we are creatures of habit. Having read Col 2:16 in English so many times, it had somehow registered in my brain in the way it is normally translated, and I had assumed that this is the way it should be translated. When looking at the Greek text, the English translation embedded in my brain acted as a lens with which to read the Greek and until now I had not been able to notice the disparity between the Greek text and the English translations. Such is the force of habit!

But now I have noticed that through the detail of ἐν μέρει, a whole new possibility in translation and exegesis opened up. Of course, the fact that two words mean something in modern Greek does not automatically mean that they meant the same thing in *koine* Greek. But I have made an important discovery and I am ready to pursue it. I open my Bible software and study carefully how μέρος is used in the LXX and NT. And to my great excitement, modern Greek is right. The word always has a partitive sense. Now, I am convinced Michael was right.

Introduction

Fast forward again a few months, maybe more. It is Sabbath morning and I am sitting in church. The realization that in Col 2:16–17, Paul is most likely arguing against sacrifices has been in my mind. I am wondering what else we may have missed in Paul's writings in translation or otherwise. The expression "works of the law" comes to my mind. "Law" in the first century mindset usually referred to the Torah, the first five books of the Bible, Genesis to Deuteronomy, the Pentateuch.

Suddenly, a thought comes to mind. I wonder if the word "works" is used in the Pentateuch to refer to sacrifices. I mean, "works of the Torah" must refer to something in the Torah, right? That would make a massive difference in interpretation. Say "works of the law" and most Christians think of trying to work your way into heaven, or at least to God's favor. It is a derogatory term. But "works of the Torah" sounds different, doesn't it? So this thought has come into my mind, and I cannot get it out. I need to know whether the use of the word "works" appears in the Torah, and if so how. It would make a big difference on the interpretation of some of the statements of Paul. The more I am thinking about it, right there, sitting in church, the more I become restless. I need to know the answer.

So I get up and walk back to our home, thankfully only a four-minute walk from the church. I get home, open my Bible software, and do a very simple concordance search on the word "works" in the Pentateuch. What I see blows my mind away. The word can refer to secular human works, to the mighty acts of God, but most commonly (nearly half the occurrences) refer to the sanctuary, from its construction to all of its ritual ministry, sacrifices included! What an amazing discovery for me. I cannot believe my eyes. I am *gobsmacked*, as they say in Britain.

Every NT student knows that "law" in the NT means Torah. And yet no one seems to have put two and two together and look what "works" the Torah is talking about, and thus properly understand the expression "works of the Law/Torah." Again, the force of habit has been holding sway. But not anymore, at least not for me. Armed with this information, I am now more convinced than ever that one of the main issues Paul was facing in his ministry was Christians who were clinging to the temple and its sacrificial system, long after the death of Jesus on the cross was supposed to have put an end to these things, at least for Christians.

I walk back to church but I am not really walking, I feel as if I am flying. This has been perhaps the greatest theological discovery of my life. I arrive at church and sit down again next to my beautiful family. There is

Introduction

a big smile on my face. They are wondering where I went to and why I am smiling. I can't wait for the service to finish to tell my wife all about it. Who says theology is boring!

The three main incidents outlined above, that first meeting with Michael, the insight on ἐν μέρει, and my new understanding on "works of the law" have changed me theologically speaking. There were other moments of discovery, perhaps less sensational. There was also a lot of painstaking study on the text of the NT. In this, my students were of great help. As an alternative way of understanding, Paul began to grow in my mind. I shared my thoughts with my students, especially those at the MA and PhD level. They became my peers and I gained valuable insights in interactions with them.

The result is this book. It was a long way coming. In the beginning, I started putting my thoughts in writing in short studies or in notes for my lectures, with a view to writing a book later on. But this "later on" always seemed to be in the distance, lost sometime in the future. Until I realized suddenly, I knew it all along of course, but it had not clicked, that 2017 marks 500 years since the Protestant Reformation when Luther nailed his 95 theses on the then wooden (now metal) door of Wittenberg Cathedral.

The Protestant Reformation was a result of Luther studying the writings of Paul and discovering that salvation is a free gift from God not something to be earned through "works of the law." He, of course, understood "works of the law" to be works of obedience to God's law or at least good works of some sort. How fitting it would be, on the 500th anniversary of the Reformation, to address some of the weak points of Luther's outlook and present a yet better model for understanding Paul.

With this realization in mind, I have spent the last short while putting together into one hopefully coherent whole, my thoughts, notes, and short studies previously prepared, together with some new research. This book is the result.

I hope that you, the reader, will read this book prayerfully and with an open mind. Much of what you read will go against theological viewpoints you have held for years, perhaps even decades. You might at times feel that you disagree, that I am wrong, that the exegesis is at times unusual. But please read on because, I am convinced, in these pages is found a model of Paul that makes better sense of all the issues that have troubled Pauline theologians for centuries, than any other model taught in seminaries around the world today.

1

Reformation Perspectives and New Perspectives

The Current Impasse

Thesis Statement—Both the Reformation Perspective on Paul and the New Perspective have gaps and fail to fully make sense of Paul. A new paradigm is needed and proposed.

PAUL'S APPARENT SELF-CONTRADICTIONS

Pauline studies are in a conundrum in a number of ways. This study will focus on one of them, Paul's relation to law. Part of it has to do with Paul's own sometimes convoluted way of thinking. Commenting on this, 2 Pet 3:15–16 writes, "And count the patience of our Lord as salvation, just as our beloved brother Paul also wrote to you according to the wisdom given him, as he does in all his letters when he speaks in them of these matters. There are some things in them that are hard to understand, which the ignorant and unstable twist to their own destruction, as they do the

Israel, Covenant, Law

other Scriptures."[1] If Peter found Paul's writings "hard to understand," we are excused to feel the same way.

Consider some of Paul's seemingly contradictory statements concerning the law (emphasis added): "But now *we are released from the law*, having died to that which held us captive, so that we serve not under the old written code but in the new life of the Spirit" (Rom 7:6).

"For he himself is our peace, who has made us both one and has broken down in his flesh the dividing wall of hostility by *abolishing the law of commandments* and ordinances, that he might create in himself one new man in place of the two, so making peace" (Eph 2:14–15).

"Now if *the ministry of death, carved in letters on stone*, came with such glory that the Israelites could not gaze at Moses' face because of its glory, which was being brought to an end, will not the ministry of the Spirit have even more glory? (2 Cor 3:7–8).

"Let me ask you only this: Did you receive the Spirit *by works of the law* or by hearing with faith? Are you so foolish?" (Gal 3:2–3).

"For *all who rely on works of the law are under a curse*; for it is written, 'Cursed be everyone who does not abide by all things written in the Book of the Law, and do them'" (Gal 3:10).

"Now before faith came, we were held captive *under the law, imprisoned* until the coming faith would be revealed. So then, the law was our guardian until Christ came, in order that we might be justified by faith. But now that faith has come, *we are no longer under a guardian*" (Gal 3:23–25).

"And you, who were dead in your trespasses and the uncircumcision of your flesh, God made alive together with him, having forgiven us all our trespasses, by *canceling* the record of debt that stood against us with its *legal demands*. This he set aside, nailing it to the cross" (Col 2:13–14).

Texts like the above appear to, and have been understood to, abolish the legal codes of the OT. Had these been the only relevant texts in relation to law, we would have been excused in thinking that Paul was an antinomian. However, Paul has numerous other texts that appear to suggest the exact opposite, namely, the OT law is binging. Consider a few examples.

"Do we then overthrow the law by this faith? By no means! *On the contrary, we uphold the law*" (Rom 3:31).

"So *the law is holy*, and *the commandment is holy and righteous and good*" (Rom 7:12).

---

1. All Scripture references are from the ESV, unless otherwise noted.

Reformation Perspectives and New Perspectives

"For *we know that the law is spiritual*, but I am of the flesh, sold under sin" (Rom 7:14).

"For *I delight in the law of God*, in my inner being" (Rom 7:22).

"*The commandments*, 'You shall not commit adultery, You shall not murder, You shall not steal, You shall not covet,' and any other commandment, are summed up in this word: 'You shall love your neighbor as yourself'" (Rom 13:9).

"For neither circumcision counts for anything nor uncircumcision, *but keeping the commandments of God*" (1 Cor 7:19).

"'Honor your father and mother' (this is the first *commandment* with a promise)" (Eph 6:2).

Reading the above texts and a number of others, one might reasonably be tempted to conclude that Paul was confused.

REFORMATION PERSPECTIVES ON PAUL AND THE LAW

Beyond apparent contradictions in the Pauline writings, there is the question of theological outlook. Theological outlooks are like a pair of glasses with which we read the text. Every NT scholar wears them. For some, the glasses are of higher diopter and for some of lower, but we all wear them. The type of glasses, the theological outlook, an exegete has will determine to some extent the way a particular text is read and interpreted. The higher the diopter the more inclined is the exegete to read texts in a way that suits a given theological outlook.

In the Protestant world, for close to five centuries, theological thinking has been shaped by the Reformation and its great teachers, chief among Martin Luther. The son of a German miner, Luther was prompted by his father towards a career in law, and to this effect he entered the University of Erfurt, graduating eventually with a Master of Arts degree. His life changed dramatically during one night in 1505 when while in a forest during a severe thunderstorm, he became so scared that he thought he would not survive the experience. In fear and trembling, he prayed that if he were to survive, he would become a monk.

Survive he did, and faithful to his promise he became a monk in the Augustinian order. There is some debate whether this was a decision of the moment or, more likely, something Luther had been contemplating for a while. His intense fear of hell and the wrath of God caused him to think that perhaps in the monastery, he could find peace and assurance of salvation. A person of continual inner reflection, once in the monastery Luther devoted himself to long hours of prayer, fasting, pilgrimages, and frequent confessions. But none of these allayed his conscience or brought peace of mind. Luther later referred to this time in the cloister as one of deep spiritual despair. After a trip to Rome that filled him with more disillusionment, he enrolled in the University of Wittenberg, excelled in his studies, and graduated as a doctor of theology, becoming in turn a professor of theology at the university.

It was while lecturing from the Epistle of Romans, around 1515, that Luther began to understand salvation as a gift from God that cannot be attained by good works or human merit. Luther projected his own troubled conscience onto Paul before the Damascus experience. His previous religious experience of prolonged prayer, fasting, pilgrimages, and activities that failed to bring him inner peace he projected upon first century Judaism with its manifold laws, traditions, and regulations that, likewise, in Luther's mind, could not bring peace. And now that he had at last understood that salvation is a free gift, he became a type of new Paul combating the "works" perversions of the gospel around him.

A whole new theological world opened up before him. God offered salvation as an act of grace. The human received it by faith. This was termed justification by faith, a term understood in a legal framework whereby God forgives the sinner who therefore stands guiltless before God. The terms, "sola gratia" and "sola fide" became rallying cries of the Reformation. Other great persons joined the ranks and Reformation became established in a large part of Europe and eventually America.

I have always held Luther in the highest esteem, and still do. One day, I hope to shake his hand in the kingdom of our Lord Jesus. He had an amazing intellect and power of the will, and left a great imprint on the history of Christianity. The concept of salvation as a free gift unmerited by human behavior is a doctrine that has bought peace to countless anguished persons. He has left an impressive legacy of love for God and for God's word, and for uplifting the crucified and resurrected Jesus as the sole hope and solution for our sinful human race.

More ambivalent was Luther's attitude towards the OT law, our topic of interest in this book. Some accuse Luther of antinomianism, while others vehemently deny the charge. Luther did not reject law altogether. He accepted a positive threefold use. First, law has a civil function. Since societies are filled with persons who are not saved, law is necessary to promote orderliness and provide a standard by which society can regulate behavior. Second, law has a pedagogical function. It convicts a sinner of sinfulness prompting him to turn to Christ and receive salvation. Third, it has a normative function. It shows what is and is not appropriate in the Christian life. This third aspect however, received less emphasis, primarily by later generations of theologians, and to a person who lives in active fellowship with God and has been justified by grace, it was considered more or less redundant.

That perhaps is a natural consequence from seeing justification primarily in terms of legal acquittal of all wrongdoing. If Jesus has paid the penalty for the sins of his followers, past, present, and future, then requirements to obedience seem to be irrelevant at worst, or secondary at best, to the standing of a person before God. Luther was no antinomian. But within the system of soteriology developed lay the seeds which could and did develop in the minds of some, of antinomian approaches to the law.

John Calvin, the younger contemporary of Luther, was the second most influential reformer. He joined the ranks of the Reformation while a young student at the University of Orleans. His most famous work, *Institutes of the Christian Religion*, was published in 1536, and aimed at systematizing the faith of the Protestant Reformation. Calvin agreed on some points with Luther, and disagreed on others. When it comes to Bible law, Calvin accepted the threefold function of law, but gave much more emphasis on the third point, the normative function of law in the life of the believer.

The legacy of the Reformation with its emphasis on grace and faith has led to an ambivalent attitude towards law that one meets in modern commentaries. Here are a few examples of apparently antinomian comments by respected theologians from commentaries on Rom 7:5 and Gal 3:23–35.

"The key to this new life is release from the law, expressed here with the aorist passive κατηργήθημεν ("we were released"), which refers to a single moment in the past of believers in which they accepted the gospel of Christ crucified and resurrected and became part of the new community of faith."[2]

"By dying to that which was once in control, the believer is now released from the law and freed to serve in a new way. Formerly we were in

---

2. Jewett et al., *Romans: A Commentary*, 437.

bondage to written regulations. Law was our old master. But now we are set free to serve our new master in a new way, in the Spirit."[3]

"How did it come about then that Christians were freed from the law? Christ's death freed them from sin by their share in baptism. Did it also deliver the Christian from the law? Paul's implied answer has been Yes."[4]

"The word is the same which, in Ro 6:6 and elsewhere, is rendered 'destroyed,' and is but another way of saying (as in Ro 7:4) that 'we were *slain* to the law by the body of Christ'; language which, though harsh to the ear, is designed and fitted to impress upon the reader the *violence* of that death of the Cross, by which, as by a deadly wrench, we are 'delivered from the law.'"[5]

"We are annulled in relation to the law, and therewith the law is annulled to us."[6]

"By saying that 'we are no longer under a custodian' (RSV) Paul is in fact speaking of 'the historic succession of one period of revelation upon another and the displacement of the law by Christ': from the vantage point of salvation history, the validity of the law ceased with the coming of faith in the coming of Christ."[7]

"On the plan of salvation-history the coming of faith coincides with the coming of Christ, in whom the parenthetic age of law was displaced by the age of faith (cf. 4:4), which fulfils the promise made to Abraham."[8]

"To the figure of a prison warden, then, Paul adds that of a slave-attendant to describe the function of the law before the gospel age. Another, but related, figure is employed in 4:1f., but first he pauses to make one of his greatest affirmations about the new order of liberated existence 'in Christ.'"[9]

"Paul continues to speak of the era of the Law, saying three things about it: (a) It was the period in which "we" existed under the Law's power; (b) it had a definite terminus, the arrival of faith (vv 23, 25; cf. the advent of the promised seed in v 19 and Christ's coming in v 24); (c) even in the era of the Law's dominion, God was on the verge of executing his ultimate purpose, thinking ahead (*mellō*) to the faith by which he would terminate it."[10]

---

3. Mounce, *Romans*, 162–63.
4. Achtemeier, *Romans*, 114.
5. Jamieson et al., *Old and New Testaments*, Rom 7:6.
6. Lange et al., *Romans*, 222.
7. Fung, *The Epistle to the Galatians*, 170.
8. Bruce, *The Epistle to the Galatians*, 181.
9. Ibid., 183.
10. Martyn, *Galatians*, 361–62.

Reformation Perspectives and New Perspectives

Many more could be added. Compare these with statements in support of the law, sometimes from the same commentators, writing, for example, on Rom 3:31.

"But, as on other occasions when Paul faces such an objection (cf. Rom. 7:7), he responds with a forthright denial: 'By no means!' He then follows this up with a counter assertion: 'Rather, we establish the law.' That Paul affirms here a continuing role for the law, despite its playing no part in justification, is clear." "Christian faith, far from shunting aside the demands of the law, provides (and for the first time!) the complete fulfillment of God's demand in his law."[11]

"He [Paul] refuses to countenance the dismissal of the Mosaic law, i.e., not just the OT in general, but the Pentateuch, the five books of Mosaic legislation."[12]

"That love is the fruit of faith itself; and so through faith the law is fulfilled; it is not nullified."[13]

"The conclusion of Paul's comments about the oneness of God and the inclusive quality of God's righteous activity in Christ is the inferential question, 'Are we then neutralizing law through this faith?' The undeniable premise of v. 30a establishes a rhetorical requirement of a negative answer to this question of whether Paul and his fellow believers are antinomians."[14]

"Third, Paul concludes (οὖν, *oun*, therefore) that faith does not nullify the law but establishes it (v. 31)."[15]

"While no law can provide salvation and while honor should no longer be attached to its compliance, Paul upholds law in a transformed and clarified state by faith in Christ crucified."[16]

"Christ's atoning death means the working out of what the law really means. When we see this, we see the place of the law—'we establish the law.'"[17]

"Finally, Paul asked if the principle of faith robs law of its rightful role. Does it 'nullify the law'? The answer is, 'Not for a moment!' (Moffatt[18]). On

---

11. Moo, *The Epistle to the Romans*, 252–53, 255.
12. Fitzmyer, *Romans*, 366.
13. Ibid.
14. Jewett et al., *Romans*, 302.
15. Schreiner, *Romans*, 200.
16. Jewett et al., *Romans*, 303.
17. Morris, *The Epistle to the Romans*, 189.
18. Mounce, *Romans*, 120.

the contrary, faith puts law in its proper place. It plays an essential role in the divine plan, but it was never intended to make it possible for a person to earn righteousness. Faith 'uphold[s] the law' in the sense that it fulfills all the obligations of the law.'"[19]

"Does this doctrine of justification by faith, then, dissolve the obligation of the law? If so, it cannot be of God. But away with such a thought, for it does just the reverse."[20]

"Paul had shown that the justification of the Gentiles, with the justification of the Jews, is to be traced back to one and the same God. By this means, he says, the law is not made void, but established."[21]

"In verse 31 Paul uses the Law as a reference to the total religious system of Judaism, which finds its visible embodiment in the Old Testament. So Paul now turns to the Old Testament itself to prove that faith does not do away with the Law but rather upholds it."[22]

"We open the door, then, to moral license? We abolish code and precept, then, when we ask not for conduct, but for faith? Away with the thought; nay, we establish Law; we go the very way to give a new sacredness to its every command, and to disclose a new power for the fulfilment of them all."[23]

Statements could be multiplied. This ambivalence that sometimes borders on theological schizophrenia has been part and parcel of the Reformation perspectives on Paul and the law. Part of this outlook has also been a disparaging of Judaism. Though the legal precepts of the OT have been considered at times abolished, at times binding, and at times both at the same time as noted above, Judaism as a faith system that purportedly relies on obedience for salvation has been considered as an ultimate other.

ANTINOMIANISM'S ACHILLES'S HEEL

While it is true that some of Paul's comments on law are difficult and appear contradictory, I believe Paul would have been unhappy and in disagreement with any antinomian interpretation of his writings.

---

19. Jamieson et al., *Old and New Testaments*, Rom 3:31.
20. Ibid.
21. Lange et al., *Romans*, 137.
22. Newman and Nida, *Paul's Letter to the Romans*, 72.
23. Moule, *The Epistle to the Romans*, 99.

Reformation Perspectives and New Perspectives

A key text in support of my assertion is 1 Cor 5:1–13, the incident of the man in Corinth living with his father's wife. I have termed this story "Antinomianism's Achilles's Heel." The great hero of Greek mythology, Achilles, appeared invincible in almost every aspect, expect his heel. But one arrow there brought him tumbling down wounded and eventually dead. It seems to me that the incident of the offending man in Corinth does just that for any suggestion of Pauline antinomianism. Let us look at some of the elements.

The first thing to note is that the offending man is obviously a practising Christian.[24] This is evident in 5:2: "Let him who has done this be removed from among you." The second personal pronoun "you" in "among you" clearly refers to the recipients of the letter, the church in Corinth. Likewise in 5:6–7, Paul uses an example from everyday life that further confirms his standing: "Do you not know that a little leaven leavens the whole lump? Cleanse out the old leaven that you may be a new lump."[25] The "whole lump" represents the church and the "little leaven" the man. Just like leaven is mixed completely into the lump, similarly this man is fully part of the church. And just as leaven can change the whole constitution of the lump, the sin of that man can pollute the whole congregation. In 5:11, Paul admits that his man is called a "brother": "But now I am writing to you not to associate with anyone who bears the name of brother if he is guilty of sexual immorality or greed, or is an idolater, reviler, drunkard, or swindler—not even to eat with such a one." This means that until the man began to live in sin, he was considered a brother and had full fellowship. In fact, he still was, and this is why Paul asks that he longer be considered so. And in 5:12, the person is considered an "insider" as far as the church is concerned—"For what have I to do with judging outsiders? Is it not those inside the church whom you are to judge?" The offender therefore, has been a member of the Corinth church in good and regular standing. We do not know for how long, but as Paul writes his letter, the man is still there.

---

24. Fee, *The First Epistle to the Corinthians*, 202. Gordon D. Fee calls the man a "fallen brother." Ibid.

25. Fitzmyer, *First Corinthians*, 240. Joseph A. Fitzmyer observes, "Paul's rhetorical question quotes a common popular proverb, as also in Gal 5:9. The proverb suggests that it takes only one small instance of improper sexual conduct to contaminate the whole community; cf. the proverb cited in 15:33, 'Bad company corrupts good habits.' Philo (De spec. leg. 1.53 §293) mentions the 'rising' effect of leaven and understands it as a symbol of arrogant conduct. The proverb is introduced by the expression, *ouk oidate hoti*, 'Do you not realize' . . . Paul thus stresses a notion plainly admitted by everybody." Ibid.

A second thing to note concerns the nature of the offense. The man has clearly done something wrong, and it is for this reason that Paul is asking the Corinthian believers to take disciplinary action. But what is his sin? There is no indication that the relationship of the man to the wife of the father is adulterous. His sin is termed not as μοιχεία, "adultery," but πορνεία, "fornication," an "unlawful sexual relation (5:1).[26] This would probably suggest that the father has died. If the father was still alive, the sin would constitute adultery, even if the father and the woman had been divorced (Matt 19:9).[27] Moreover, it seems that the offending man is not simply cohabiting with the woman or involved in an illicit relationship, but is married to her. This is suggested by the phrase γυναῖκα . . . ἔχειν (5:1; e.g., 1 Cor 7:2, 12, 13, 25).[28] The more likely scenario then is that the father has died and the man has married his step-mother.

A relation of any sort to a step mother is a violation of Lev 18:8 which prohibits sexual relations with the wife of a man's father: "You shall not uncover the nakedness of your father's wife; it is your father's nakedness."[29] Punishment for such an offense was for the offender to be "cut off" from among the people (Lev 18:29). According to Leviticus, such sins polluted not only the offender but the whole community and indeed the land. It was for this reason that such offenses had to be dealt with promptly and

26. Robertson and Plummer, *First Epistle of St. Paul to the Corinthians*, 95–96. Archibald Robertson and Alfred Plummer define πορνεία as "illicit sexual intercourse in general" and note: "In Rev. 19:2, as in class. Grk., it means prostitution: in Matt. 5:32, 19:9 it is equivalent to μοιχεία, from which it is distinguished Matt. 15:19 and Mark 7:21: cf. Hos. 3:3." Ibid.

27. There is a possibility that the father has divorced the woman and the offender has ongoing sexual relations with her. Fitzmyer comments, "Theoretically, this might mean that after the father's death his son has married the widowed second wife. . . . It is, however, much more likely that the son has entered into a continuous union with his father's second wife, who is separated from him, while he is still alive," which then would be breach of Roman law, according to Fitzmyer. Fitzmyer, *First Corinthians*, 234. If that were the case, the offense would constitute adultery not fornication and the offender would be culpable to public courts, not just church polity.

28. Fitzmyer writes, "The expression *gynaika echein*, "have a wife," denotes a continuous state of union, not a casual adulterous act, as also in 7:2, 12, 13, 29; Gal 4:27 (quoting LXX Isa 54:1); John 4:17–18." Fitzmyer, *First Corinthians*, 233. I would add that the way the noun γυναῖκα is used indicates that the woman has been the wife of two men. First, she has been the wife of the father as evidenced by the phrase γυναῖκά τινα τοῦ πατρὸς, the "wife of the father." But it seems that she has become the offender's wife too from the infinitive ἔχειν: γυναῖκα . . . ἔχειν.

29. "The language 'father's wife' is taken directly from the LXX of Lev. 18:7–8, where this specific sin is forbidden." Fee, *First Corinthians*, 200.

forcefully: "Do not make yourselves unclean by any of these things, for by all these the nations I am driving out before you have become unclean, and the land became unclean, so that I punished its iniquity, and the land vomited out its inhabitants" (Lev 18:24–25); "everyone who does any of these abominations, the persons who do them shall be cut off from among their people" (Lev 18:29).

The offender has broken one of the Levitical laws and now Paul is asking that he receive a punishment like the one prescribed in Leviticus, namely, that he be removed from the congregation of believers. Is this not strange? Perhaps it would have been conceivable if the man had committed a flagrant violation of one or more of the Ten Commandments; or some of the words of Jesus; but Leviticus? If OT law has been abolished, or part of OT law has been abolished, is it not strange to see a man condemned for breaking one of the prohibitions of Leviticus and suffering the penalty prescribed in Leviticus?

It could be counterargued that according to the Jerusalem Council, immorality of all kinds was to be frowned upon by Gentile Christians. Indeed, the background of that prohibition, and the other three mentioned, draws from Lev 17 and 18. So it could be argued that of all the OT laws, only the four mentioned in Acts 15 have been retained, and that the man in Corinth was in breach of one of them. This is certainly arguable. However, Paul gives a different explanation as to why the man is culpable: "It is actually reported that there is sexual immorality among you, and of a kind that is not tolerated[30] even among pagans" (1 Cor 5:1).[31] The word translated "pagans" is ἔθνεσιν, from ἔθνος, literally "nations" or "Gentiles." In his statement, there is a clear juxtaposition between the customs of Gentiles on the one hand, and the kind of morality expected of believers on the other. What Paul is doing is drawing a line between them, Gentiles, and us, believers. They do not do anything like that, how much more should we not.

---

30. The verb "tolerated" is not in some of the earliest manuscripts. For possible readings, see Thiselton, *The First Epistle to the Corinthians*, 385.

31. Paul says that something like that was unknown even among the nations. In actual reality, while not common, it did happen sometimes within royal families for purposes of inheritance or royal continuity. There is also a biblical precedence when Adonijah, the son of David, wanted to marry Abishag the Shunammite who had been a concubine of David (2 Kgs 1:3–4; 2:13–25). There is difference in that David had not had any sexual relations with Abishag, in contrast presumably to the father of the Corinthian man. Nonetheless, Solomon perceives the request of Adonijah as an attempt to get the throne from him and commands the death sentence for Adonijah.

Israel, Covenant, Law

Evidently, through this juxtaposition, Paul considers the man (and the church as a whole) to be no longer Gentile but part of Israel, and therefore bound to live by the precepts of Israel. That is not to say that the man is of Jewish ancestry. Marrying a step mother would have been an abomination to any self-respecting Jew and it is unlikely that he would have engaged in it had he grown up within the Jewish community. More likely the man is a Gentile Christian who, having lived before his conversion in the permissive moral fabric of Corinthian society, did not take seriously the immoral and antibiblical nature of his actions.[32] Hays concurs, "The word *ethnē*, translated by NRSV and most English versions as 'pagans,' is Paul's normal word for 'Gentiles' (i.e., non-Jews). His use of this term here offers a fascinating hint that he thinks of the Gentile converts at Corinth as Gentiles no longer (cf. 12:2, 13; Gal. 3:28). Now that they are in Christ, they belong to the covenant people of God, and their behavior should reflect that new status."[33] So though a Gentile Christian, Paul considers him part of the faith of Israel (more about this in Chapter 2) and therefore obliged to obey the laws of Israel.

Of interest is also the nature of the punishment Paul envisages. First, he asks the church to cast the man out of the congregation: "let him who has done this be removed from among you" (5:2); and "cleanse out the old leaven [the offending man] that you may be a new lump, as you really are unleavened" (5:7); and "but now I am writing to you not to associate with anyone who bears the name of brother if he is guilty of sexual immorality or greed, or is an idolater, reviler, drunkard, or swindler- not even to eat with such a one" (5:11); and "purge the evil person from among you" (5:13). Very strong language. It harkens back to the penalty for such violations prescribed in Leviticus, as noted above.

There is however, one more statement by Paul that leads some commentators to think that he is not being too harsh on the offender after all, and that the discipline prescribed is for the man's good. 1 Cor 5:5 states, "You are to deliver this man to Satan[34] for the destruction of the flesh, so

---

32. "From 6:9–10 we learn that sexual immorality had been part of the Corinthians' previous lifestyle; on the basis of 5:9, 6:12–20, 7:2, and 10:8 (cf. 2 Cor. 12:21), we may deduce that they had carried that lifestyle into their new existence in Christ." Fee, *First Corinthians*, 197.

33. Hays, *First Corinthians*, 81.

34. "This means solemn expulsion from the Church and relegation of the culprit to the region outside the commonwealth and covenant (Eph. 2:11, 12), where Satan holds away. We have the same expression 1 Tim. 1:20. It describes a severer aspect of the

that his spirit may be saved in the day of the Lord." Whatever discipline, it would result in the man's eventual salvation, or so the argument goes.[35]

Though this is a common way to interpret this text, I think it is a wrong one. First, the pronoun "his" in the phrase "that his spirit may be saved" is not in the Greek text. So the proper translation is, "that the spirit may be saved," not "his spirit." Second, it is hard to see how handing over a person to Satan could lead to salvation. Third, it is hard to see how casting the offender out of the church of Corinth could result in the "destruction of the flesh."[36] The proposed salvific nature of the discipline is weak. Instead, I want to propose the following considerations. First, the "destruction of the flesh" refers to the final judgment. The word translated "destruction," ὄλεθρος, is elsewhere in the NT used only by Paul (1 Thess 5:3; 2 Thess 1:9; 1 Tim 6:9), and only in relation to the destruction of the wicked on the Day of Judgment. Consistency would suggest that the same use is in view here. After all, there is no reason why the man should be "destroyed" when expelled from the church; the destruction would come in the judgment. Second, the "spirit" to be saved in the judgment is not that of the offender but of the church. In fact, throughout this pericope, Paul is more upset with the church who has tolerated the offender and the offense, than about the offender himself[37] who, as far as Paul is concerned, has already been condemned: "I have already pronounced judgment on [him]." There is a string of strong warnings to the church (emphasis added): "It is actually reported that there is sexual immorality *among you,* and of a kind that is not toler-

---

punishment." Robertson and Plummer, *First Epistle of St. Paul to the Corinthians*, 99.

35. E.g., Ellingworth et al., *Paul's First Letter to the Corinthians*, 114: "In any case, the purpose of punishing him physically now is that he may be spiritually saved when Christ returns in judgment (see 3:13)"; Jamieson et al., *Old and New Testaments*, 1 Cor 5:5, first not the heinous nature of the sin and the severity of the punishment, "Besides excommunication (of which the Corinthians themselves had the power), Paul delegates here to the Corinthian Church his own special power as an apostle, of inflicting corporeal disease or death in punishment for sin ("to deliver to Satan such a one," that is, so heinous a sinner);" but then revert to the idea that the disease and even death of the sinner will somehow save him.

36. Robertson and Plummer, *Corinthians*, 99: "The sinner was handed over to Satan for the 'mortification of the flesh,' *i.e.* to destroy his sinful lusts.... But so strong a word as ὄλεθρος implies more than this. 'Unto destruction of the flesh' includes physical suffering, such as follows spiritual judgment on sin (11:30; Acts 5:1 f., 13:11)." Popular though such suggestions might be, they are not even hinted at in the text.

37. Fee writes, "The two sides to the problem are expressed in vv. 1–2. V. 1 indicates the nature of the deed itself; v. 2 moves on the greater issue, the church's response—or lack thereof—to this sin in their midst." Fee, *First Corinthians*, 199.

ated even among pagans" (5:1); "Ought *you* not rather to mourn?" (5:2); "*Your* boasting is not good" (5:6); "Is it not those inside the church whom *you are to judge?*" Paul is then suggesting that though it is the offender who has sinned, it is the church who is in danger because of her inaction in the face of gross sin. The danger is that the church as a whole will become polluted: "Do you not know that a little leaven leavens the whole lump?" (5:6). This again points back to Leviticus, as noted above, where individual sin could pollute the land and the nation. Unless the leaven, the offender, is cast out, the whole lump, the whole church, will be in danger. Paul's warning therefore to cast the man out so that "the spirit may be saved in the day of the Lord" has in mind the protection and salvation of the church, not the offender, and it is the spirit of the church that he wants to save in the judgment. If the offender also repents in the process, it is perhaps an added bonus; but Paul's concern is for the salvation of the church.

Even if someone does not agree with every point in my analyses above, two things are evident. First, Paul considers the prohibition of Lev 18:8 (and presumably many others) binding on Christians. Second, breach of such prohibitions calls for strong disciplinary measures modeled after the discipline envisaged in Leviticus, the "cutting off" of the offender from the congregation.

How does this incident impact the Reformation view of justification and soteriology? Simply put, it does not fit the picture comfortably. Reformation soteriology sees justification as an accomplished legal act. Obedience to biblical law might be a good life habit but it has no bearing on one's salvation. Paul, by contrast, considers believers as operating within a legal framework defined by biblical Israel, considers at least some of Israel's laws binding, and severe and open breach of one of them causes him to demand the punishment of the offender, possibly with a view to his repentance, but more likely in the final judgment and warns that failure to do so will endanger the spiritual well-being of the church in the judgment. The outlook reflected in 1 Cor 5:1–13 seems to be at variance with Reformation soteriology. All suggestions of abolition of OT law sound strange against such a background.

Achilles had two heels but only one was vulnerable. Antinomianism has two heels, or perhaps more, and they are all vulnerable. We looked at the incident of the offender of Corinth. Let us look at one more piece of evidence that makes antinomianism feel out of place for Paul. This second heel is the noun ἀνομία, and the cognate adjective ἄνομος. Both words are compound of the noun νόμος, "law," and the negating particle, -α. The literal meaning is therefore, "a lack of law" or "absence of law," and the two words are usually translated "lawlessness" for the noun and "lawless" for the adjective. Paul uses the noun seven times (Rom 4:7; 6:19 [x2]; 2 Cor 6:14; 2 Thess 2:3, 7; Titus 2:14), and the adjective six times (1 Cor 9:21 [x4]; 2 Thess 2:8; 1 Tim 1:9), always in a negative light. Of interest are the uses of 2 Thess 2:3, 7, 8 where noun and adjective describe the "man of lawlessness" an antichrist persona. Moreover, in Titus 2:13–14 Paul declares, "Waiting for our blessed hope, the appearing of the glory of our great God and Savior Jesus Christ, who gave himself for us to redeem us from all lawlessness [ἀνομία] and to purify for himself a people for his own possession who are zealous for good works."

One would have thought that if biblical law had been abolished by the gospel, or at least rendered pleonastic, ἀνομία and ἄνομος would have been fair descriptive terms to designate the new lawless realities of the gospel. The fact that they are not but instead represent the worst opposition and attack Paul could envisage against the Christian church strongly suggests, in my view, that any soteriological system that touches even remotely on antinomianism has taken a wrong turn.

THE NEW PERSPECTIVE AND THE LAW

Reformation theology and the key doctrine of justification by faith as developed by Luther and other Reformers held sway in Protestant circles for the better part of 500 years. But a challenge has recently appeared and it is directly relevant to our topic of study. The year is 1977 and E. P. Sanders' book, *Paul and Palestinian Judaism*, comes out of the printing presses of Fortress Press to stir the waters.[38] Sanders challenged several of the foundational tenets of Reformation theology, including the notion that first century Judaism was a works-oriented religion. Sanders maintained that for Jews, salvation was offered by grace but that once in the covenant, Jews had to keep the covenant laws. This was termed *covenantal nomism*.

It seems that one of the main concerns of Sanders was to debunk the intense disapproval by Protestant Christianity of the Jewish emphasis on obedience and law and as such bring the two faith systems closer together. Sanders found ready audiences and soon other theologians joined the frame. The new movement was called the "New Perspective" on Paul,

---

38. Sanders, *Paul and Palestinian Judaism*.

though as with Reformation theology there are variant approaches by different proponents and some prefer the term New Perspectives. The two key apologists of the New Perspective are two well-respected British theologians, both associated with Durham, England; N.T. Wright,[39] and James Dunn,[40] in front of whose office I passed every time I visited the theology school in Durham University where I did my PhD (but never had the privilege to meet him in person).

The New Perspective takes a much more positive view of biblical law. In contrast to Reformation outlooks, it views Paul's attacks on the law not as attacks on law as a moral entity, neither on good works in an attempt to earn the favor of God, but rather on law as a social reality whereby Jews considered themselves as superior to others and separated on account of their possessing and adherence to the law.[41] Within the law were what Dunn called "boundary markers," commands that aimed to separate the Jew from the Gentile. Now that the gospel was to go to all the nations, such boundary markers were no longer necessary; quite the contrary, they were stumbling blocks for the nations to come to faith. As such they were redundant. But some Jewish believers wanted to retain them and this explains Paul's vehement attack on these Jewish Christians and on these boundary markers themselves. The New Perspective therefore offers an ingenious way of dealing with Paul's apparent antinomian statements—they attack not biblical law as such, but the specific aspects just described. Beyond the boundary marks, law is good and obedience required. Indeed, Wright points to Rom 14:10–12, 2 Cor 5:10, and especially Rom 2:1–16 to demonstrate that judgment will be on the basis of works, presumably works of obedience to divine law.[42]

---

39. See Wright, *Justification*; Wright, *Paul and His Recent Interpreters*; Wright, *What St. Paul Really Said*.

40. See Dunn's most complete treatment is the compilation. Dunn, *The New Perspective on Paul*.

41. Dunn observes, "The solution suggested by the above analysis is that it is the law in its social function which draws a large part of Paul's critique. The law as fixing a particular social identity, as encouraging a sense of national superiority and presumption of divine favour by virtue of membership of a particular people—that is what Paul is attacking in the passages mentioned above. Divorced from that perspective, as the law understood in terms of faith rather than in terms of works, it can continue to serve in a positive role." Dunn, *New Perspective*, 131.

42. Wright, "New Perspectives on Paul."

In the list of boundary markers, the following three are usually listed: the Sabbath, food-laws, and circumcision.[43] Looking at the list, I have two serious problems. First, is this a comprehensive list? Is it somewhere stated in the OT or the NT, or in Jewish writings for that matter, that these three specifics are boundary markers, or something equivalent, and others are not? Would an NT Christian or Jew reading Paul's Epistles know that Paul has a specific corpus in mind and that this corpus has a specific set of laws, the three mentioned above?

Dunn has done most work in this area[44] and Wright simply accepts Dunn's conclusions. But on closer scrutiny, this list is problematic. In defining the boundary markers, Dunn first cites 1 Macc 1:6-63 where circumcision and the law of clean and unclean meats are mentioned as two laws, obedience to which qualified someone to be persecuted and even killed by the soldiers of Antiochus. These were therefore boundary markers in the eyes of Antiochus to single up practicing Jews for persecution. Dunn then assumes that these two were also the issues behind the conflict described in Gal 2:1-14.[45] However, Galatians mentions table fellowship but nothing about unclean meats. Jewish food laws were not limited to the type of meat served (clean or unclean animal) but whether an animal had been properly slaughtered (Lev 17:15) and the blood drained out (17:10), whether the fat had been removed (7:23), whether the animal had been slaughtered in front of an idol (17:2-9), not to mention rabbinic traditions on foods made common by association (e.g., Mark 7:1-4). Moreover, Jews were not allowed to associate closely with Gentiles whether over a meal or in other contexts.[46] It was most likely this last prohibition that is at work in Gal

---

43. E.g., ibid.

44. See the discussion in Dunn, *New Perspectives*, 121-52.

45. Ibid., 123.

46. See for example the incident of Jesus offering to go to the centurion's house to heal his servant only for the centurion, aware of Jewish scruples of entering into the house of a Gentile, requests that instead Jesus say a word and the servant will be healed from a distance (Matt 8:8-13; Luke 7:2-10); or that of the Syrophoenician woman whom the disciples ask that Jesus send away and who is compared to a dog, as Gentiles were often considered to be by some Jews (Mark 7:26-30); or the Jewish leaders who did not want to enter Pilate's house "so that they would not be defiled," and be prohibited from eating the Passover (John 18:28); or Acts 10:28 where Peter declares, "You yourselves know how unlawful it is for a Jew to associate with or to visit anyone of another nation, but God has shown me that I should not call any person common or unclean." George R. Beasley-Murray comments on John 18:28: "The Jewish deputation refuses to enter the governor's residence in order to avoid contracting defilement, and thereby disqualify

2:1–14. When the delegation from Jerusalem arrives, Peter withdraws from table fellowship with Gentile believers. Had the issue been an issue of food, whether unclean meat or food not prepared in a Levitically appropriate way, Peter could have conceivably asked the cook to prepare something else (vegetables) and resolve the problem without friction. By contrast, if we assume that the problem was association with uncircumcised persons, the Gentile believers, then there was no easy solution and Peter inappropriately, feels he has no other recourse but to remove himself from fellowship with them. The attempt to connect 1 Maccabees to Galatians is thus not convincing.

Dunn then mentions Philo (*Mos.* 1.278): "Israel cannot be harmed by its opponents so long as it is 'a people dwelling alone' (Num 23.9), 'because in virtue of the distinction of their peculiar customs they do not mix with others to depart from the way of their fathers.'" The "peculiars" Dunn gleans from Philo here are "circumcision, *kashrut*, Sabbath observance, and avoidance of civic rituals which implied recognition of pagan gods."[47] He then cites Aristeas who states that God hedged Israel in with "rules of purity, affecting alike what we eat, or drink, or touch, or hear, or see."[48] Aristeas's list is much more inclusive than Philo's, which is more inclusive than 1 Maccabees, which is less inclusive than the one cited by Wright above. Suddenly, the concept of "boundary markers" becomes somewhat nebulous. Yes, there were laws which set Israel apart but which laws exactly should be included? Did Paul have a specific list? Or his audience? Not that we know of. Perhaps interpretation was to be left to the discretion of the audience? Quite unlikely.

Second, and congruent to the above, is the question of what designates an OT law as a boundary marker. Take circumcision for example. Was it a boundary marker? It was, if we look at circumcision in the sense that every male person who wanted to join the covenant of Israel had to circumcise. And it was if we are to set Israel apart from Romans and Greeks. But was

---

themselves from sharing in the passover meal. They are acting in accordance with the dictum, 'The dwellings of non-Jews are unclean,' *Ohol.* 18:7." Beasley-Murray, *John*, 327. Hendriksen and Kistemaker write, "The 'venerable' members of the Sanhedrin who were in the procession which delivered up their prisoner had religious scruples against entering the dwelling-place of a heathen! They did not desire to be defiled. They apparently regarded ceremonial defilement to be a much more serious matter than moral defilement." Hendriksen and Kistemaker, *Exposition of the Gospel According to John*, John 18:28.

47. Dunn, *New Perspectives*, 125.
48. Ibid.

it a marker in the sense of setting Israel apart from other nations in a more universal way? The answer is a resounding, No! Many nations in antiquity practiced circumcision. In fact, among the Canaanites and other peoples of the Near East during OT times, more nations/tribes practiced it than did not.[49] It was indeed abhorrent to Romans and Greeks who considered it a form of bodily mutilation. But Romans and Greeks were relative newcomers to the area. To call circumcision a boundary marker in the sense of setting Israel apart from other nations is to disregard the clear evidence of history that it was not unique to Israel.

With regards to the Sabbath, it is true that there was no immediate counterpart in the surrounding cultures of Israel. However, regular days on weekly or monthly intervals, whether for rest, festivities, or other reasons, were not unknown. The Babylonians marked off the seventh, fourteenth, twenty-first, and twenty-eighth day of the month; the Romans, the first, seventh, and fifteenth. The weekly cycle as we now know it was coming into use by the first century BC.[50] Maybe none of these was a direct counterpart to the Sabbath but the concept of a regular cycle was not unique to the Jews. Moreover, if we take the Sabbath to include not only the weekly Sabbath but the annual festal calendar of Israel, then all nations had their annual feasts and festivals. They were not identical to Israel's but like Israel's, there were festivals that were based on the agricultural cycle.[51] So I would be interested to know, from a New Perspective perspective, which of the festivals of Israel were boundary markers? Was it only the weekly Sabbath? Or were the monthly and annual festivals too? And they were boundary markers vis-à-vis who? And would the Galatian readers of Paul's Epistle know which feasts constituted boundary markers? The whole arrangement seems nebulous.

---

49. See for example Hall, "Circumcision," 1025–31. He notes, "In the ancient Near East circumcision was widely practiced." Ibid., 1025.

50. It seems that the Babylonians had some kind of weekly cycle of seven days based on the lunar with added days every four weeks to make up the extra day of the lunar cycle, and where certain days were considered special; see for example, Pinches, "Sabbath (Babylonian)." The Roman calendar originally had a weekly cycle of eight days. Evidence for a seven-day week exists as early as the first century BC. There were at least three special days in a month: *Kalendae* on the first of each month; *Nonae* sometimes on the seventh day, sometimes on the fifth; and *Idus* on the thirteenth of fifteenth day; see Beck, *On the Roman Calendar*; Odom, *Sunday in Roman Paganism*, 31–124; Rüpke, *Roman Calendar from Numa to Constantine*, 162.

51. See the discussions of Rochberg-Halton and Vanderkam, "Calendars," 810–19.

There is also a problem in the reverse direction. There is one boundary marker that is never designated as a boundary marker by the New Perspective, namely, the second commandment: "You shall not make for yourself a carved image, or any likeness of anything that is in heaven above, or that is in the earth beneath, or that is in the water under the earth. You shall not bow down to them or serve them, for I the LORD your God am a jealous God, visiting the iniquity of the fathers on the children to the third and the fourth generation of those who hate me, but showing steadfast love to thousands of those who love me and keep my commandments" (Exod 20:4–6). Every non-Israelite religion of antiquity had images, statues, and idols of all sorts, and this was especially true of Greek and Roman religion. The faith of Israel was the only one (to my knowledge) that had a prohibition against such. This would then make the second commandment the boundary marker par excellence, more exclusive to Israel than the food laws, Sabbath, or circumcision. Yet nowhere is it designated as such in New Perspective literature. Is this an oversight? Not only is the literature silent on this marker but Paul, quite on the contrary, seems not to have been against this marker because he repeatedly argues against any form of idol worship that seems to confirm that for him the second commandment was still valid (e.g., 1 Cor 5:10, 11; 6:9; 10:7; Eph 5:5).

It seems to me therefore that the boundary markers identified by Dunn and Wright are not a coherent biblical list but one of convenience that they have subjectively identified in their mind without an attempt to properly substantiate exegetically what it consists of and why. The whole concept is arbitrary and without foundation. If the boundary markers go, the position of the New Perspective and its interpretation on Paul's attitude to the law becomes tenuous at best if not completely redundant.

TOWARDS A THIRD PERSPECTIVE ON PAUL

In this book, I want to present what I believe is a better paradigm for understanding Paul, a Third Perspective so to speak. Most of what will be presented in the following four chapters is not new. But as a package, it certainly is. It stands on three premises.

The first premise is that, in Paul's mind, the Christian church is the natural continuation of Israel, at least theologically. I will develop this idea in Chapter 2. While many Christian writers have identified the church as a "spiritual Israel" or a "new Israel," words like "spiritual" and "new" imply a

Reformation Perspectives and New Perspectives

break between the old and the new, or the supposed "physical" Israel of the OT and the spiritual of the NT. There are assumed elements of discontinuity that I believe Paul did not envisage. A natural continuation of Israel, by contrast, stresses much more the element of continuity than discontinuity. If the church is the continuation of the faith of Israel, it follows that antinomianism has no place in it.

The second premise, congruent to the first, is that the covenants of Israel apply to the church. This includes the Sinai Covenant with the Ten Commandments and the Book of the Law. The key difference between the Sinai Covenant and the New is not in the legal dimension, but in the ritual. The sacrifice of animals and circumcision of the flesh are replaced by the sacrifice of Jesus and circumcision of the heart. The legal continuity between the covenants explains why Paul was so upset at the offender in Corinth who had violated one of the Levitical laws concerning appropriate and inappropriate sexual behavior. I develop the concept of covenant in Chapter 3. My approach has similarities but is not identical to Calvinist covenantal theology.

The third and most important premise is that Paul's attacks on the law in Galatians and elsewhere are not targeting a legal code as such but the ritual entailed in the Abrahamic and Sinai covenants: namely, circumcision and sacrifice. I develop this premise exegetically in Chapters 4 and 5.

You, the reader, reading the above three paragraphs may jump to the conclusion that my approach is more arbitrary than, say, what I make out the New Perspective's boundary markers to be. If you feel this way, it is fine. But please read the chapters that follow, or at least peruse them. I think that while my exegesis on several occasions departs from, and even goes against how texts are traditionally interpreted, taken together there is a certain force in my arguments that will be difficult to dismiss. While it is my hope that I will convince many, even those not convinced should be at least made aware that there is an alternative way of reading Paul that can be well argued from the text. A Third Perspective has come, and I hope it has come to stay.

2

Paul and Israel

Towards an Understanding of Early Christian Self-Identity

Thesis Statement—For Paul, believers in Christ of any national background are the natural continuation of Israel, a true Israel.

The question of the relations between Israel and the church is wrought with challenges. Though initially Christian ministry focused on Jews (e.g., Acts 1:1–12:26), and Christianity was perceived as a sect of Judaism (e.g., Acts 5:34–42; 18:15; 19:23; 22:4; 24:14, 22; 28:17–27), from a very early time the preaching of the apostles about the crucified and risen Messiah elicited opposition which in time led to a parting of ways. Christianity and Judaism became antagonistic religious systems and such antagonism at times turned into acrimony.

Approaching the topic of Paul's self-identity as a believer in Jesus vis-à-vis Jews who did not, is a difficult task because the modern scholar is challenged by these two millennia of antagonism. It is important however, as much as possible, to put historical and contemporary issues aside and approach the topic from the biblical text in order to understand Paul's description of the identity of the early church.

Paul and Israel

When Paul wrote his Epistles, Christianity was a small minority in a vast Roman Empire, barely noticed and with minimal influence in society. By most of those few who were aware of its existence, it was considered a sect of Judaism, and indeed initially it was. Even within Judaism with its several sects, groups, and variant approaches, Christianity initially raised few eyebrows outside the immediate environs of Jerusalem and Judea. When Paul is writing therefore, he is endeavoring to biblically define for this small group of believers their status in the world of Judaism, and indeed in the bigger picture of God's plan for the world.

It is also important to know that when Paul wrote, there was no Israeli-Palestinian conflict over who will possess the land variously designated today (depending on who you ask) as Israel, Palestine, or Holy Land; no terrorism in the way we know it today or settlements in occupied land as defined by the UN; and no holocaust or centuries of pogroms, massacres, and hatred of Jews by the Christians (and perhaps, vice versa). Had there been, it is probable that Paul would have expressed himself differently. But such things had not happened yet, and Paul expressed himself in the way he did. His writings need to be studied and analyzed in their historical context rather than through the lenses of the modern political arena.

As stated in my thesis statement above and as I will endeavor to demonstrate below, Paul considered the nascent church to be the true Israel. In this, he was in no way a pioneer. Other sects within Judaism—like the Maccabees and their followers in the context of the Hellenism that was spreading quickly in Jerusalem; the Pharisees, or "set apart ones,"[1] who wanted to separate themselves from those who had compromised their faith; and the Essenes, many of who retired to Qumran so as not to be part of corrupt priestly establishment of Jerusalem—all in some form or other considered themselves as the true keepers of the flame, the true holders of the identity of Israel. Paul believed exactly the same about those who believed in Jesus as the Messiah. The main difference between him and others before him was not in their self-identity, but in the fact that in the nascent church, a large number of Gentiles began to flock in. But even for this, there was a theological and historical precedent, as we will see. So in understanding the early church as a faithful remnant of Israel, Paul was operating within well-established patterns of Jewish thought.

So though what I will present below is at variance with the views most scholars hold today, in Paul's world would have been considered a fairly

---

1. C. Brown, "Pharisees," 810.

normative approach to self-identity. This chapter will be divided into four parts. First, we will explore issues of identity in the OT and the Second Temple Jewish mindset. Second, we will discuss some key Pauline texts that address the issue of identity. Third, we will explore other passages in the NT that evidence a similar outlook. Fourth, we will bring the discussion together.

ISRAEL AS A SPIRITUAL ENTITY—AN OLD TESTAMENT AND EARLY JEWISH OVERVIEW OF THE IDENTITY OF ISRAEL

Today Israel is commonly perceived as the physical descendants of Abraham, through Isaac and Jacob. While this is an accurate understanding of the origins of the term, as history unfolds the picture becomes more complex.

Of Abraham, it is stated in Gen 18:19: "I have chosen him, that he may command his children and his household after him to keep the way of the LORD by doing righteousness and justice, so that the LORD may bring to Abraham what he has promised him." The word בַּיִת, "household" can have a variety of meanings ranging from a physical dwelling place, the house, to an extended family.[2] Abraham's household included not only his son through Sarah, Isaac, who at that stage had not even been born yet. It included anyone living with him, including his servants, as is evident from the fact that one of his servants was due to inherit him (Gen 15:2). In one instance, Abraham was able to arm 318 of his servants (Gen 14:14)[3] and form a small army with which he rescued Lot. Evidently, Abraham's "household" probably numbered as many as 1000 persons or more. This household Abraham was to teach so that the Lord might fulfill what he had promised.

This inclusiveness and openness are evident in the later history of Israel. When God made the covenant with Israel at Sinai, participation in the

---

2. Köhler, "בַּיִת," 125. BDB 109–10.

3. Victor P. Hamilton states, "Here yālîḏ does not refer to physical descent; rather, it designates membership in a group by a means other than birth. Here in particular the term is applied to a slave or servant whose major function is to provide military assistance." Hamilton, *The Book of Genesis*, 406–7. Compare with E. A. Speiser, "As opposed to slaves obtained through purchase, this class ranked close enough to members of the family to be entrusted with tasks of considerable importance and responsibility." Speiser, *Genesis*, 104.

covenant was not based on descent. Numerous individuals not descended from Abraham became part of the covenant. Joseph had married an Egyptian woman (Gen 41:45); Moses a Midianite (Exod 2:16-21) whose family was invited to join Israel, but declined (Num 10:29-30). Caleb was a Kennizite (Num 32:12); Rahab, a Canaanite (Josh 2:1); Ruth, a Moabite (Ruth 1:4); Uriah, a Hittite (2 Sam 11:3). King David himself was only partly Israelite (Ruth 4:17).

Not only individuals but whole groups of foreign people joined the covenant. When Israel left Egypt a "mixed multitude" (Exod 12:38)[4] joined and partook fully of the covenant. Canaanites not destroyed or expelled, were eventually integrated, with the Rechabites becoming especially respected for their fidelity to God (Jer 35:1-19).[5] David's elite bodyguards were Philistines (1 Chron 18:17) who presumably had converted, for it is hard to imagine David's palace filled with pagans. Throughout the monarchy there were thousands of foreigners in Israel (e.g., 1 Chron 22:2; 2 Chron 30:25) whom the LXX calls προσήλυτοι, "converts."[6] In Solomon's time, their number was 153,500 (2 Chron 2:17). Of pagans in the Persian Empire, Esth 8:17 declares, "Then many of the people of the land became Jews," while 9:27 indicates that people continued to join the faith even after the momentous events described there.

When Ezra returned from Babylon, he was authorized by the king of Persia: "And you, Ezra, according to the wisdom of your God that is in your hand, appoint magistrates and judges who may judge all the people in the province Beyond the River, all such as know the laws of your God. And those who do not know them, you shall teach" (Ezra 7:25). It is not clear whether those "who do not know" the laws of God meant only Jews who had lapsed from the faith, or included a mandate for proselytism among the non-Jews. Most commentators opt for the former, though the latter possibility should not be excluded.[7]

During the intertestamental period, John Hyrcanus converted the whole nation of the Idumeans (Edomites) to Judaism on the point of the

---

4. "That there were many who became Israelite by theological rather than biological descendancy is many times referred to in the OT and is the occasion for such requirements as those set forth in vv 43-49 of this composite." Durham, *Exodus*, 172.

5. See Thompson, *Book of Jeremiah*, 616-17.

6. LSJ, s.v. "προσήλυτοι."

7. Myers, *Ezra, Nehemiah*, 62. Cf. Williamson, *Ezra, Nehemiah*, 104. See also Fensham, *The Books of Ezra and Nehemiah*, 108; Batten, *The Books of Ezra and Nehemiah*, 314.

Israel, Covenant, Law

sword.[8] Out of them came the notorious family of Herod.[9] While both the family of Herod and the Idumeans were looked upon with suspicion by mainstream Jews, this had less to do with their racial background and more with the suspicion, most true in the case of Herod and probably many (most?) other Idumeans that their "conversion" was skin deep and that in practice they continued in their pagan ways.[10] Idumeans joined other Jews in the defense of Jerusalem against the Romans in the siege of AD 70 and played a pivotal part in those dramatic events.

In NT times, the Pharisees were well known for their missionary zeal (Matt 23:15). Martin Goodman has argued that Pharisees were not interested in converts from among the nations, but rather that they were trying to convert other Jews into their own stream of Judaism.[11] This is a possibility, though others disagree.[12] Whichever the case, the appeal of Judaism among Gentiles is well documented and not limited to Matt 23:15. We know from other statements that synagogues were filled with foreign converts or God-fearers (e.g., Acts 13:15, 26; 16:14; 17:17). Foreigners flocked to Jerusalem to worship during the feasts (John 12:20)—with 15 nations mentioned, "Jews and proselytes" in Acts 2:9–11—as participating in the feast of Pentecost. Some of the converts, or at least sympathizers, were from

---

8. Schürer, Vermès, and Millar, *Jewish People in the Age of Jesus Christ*, 207.

9. Freedman, "Herod," 161.

10. There is an interesting and directly relevant story in *m. Sotah* 7:8 about Herod Agrippa: "The synagogue attendant takes a Torah scroll and hands it to the head of the synagogue. The head of the synagogue in turn hands it to the deputy [of the High Priest], who in turn hands it to the High Priest, who hands it to the king. The king stands and receives it, but reads sitting. King Aggripas stood and received it and read standing, for which act the Sages praised him. When he reached, 'You may not put a foreigner over you,' (Deuteronomy 17:15) his eyes ran with tears [because on his father's side he was not of Jewish descent]. They said to him, 'Fear not Agrippas, you are our brother, you are our brother, you are our brother!'"

11. Goodman, *Judaism in the Roman World*, 99–101.

12. Willoughby C. Allen, though acknowledges that perhaps Pharisees wanted to make other Pharisees, notes the extensive missionary work of Jews among Gentiles: "Whilst the number of heathen attracted to Judaism at this period was very great, a comparatively small proportion would have been regarded by the Pharisees as satisfactory converts. The Hellenistic Jewish literature, e.g. the writings of Philo and the Sibylline Oracles (Book iii.), are evidence of the zeal of Jews of the Dispersion to attract Gentiles to the worship of the one God." W. Allen, *The Gospel According to S. Matthew*, 246. "Their zeal extends even beyond their primary charge, the people of Israel, to the gaining of proselytes from among other nations." France, *The Gospel of Matthew*, 870.

the upper echelons of society and included the wife of Nero[13] and Helena, Queen of Adiabene.[14] Such an outlook is already reflected in the OT: "My house shall be called a house of prayer for all nations" (Isa 56:7). The very fact that for few, like the Moabites, there were certain limitations on when they could enter the covenant (Deut 23:3) indicates that for others, access was unhindered.

This willingness to accept converts persisted through history and is a reality down to our time. The story of the Khazars, a semi-nomadic Turkic people living in the Middle Ages north and east of the Crimea, stands out. Though the historicity of the account is sometimes disputed,[15] it appears that sometime between the eighth and tenth centuries, the royal family, the nobility, and perhaps a part of the population converted to Judaism.[16] And there are groups of people who claim to descend from ancient Israel in different parts of the world who are accepted as Jews by the rabbinate in Israel, but who are so considered primarily on grounds of religion rather than a tenuous and largely imaginary physical descent from Abraham.[17]

Not only could any person of any background join the covenant, but those within it could opt out or be forcefully ejected. To be "cut off" from the people of Israel was a punishment for a number of sins (e.g., Exod 30:33, 38; 31:14; Lev 7:20, 21, 25, 27).[18] To what extent this was carried out we do not know. But the provision was there. The word "apostasy," or "falling away from the faith,"[19] is not uncommon in the LXX to describe Israel's sometimes rebellious attitude towards God (e.g., Josh 22:22; 2 Chron 29:19).

It is patently evident that any person of any background could join the covenant and many did throughout Israel's history; and that anyone of whatever background could choose to exit the covenant. In today's language we could say that Israel functioned in many ways like an ἐκκλησία

---

13. See Kohler and Neumann, "Poppaea Sabine," 129: "She had a certain predilection for Judaism."

14. See Gottheil and Seligsohn, "Helena," 334.

15. Rosensweig, "The Origins of East European Jewry," 139–62.

16. See the complete description of this theory by Koestler, *The Thirteenth Tribe*.

17. See for example, Bruder, *The Black Jews of Africa*, 133–86.

18. Robert M. Good is of the opinion that to be "cut off" means execution. Good, *The Sheep of His Pasture*, 85–90. Rodney R. Hutton notes that execution is usually expressed by a different term. According to Num 19:13, it could mean, "to become unclean." Hutton, *Declaratory Formulae*, 138–42. For a fuller discussion, see Hartley, *Leviticus*, 100. John E. Hartley observes that one cannot be certain of the meaning.

19. LSJ, s.v. "ἀποστασία."

or a church—people joining and people leaving. Indeed, ἐκκλησία is the very word Peter chose to describe Israel of old: "This is he who was in the congregation [ἐκκλησία] in the wilderness" (Acts 7:38). And lest one be tempted to consider this an exceptional example, the LXX uses ἐκκλησία 77 times, almost exclusively as a reference to Israel.

This brief background discussion is important in order to understand the identity Paul ascribes to the early church.

PAUL AND EARLY CHRISTIAN IDENTITY

Space does not permit a full analysis of all the relevant Pauline passages that tackle the question of early Christian identity. What we will do instead is focus on selected passages that demonstrate, fairly clearly in my view, the thesis statement presented above.

The Parable of the Olive Tree

Paul's best known and most clear analysis is the parable of the olive tree in Rom 11:15–24. The parable draws from Jer 11:16–23 where Israel is described as a "green olive tree, beautiful with good fruit" (Jer 11:16).[20] However, the Lord would set fire to it and its branches would be destroyed (11:16), not only because Israel worshiped Baal (11:17), but also because they rejected the ministry of Jeremiah who was "like a gentle lamb led to the slaughter" (11:19), imagery used in the NT of Jesus (John 1:29, 36; Acts 8:32; 1 Pet 1:19; Rev 5:6, 9, 12; 13:8; cf. Isa 53:7).[21]

Paul's argument begins already from chapter 9. There Paul declares his sincere pain for his brothers, fellow Jews, who do not follow Jesus (Rom 9:2). But then he makes an interesting statement that will be programmatic, a guide for the rest of his argument: "Not all who are descended from Israel belong to Israel" (Rom 9:6). What Paul is saying here is that not everybody who carries the name Israelite belongs to God's actual people. God's people

---

20. L. Allen, *Jeremiah*, 141.

21. William Lee Holladay and Paul D. Hanson note that in most cases (111 out of 116), the word used here for "lamb" refers to a sacrificial animal, and they write, "The symbolism of Jrm as a lamb led to slaughter entered into the symbolism of Deutero-Isaiah in Isa 53:7 (though the word for lamb there is different . . .) and ultimately into the Johannine metaphor of Christ as the Lamb of God (John 1:29, 36; 27 times in Revelation)." Holladay and Hanson, *Jeremiah 1*, 372.

are in fact only those who follow God faithfully, a true Israel so to speak. This means that for Paul, the concept of Israel is more than that of blood relations, or declared identity. It has to do with faith and practice. In order to support his claim, Paul gives two examples. First, he shows that although Abraham had many sons[22] only Isaac's seed is considered as the line from where Abraham's elect sons descend. Likewise, although Isaac had two boys, only Jacob was the one God loved. Paul's point is not that only Israel is God's people but rather that it is not simply blood relations that determine who truly God's child is.

This idea that true Israel is not the totality of natural Israel but the totality of the believers comes not from Paul but from the OT concept of a remnant. The prophets repeatedly spoke of a faithful remnant that will remain whereas the rest will perish. It is interesting that Paul clearly subscribes to that idea when he quotes Isaiah in Rom 9:27: "And Isaiah cries out concerning Israel: 'Though the number of the sons of Israel be as the sand of the sea, only a remnant of them will be saved.'"

The same concept is present in Rom 11:1–5. There Paul speaks of how among the multitudes of Israel at the time of Elijah, only 7,000 had not bowed to Baal. For Paul, these 7,000 constituted the true people of God, the true Israel. Paul then takes this event from history and in 11:5, applies it to his current situation: "So too at the present time there is a remnant [λεῖμμα], chosen by grace." The *remnant* is composed of those who, like Paul, have believed in Jesus. Paul's next argument attempts to make sense of Israel's unbelief. He concludes that the failings of Israel brought riches to the Gentiles (11:12); in other words, it opened the road for the Gentiles to be evangelized. Paul however, being a Jew, had a special love for his own people. This is why he hoped that helping lead the Gentiles into the kingdom, he would make his own people jealous so that he could "save some of them" (11:14).

With this brief discussion of the context, we move to the parable, the basic elements of which are as follows. We will see that the parable fits neatly into the context discussed above. The olive tree is "cultivated" (ESV, RSV, NIV, NKJV) or "good" (KJV; Rom 11:24). It has a "holy" (11:16) and healthy root that supports and nourishes the tree (11:17–18). Some of the branches, however, have been broken because of unbelief (11:17).

---

22. The designation son, or less frequently, daughter of Abraham, was a common designation referring to a person belonging to God's chosen nation (e.g., Luke 19:9; 13:16).

By contrast, other branches, from wild olive trees, have been "grafted in" among the remaining branches of the tree (11:17).

Who are the branches broken off because of unbelief? Clearly, they are Jewish people who have rejected the ministry of Jesus.[23] These are the ones Paul mentioned in 11:14, his fellow but unbelieving Jews, whom he desires to save. "For if their rejection means the reconciliation of the world" (Rom 11:15) parallels 11:17, "But if some of the branches were broken off." Failure to believe in Jesus causes these branches to be broken off. These broken branches may be grafted back onto the tree provided "they do not continue in their unbelief" (11:23).

The wild branches that have been grafted in, in the place of the branches that were broken off, are clearly Gentile believers.[24] Paul addresses them in 11:13: "Now I am speaking to you Gentiles." In 11:20, he explains that Gentiles have been grafted onto the tree because of their faith. Their position on the tree should not lead to pride (11:20) or to contempt for the broken branches (11:18) because the wild branches have been graciously grafted onto the root that supports them and on which the broken branches once where (11:18). Indeed, such an attitude could mean that the grafted in branches could also in turn be broken off (11:21).

It is important to point out a dimension of Paul's outlook as expressed in 11:17 and 18: "and you, although a wild olive shoot, were grafted in among the others and now share in the nourishing root of the olive tree" and "remember it is not you who support the root, but the root that supports you." It is the root and the trunk, historical Israel, which provide the nourishment, the theological context of existence for the early church. Rather than Gentiles departing from the faith of Israel to form a new reality, Paul envisages here a movement in the exact opposite direction, Gentiles coming to Israel not only in their sense of identity, but also in the source from which they receive spiritual nourishment and support.

There is a further detail that perhaps adds some light into the meaning of this parable. It has been noted by numerous authors that the normal agricultural practice would be to graft cultivated olive branches onto wild olive trees so as to make them cultivated. Paul presents here the exact opposite, wild branches grafted onto cultivated trees. It is unlikely that Paul was not aware of simple agricultural realities. This leaves us with two possible options. Either Paul chose to ignore normal agricultural practice or indeed

23. Fitzmyer, *Romans*, 614.
24. Moo, *The Epistle to the Romans*, 701–2.

reversed it to make a theological point; or there is evidence that it was not uncommon among farmers of olive trees to graft wild olive branches onto cultivated olive trees that were becoming aging and unproductive in order to reinvigorate them. The second option is the more likely and is the one preferred by most commentators.[25] If that is indeed the case, Paul's parable takes an even more dramatic tone. The Gentiles, wild olive branches, not only gain the privilege to become part of Israel, the cultivated olive tree, but add new life and vigor to this tree. Gentiles then become a force that does not replace Israel but reinvigorates it.[26]

There are some very simple and yet profound theological implications that can be drawn from this simple analysis, and which contemporary Christian theology finds hard to understand. The first is that the tree, Israel, continues to exist. God does not reject the tree; why would he since the tree is called "holy" and the root is healthy and nourishing. Only branches are rejected or broken off. This means that Israel continues to be God's favored entity. It is not Israel who is rejected, it is unbelieving individuals. Second, Gentiles who come to faith in Jesus are grafted onto this one tree, Israel. They are now part of Israel. They are not a new Israel. Rather, they become as much part of the historical tree as Rahab, Ruth, and Uriah before them. And they find their nourishment and theological foundation in the faith of Israel.[27] Third, Jews who have failed to believe and persist in unbelief are no longer part of the tree. For Paul therefore, believers in Jesus are the real Israel, the continuation of the Israel of the OT.

It is important at this stage to compare Paul's outlook of the church as the natural continuation of Israel with traditional and modern Christian theological outlooks. Replacement (Supersessionist) theology in all its forms and variants entails a break between the Israel of the OT and the Christian church; the Christian church replaces historical Israel[28] and in the process, much that belonged to historical Israel. Dispensationalist models see God as having two special peoples: Israel and the church. If we were to apply these models to the parable of the olive tree, Replacement theologies would have God uprooting the one tree (Israel) and planting a new one

---

25. For instance, Morris, *The Epistle to the Romans*, 412. Additional evidence is given in Baxter and Ziesler, "Paul and the Arboriculture," 31.

26. Baxter and Ziesler, "Paul and the Arboriculture," 27–28.

27. Leslie C. Allen describes the tree after the incoming of the Gentiles "the ongoing community of faith." L. Allen, *Jeremiah*, 141.

28. Diprose, *Israel and the Church*.

(the Christian church). Dispensationalist models would have God leaving the one tree as is (Israel), without perhaps even pruning it, and planting a second one alongside it (the Christian church).[29] Neither model fits Paul's paradigm. God neither uproots nor plants another tree, he simply prunes the existing one and it continues to exist and represent God on earth. For Paul then, the church is the natural continuation of historical Israel.

The Parable of the Half Empty Cauldron— "All Israel Will Be Saved"

Paul follows the parable of the olive tree with another one (Rom 11:25–26). It depicts an empty item of some sort being filled. Since Paul does not specify what is the object being filled I will take a liberty and call it, a cauldron. Whatever it is, it is a symbol of Israel.

Paul begins by stating that πώρωσις ἀπὸ μέρους τῷ Ἰσραὴλ γέγονεν, "a partial hardening has come upon Israel." The expression ἀπὸ μέρους suggests that one part of Israel was hardened and one not.[30] The hardened ones parallel the broken branches and are the ones who have failed to believe. The ones not hardened are the ones who have believed. Paul is therefore expressing the same reality he was experiencing in the parable of the olive tree.

How does God deal with this situation? Paul declares that this situation will last ἄχρι οὗ τὸ πλήρωμα τῶν ἐθνῶν εἰσέλθῃ, "until the fullness of the Gentiles has come in" (11:25). Πλήρωμα[31] is a verbal noun that describes one entity filling something, in this case the Gentiles coming in to fill a void left by the rejected, hardened Israelites. The void is a void in Israel, left by those whose hearts were hardened. If we can imagine a cauldron that represents Israel, it was once full and complete. The hardening of some and their resulting exclusion leave a void. The Gentiles come in to fill this void, just as the wild branches filled the void left by the broken branches in the parable of the olive tree.

Paul concludes by saying, "and in this way all Israel will be saved" (11:26). The opening phrase, καὶ οὕτως, "and in this way" implies an inference,[32] a conclusion of what was said in 11:25: namely, all Israel, minus

29. DeWitt, *Dispensational Theology in America*.
30. Morris, *The Epistle to the Romans*, 420. Against Dunn, *Romans 9–16*, 679.
31. Danker, Bauer, and Arndt, "Πλήρωμα," 829.
32. Against Jewett, Kotansky, and Epp, *Romans*, 701. They assume a temporal sense.

those hardened plus the Gentiles coming into Israel, equals all Israel; or a once full cauldron, Israel, becoming partially empty because of those who have not believed, but becoming full again as the πλήρωμα of the Gentiles comes in to fill the void. It is this body of believers, this new totality, irrespective of ethnic background, that is designated as "all Israel" and will be saved.[33]

Paul adds, "as it is written, 'The Deliverer will come from Zion, he will banish ungodliness from Jacob'" (11:26). This is a quotation from Isa 59:20. The context of the quotation is important because 59:18–19 depicts people from the coastlands and from east and the west, some being punished for their sins and some coming to the Lord: "According to their deeds, so will he repay, wrath to his adversaries, repayment to his enemies; to the coastlands he will render repayment. So they shall fear the name of the LORD from the west, and his glory from the rising of the sun." This statement highlights four things. First, it is in harmony with the parable of the olive tree and the half empty cauldron both of which depict Gentiles being welcomed into Israel, the family of God. Second, deliverance or salvation is only connected to the Deliverer, Jesus Christ. Those who accept him are in the family, irrespective of race. Third, ungodliness is banished and so are those who practice it again irrespective of race. Fourth, the community of the saved is still designated as Zion and Jacob.

We have discussed two fairly-straight forward and simple passages that concern Paul's depiction of the identity of the early church. How does the picture outlined above tally with other Pauline discussions on the same topic? We will now see that Paul's outlook was consistent and pervasive. We will explore three other passages that deal with the question of identity, and then will explore some other random statements.

Two Wives Two Sons—
Galatians 4:22–31

The first passage is Gal 4:22–31, the parable/allegory of Isaac and Ishmael as representing two covenants: "For it is written that Abraham had two

---

33. Most scholars disagree with this statement and for them an ethnic element is always present. E.g., Moo, *The Epistle to the Romans*, 723; Fitzmyer, *Romans*, 623; Dunn, *Romans 9–16*, 681–82; Cranfield, *The Epistle to the Romans*, 576.This reflects a failure to understand the concept of Israel as developed by biblical writers, especially Paul. Cf. The discussion on Gal 3 below.

sons, one by a slave woman and one by a free woman.... Now this may be interpreted allegorically: these women are two covenants. One is from Mount Sinai, bearing children for slavery; she is Hagar. Now Hagar is Mount Sinai in Arabia; she corresponds to the present Jerusalem, for she is in slavery with her children. But the Jerusalem above is free, and she is our mother" (Gal 4:22, 24–26).

There are a number of issues that are worth discussing in this passage, and we will return to it both when we discuss the concept of covenant in the next chapter, and also when we discuss the concept of law, in the fifth chapter. For the time being, we will only focus on what it says about early Christian identity.

Paul takes the story of Abraham and turns it into an allegory of the status of Jews and Christians before God in his time. Let us remind ourselves of the main outlines of the story of Abraham. Abraham has one wife, Sarah. God promises him a son. As the promise delays, Abraham, at the instigation of Sarah, takes his slave woman Hagar and through her has a son, Ishmael. Ishmael was born according to "the flesh" (Gal 4:23), meaning according to human will and desire. By contrast, Isaac was the one promised by God and the one who eventually inherited Abraham.

Paul makes some amazingly impressive statements. He declares that the free woman, Sarah, represents the heavenly Jerusalem, and is "the mother of us all" (Gal 4:26). The "us all" refers to the community of believers in Galatia and by implication, all Christian believers. There is a general consensus that the church in Galatia was composed primarily of believers of Gentile background.[34] Paul therefore declares that these Gentiles, together of course with believing Jews, are the children of Sarah and Abraham, the descendants of Isaac, not by physical descent but because they have believed the promise. They are citizens of the heavenly Jerusalem; therefore, part of a true Israel in the fullest sense of the term. Incidentally, according to Heb 11:9–10, the inheritance to which Abraham looked forward to was not an earthly one, but the "city that has foundations, whose designer and builder is God," the heavenly Jerusalem of course.

Paul then makes another impressive statement. Those who have not believed in Jesus, but who want to be justified under the Sinai Covenant and who have their hope and focus on the earthly Jerusalem, are children of Hagar. Paul is here clearly speaking about Jews who have not believed in Jesus. Though they might count themselves as descendants of Abraham

---

34. Martyn, *Galatians*, 116–17.

(physically, or more likely spiritually or perhaps both) and consider Abraham their father, this descent is of no spiritual value.[35] They are children of the slave woman and therefore not heirs to the promise. This parallels the language of Rom 11 and the parable of the olive tree where the natural branches of the tree were broken because of unbelief. Paul then declares of them: "But what does the Scripture say? 'Cast out the slave woman and her son, for the son of the slave woman shall not inherit with the son of the free woman'" (Gal 4:30). In the allegory of the two women and their offspring therefore, the true descendants of Abraham and Sarah are believers in Jesus, the nascent church.

The Real Children of Abraham— Galatians 3:26–29

Paul makes the same point again in Gal 3:26–29 where he discusses who are the true descendants of Abraham. Abraham was the father/ancestor of Isaac, Jacob, and Israel. When he talks of the children of Abraham therefore, Paul is answering the question of who the real Israel is. Galatians 3:26–29 tackles a number of issues, including the works of the law, and as with Gal 4:23–31, we will return to it again in the following chapters, when we discuss covenant and law. At this point, our sole interest is to understand Paul's view on Christian identity.

Paul declares, "Abraham 'believed God, and it was counted to him as righteousness?' Know then that it is those of faith who are the sons of Abraham (Gal 3:5–7). In these two verses, Paul outlines two simple realities. First, those who have faith (in Jesus) are sons (and daughters) of Abraham irrespective of racial background. This thought is repeated and amplified in 3:28–29: "There is neither Jew nor Greek, there is neither slave nor free, there is neither male nor female, for you are all one in Christ Jesus. And if you are Christ's, then you are Abraham's offspring, heirs according to promise." Faith is therefore the sole criterion in determining sonship into Abraham's family and participation in the promises made to him.[36] Second, and by implication, those who have no faith in Jesus are not sons of Abraham, again irrespective of racial or religious background.

Paul explains how this happens in 3:16: "Now the promises were made to Abraham and to his offspring. It does not say, 'And to offsprings,' referring

---

35. Fung, *The Epistle to the Galatians*, 209.
36. Ibid., 176.

to many, but referring to one, 'And to your offspring,' who is Christ." Paul here engages in a bit of ingenious midrashic exegesis.[37] He takes the promise of an offspring to Abraham given in Gen 12:7 and applies it to Christ. In Gen 12:7, the word for seed, σπέρμα, is in the singular. In context, it refers to Isaac, Abraham's only son with Sarah, and by implication his descendants who would inherit Canaan, as indeed happened. But for Paul the true seed is none other than Jesus, the most important descendant of Abraham, the Seed, so to speak; and the focus is certainly not the earthly Canaan and Jerusalem, then occupied by the Romans, but the heavenly one in line with what was already discussed above. It follows then that those who have failed to attach themselves to Jesus are not children of Abraham in the fullest sense of the term.

Citizenship of Jerusalem and Access to God's Temple—Ephesians 2:11–22

Paul tackles this topic again in Eph 2:11–22 while addressing believing Gentiles in Ephesus. In 2:11–12, he begins with the following words: "Therefore remember that at one time you Gentiles in the flesh, called 'the uncircumcision' by what is called the circumcision, which is made in the flesh by hands—remember that you were at that time separated from Christ, alienated from the commonwealth of Israel and strangers to the covenants of promise, having no hope and without God in the world." The words "in the flesh" here refers to circumcision or lack of it.

Paul describes the status of Gentiles before faith using three phrases: "separated from Christ," "alienated from the commonwealth of Israel," and "strangers to the covenants of promise." The three phrases complement each other. Being separated from Christ means being separated from Israel. So, the commonwealth of Israel only finds meaning in Christ, and so do the covenants. Israelite identity for Paul therefore, finds meaning in Christ. Gentiles before faith were outside this spiritual family.

But then comes a change. "But now in Christ Jesus you who once were far off have been brought near by the blood of Christ" (Eph 2:13). The words "but now" imply a change of circumstances that has happened when these Gentiles believed in Jesus. This change is expressed in spatial terms. The Gentiles, who were once far, have now been "brought near."

---

37. Dunn, *The Epistle to the Galatians*, 184.

"Near to what?" one might ask. Paul himself gives the answer in 2:19–21: "So then you are no longer strangers and aliens, but you are fellow citizens with the saints and members of the household of God, built on the foundation of the apostles and prophets, Christ Jesus himself being the cornerstone, in whom the whole structure, being joined together, grows into a holy temple in the Lord." Paul has mentioned the commonwealth of Israel; now he adds citizenship, membership in the household of God, and a temple.

The commonwealth of Israel is the whole family of God from which Gentiles were excluded from before faith but now have been incorporated. Citizenship implies a city. Of which city would Christians be considered citizens? Of Jerusalem of course. But which Jerusalem? Paul has answered this question already in Gal 4:22–31 discussed above, the heavenly, or true Jerusalem. After all, most Gentile Christians never lived in the earthly Jerusalem and never became its citizens. As such, these Gentiles who were once strangers to the commonwealth of Israel have now became partakers not only of Israel but of the city of heavenly Jerusalem itself.

But not only are believers citizens of Jerusalem, but also members of the household of God, οἰκεῖοι τοῦ θεοῦ. A household implies a house, an οἰκεῖος an οἶκος. The house of God, ὁ οἶκος τοῦ θεοῦ, is nothing less than the temple.[38] Paul depicts identity in three concentric circles: the temple in the middle, Jerusalem built around it, and the commonwealth of Israel spread beyond. The Gentiles, being Gentiles, were far removed from these concentric circles. But now that they have believed in Jesus not only have they become members of the commonwealth of Israel, but citizens of Jerusalem and indeed part of the very family of the house of God, having access to the temple of God. They have reached the very core of what it meant to be an Israelite. The reality Paul describes perhaps reflects the promise in Isa 56:7 that if Gentiles would take hold of God's covenant, God would "bring to my holy mountain, and make them joyful in my house of prayer."[39] The

---

38. See Matt 21:13; 23:38; Mark 11:17; Luke 13:35; 19:46; 1 Pet 2:5.

39. Oswalt, *The Book of Isaiah*, 460–61. "Not only will they be permitted to come, but the Holy God himself will conduct them, just as he brought his own people back from the land of exile. There he will treat them just as he would any believing Israelite. They will have the privileges of having their sins atoned for (whole burnt offerings and sacrifices) and of having instant access to God in prayer. This is what Solomon had envisaged long before (1 K. 8:41–43), and what Malachi would see as inevitable (1:11). God had not chosen Israel and given them all that he did in order to shut out the world, but to bring in the world." Ibid.

coming of faith of the Gentiles is therefore the fulfillment of the promises given to Israel.

The temple, city, and commonwealth that Paul has in view, of course, are not the earthly ones. In another study, we have explored the concept, common in both the OT and NT as well as extra biblical literature, that earthly temples in general (in pagan cultures) and the temple in Jerusalem in particular, were considered copies of inferior status of a heavenly archetypal where the true dwelling place and throne of deity were located.[40] That Paul has the heavenly temple in view is evident in that just before he mentions the temple, he declares that through the blood of Christ we "both have access [προσαγωγὴν] . . . to the Father" (2:18). The Greek προσαγωγή, compound of πρός, "to" or "towards" and ἀγωγή, "to lead someone," has the idea of being lead into the presence of someone.[41] To be led before God's throne means to appear before him in heaven. The noun has a locative dimension. For Paul therefore, in Christ believers do not only become part of the true Israel, but gain access right into the very heavenly throne room of God.

PARALLEL OUTLOOKS IN THE NEW TESTAMENT

This outlook is not unique to Paul. Repeated references in the rest of the NT present a similar outlook. We will peruse a few without detailed analysis.

Perhaps the most important is the covenant language of Heb 8:8: "For he finds fault with them when he says: 'Behold, the days are coming, declares the Lord, when I will establish a new covenant with the house of Israel and with the house of Judah" and 8:10: "For this is the covenant that I will make with the house of Israel after those days, declares the Lord: I will put my laws into their minds, and write them on their hearts, and I will be their God, and they shall be my people." The covenant the writer of Hebrews is writing about is the new covenant in Jesus Christ. Yet, in both these texts and others that will be discussed in more detail in the next chapter, the new covenant is made with the house of Israel and the house of Judah. It follows that those who are under the new covenant belong to Israel/Judah. Indeed, this is the only covenant available to humanity: "In speaking of a new covenant, he makes the first one obsolete. And what is becoming obsolete and growing old is ready to vanish away" (Heb 8:13).

40. Papaioannou and Giantzaklidis, *Earthly Shadows, Heavenly Realities*.
41. BDAG 876.

In Matt 3:7–9 (cf. Luke 3:7–8), John the Baptist tells the Pharisees: "You brood of vipers! Who warned you to flee from the wrath to come? Bear fruit in keeping with repentance. And do not presume to say to yourselves, 'We have Abraham as our father,' for I tell you, God is able from these stones to raise up children for Abraham." For one to qualify as a child of Abraham from the perspective outline here, one must evidence the fruit of Abraham. Else the fate of a fruitless tree awaits, fire and destruction (Matt 3:10, 12). Jesus makes a similar point in John 8:39: "They answered him, 'Abraham is our father.' Jesus said to them, 'If you were Abraham's children, you would be doing what Abraham did' (John 8:39). And then adds the following sober and hard-hitting words: "You are of your father the devil, and your will is to do your father's desires." Conversely, God has the ability to produce children for Abraham even from stones. The stones in question probably represent the Gentiles who later came to faith in large numbers at the preaching of the apostles.[42] Believing Gentiles are therefore children of Abraham in the fullest sense of the term.

The incoming of the Gentiles to the faith is also depicted in John 10:16: "And I have other sheep that are not of this fold. I must bring them also, and they will listen to my voice. So there will be one flock, one shepherd." The first set of sheep Jesus refers to are clearly those within Israel that believe. But Jesus declares that he has other sheep from other folds, clearly Gentiles.[43] When these other sheep hear his voice, he will "bring them also" into his fold. The Gentiles come and join the fold of Israel and its true Shepherd, Jesus.

In Matt 8:11–12 (Luke 13:28–29), Jesus describes an eschatological banquet: "I tell you, many will come from east and west and recline at table with Abraham, Isaac, and Jacob in the kingdom of heaven, while the sons of the kingdom will be thrown into the outer darkness. In that place there will be weeping and gnashing of teeth." Those who have been considering themselves sons of Abraham, the "sons of the kingdom," will no longer be considered sons but will be thrown out. Conversely, Gentiles coming from the east and west will join Abraham and the other patriarchs of Israel taking the place of the expelled sons.[44] In order to sit and have table fellowship with the patriarchs, it follows that they have been incorporated, adopted

---

42. Nolland, *The Gospel of Matthew*, 145.
43. Bernard and McNeile, *The Gospel According to St. John*, 362–63.
44. Nolland, *The Gospel of Matthew*, 357.

into their family, and are no longer "strangers" to the commonwealth of Israel (Eph 2:12).

Likewise, in Matt 19:28 (cf Luke 22:13) we read, "Truly, I say to you, in the new world, when the Son of Man will sit on his glorious throne, you who have followed me will also sit on twelve thrones, judging the twelve tribes of Israel." What gives the apostles, and perhaps by extension other followers of Jesus, the right to judge the twelve tribes of Israel? The very fact that by following Jesus, they are part of the true Israel and therefore in a position to judge Israel.

Relevant are also the multiple references to Jesus as King of Israel or King of the Jews. When Nathaniel first meets Jesus he declares, "Rabbi, you are the Son of God! You are the King of Israel!" (John 1:29). When Jesus is crucified, Pilate orders that a sign be placed on the cross: "Jesus of Nazareth, the King of the Jews" (John 19:19; cf. Matt 27:37; Mark 15:26; Luke 23:38). The Jews object, "Do not write, 'The King of the Jews,' but rather, 'This man said, I am King of the Jews'" (19:21). But Pilate refuses to alter the sign, and this refusal appears as a confirmation of the kingship of Jesus over Israel.

This title of Jesus is affirmed in numerous other texts. In Matt 2:2 the wise men ask, "Where is he who has been born king of the Jews? For we saw his star when it rose and have come to worship him." When Pilate asks Jesus if he is the King of the Jews, Jesus does not refuse the title: "The governor asked him, 'Are you the King of the Jews?' Jesus said, 'You have said so'" (Matt 27:11; cf. Mark 15:2; Luke 23:3). Beyond the importance of such statements in their original context, for the evangelists writing decades later they serve as an affirmation that Jesus was indeed King of Israel/the Jews. But how could this be, if the leadership of the Jews had rejected him? It could only be a reality for the apostles, if they considered believers to be a true Israel. Else the title is void of meaning and a misnomer—it would make Jesus a King without the subjects defined in the title but with other subjects not defined in the title as his real subjects. The title only makes sense if the subjects of the kingship of Jesus, believers of any national background, are indeed the subjects defined in the title.

Perhaps most impressive is the language of 1 Pet 2:9–10: "But you are a chosen race, a royal priesthood, a holy nation, a people for his own possession, that you may proclaim the excellencies of him who called you out of darkness into his marvelous light. Once you were not a people, but now you are God's people; once you had not received mercy, but now you have received mercy." Two things are worth noting here. First, Peter uses the very language God used in Exod 19:6 when he made the covenant with Israel at Sinai. That Peter applies this language to believers in Jesus indicates that for him such believers are a true Israel. Second, the language of 1 Pet 2:9–10 is not applicable only to Christians of a Jewish background; the fact that in 2:10 he states that his audience "once . . . were not a people," most likely indicates that he has Gentile Christians in mind.[45] For Peter therefore, believers in Jesus of any background constitute the true Israel.

CONCLUSION

We have traced briefly the question of identity through the OT and noted that biblically speaking, participation in the covenant was open to people of diverse nationalities even if originally established with Abraham and his biological son and grandsons. We noted that first century Judaism was fully cognizant of this reality, and Jews remain so until today.

We then explored key passages in Paul and it became fairly evident that for him, faith in Jesus does not signify a break from Israel, but rather its fulfilment. Jesus is the Seed promised to Abraham and in him Israel finds meaning. Therefore, any believers in Jesus are children of Abraham, Israelites, in the fullest sense of the term. We also noted that this outlook is not unique to Paul but common among different writers of the NT.

How does this outlook fit the Reformation and New Perspectives on Paul? Christians of different affiliations have often understood the church as a New Israel, or a Spiritual Israel.[46] The emphasis is on the words New or Spiritual, and they are contrasted with the Old or Physical Israel. While the retention of the word Israel in Christian self-designations implies a sense of continuity with the Israel of the OT, there is more discontinuity than continuity. For Luther, first century Judaism was the absolute other, a group of people who endeavored to earn their salvation through good works. He identified their outlook with his before his liberating understanding of justification by faith. It is no surprise then that Luther was very anti-Jewish, theologically. He also had a noted dislike, as discussed in the previous chapter, against the laws of Israel. The coming to faith of the Gentiles was a decided move away from historical Israel.

Contrast this with Paul's attitude (and that of other NT writers) whereby the coming to faith of Gentiles marks not a move away from Israel

---

45. Jobes, *1 Peter*, 163–64.
46. For instance, Ladd, *A Theology of the New Testament*, 583.

but a move from afar towards Israel. The direction of movement understood by the Reformers is the exact opposite from that understood by Paul. In this context, Reformation antinomianism seems out of place. A move away from OT Israel could imply and partly justify a move away from the legal framework of Israel. But if for Paul, the movement was in the opposite direction, Gentiles coming from afar and joining Israel, how could biblical Israel's legal framework become entirely or largely redundant? It seems hardly likely.

While the New Perspective takes a gentler approach to both biblical Israel and Israel's legal framework and is not characterized by the antinomianism of some of the Reformation theology, there is still a problem. For Wright, the works of the law against which Paul argued in Galatians and Romans were the things that made Israel distinct from other nations—circumcision, the Sabbath, and the food laws—are the main usually mentioned. But how can Gentiles become Israel, if the very things which supposedly characterize Israel are no longer valid? How can they take on the identity of Israel if the very identity markers have ceased to have meaning? There is a logical gap in this hypothesis. It does not make sense.

3

Paul and the Covenant
The Ritual Dimension of Covenant

Thesis Statement—The key difference between OT covenants and the new covenant is the difference in ritual, the sacrifice and blood of animals in OT covenants versus the sacrifice and blood of Jesus in the New. Paul accepts both the Abrahamic and Sinai Covenants as valid for believers with the exception of the ritual dimension.

Covenant is a fairly common term when it comes to discussions of Pauline theology. The New Perspective speaks of covenantal nomism—the requirement of those in the covenant of Israel to obey the laws of the covenant—and covenantal or boundary markers, legal aspects of the covenant that were intended, according to New Perspective outlooks, to make Israel stand apart from other nations. Reformed and Lutheran theologians alike speak of the Covenant of Law (Sinai Covenant) and the Covenant of Grace, the new covenant established by Jesus.

A covenant is an agreement; one that brings two or more individuals into a relationship. While there are several types of covenant, the most common both in the Bible and the ancient Near East is the marriage covenant—two individuals who unite their lives and become one.[1] It is evident

---

1. Brueggemann, *Genesis*, 47.

Israel, Covenant, Law

that there is a very strong relational aspect to the concept of covenant. The marriage covenant is used consistently to represent God's relation to humankind[2] and both Israel and the church are very often depicted as the bride of God.[3]

Covenant dates to the earliest of times. Adam was in a covenant relationship with God (Hos 6:7)[4] and enjoyed face to face communion (Gen 2:21; 3:8–11). That covenant was broken with the fall (Hos 6:7). Fellowship was replaced by fear (Gen 3:10). When, therefore, God invites humans to enter into a covenant relationship with him, he endeavors to restore the kind of fellowship that was once experienced with Adam and Eve. A covenant is all about restoring humanity to harmony with God.

Discussions on covenant focus primarily on the legal aspects of covenants, what laws they contained and how they were intended to be kept. Covenants however also had an important ritual aspect that is often overlooked. Indeed, sacrifice and blood are foundational to covenant making.[5] What hinders a relationship between God and humans is sin: "But your iniquities have made a separation between you and your God, and your

---

2. Larsson, *Bound for Freedom*, 151.

3. See Isa 49:18; 61:10; 62:5; Jer 2:32; 7:34; 16:9; 25:10; 33:11; Joel 2:16; John 3:29; Rev 18:23; 21:2, 9; 22:17.

4. Ward, *Hosea*, 129; Douglas, *New Commentary on the Whole Bible*, 1216. There is some uncertainty as to the function of the noun + prefixed preposition כְּאָדָם in Hos 6:7. Three possibilities exist: (a) the most accepted is to translate כְּאָדָם as "like Adam" (so e.g., ESV, NIV); (b) to translate כְּאָדָם as "like men" since the Hebrew *adam* can be either a proper name, that of the patriarch Adam, or a common noun denoting men in general (so KJV, NKJV); (c) to assume that כְּאָדָם is a secondary reading, the original being, בְּאָדָם, in/at Adam (so RSV), since in Hebrew the letters *bet* and *kaph* are very similar, thus, supposedly, resulting in a mix up here. In the third case, Adam would be a place name and an antecedent to the "there" that appears in Hos 6:7b: "there they dealt treacherously with me." Textual evidence for בְּאָדָם is extremely weak, only a late medieval manuscript, not even given as an option in the *Biblia Hebraica Stuttgartensia* and *Biblia Hebraica Quinta*. Moreover, though a place named Adam is mentioned in Josh 3:16, there is no evidence that any faithlessness towards God was manifested there, such that would warrant the rebuke of Hos 6:7. So the third option remains shaky. Between the first two options, (a) is preferable. It is pointless to say that Israel "like men . . . transgressed the covenant." כְּאָדָם is better understood as a reference to the fall of Adam, in which case the "there" of Hos 6:7b could be a reference to Eden.

5. See Gen 15:10–11, 18; 17:1–14; Exod 24:8; Lev 2:13; Ps 49:5; Isa 56:4–7; Dan 9:24–27; Zech 9:11; Mal 2:4–5; Matt 26:28; Mark 14:24; Luke 22:20; Acts 7:8; Rom 11:27; 1 Cor 11:25; Heb 8:6–13; 9:15–22; 10:16–17, 29; 12:24; 13:20; (in some of these texts, the word "blood" does not appear but is implied when sacrifice is there or when the forgiveness of sin is mentioned).

sins have hidden his face from you so that he does not hear" (Isa 59:2). In order for the relationship between God and man to be restored, the problem of sin needs to be dealt with, which, biblically speaking, is dealt with the shedding of blood: "For the life of the flesh is in the blood, and I have given it for you on the altar to make atonement for your souls, for it is the blood that makes atonement by the life" (Lev 17:11); and "indeed, under the law almost everything is purified with blood, and without the shedding of blood there is no forgiveness of sins" (Heb 9:22).[6] So, no understanding of the concept of covenant can be complete without an understanding of the ritual dimension.

There are several covenants in the OT. In this chapter, we will first explore two, the Abrahamic and Sinai, since these are the two key ones discussed by Paul. Then, we will look at the promise of a new covenant as described in Jeremiah, which is also addressed by Paul. We will touch briefly on the legal dimension of covenant but will focus primarily on the ritual dimension. We will first discuss the covenants as they appear in the OT and then explore how Paul (and other NT writers) viewed them. In our discussion of both OT covenants, a repeated pattern occurs whereby the covenant is established, broken, and then re-established. We will also see that in contrast to commentators who see the OT covenants—especially the Sinai Covenant—as completely different to the new covenant,[7] the relationship is rather that of shadow to reality whereby the New brings to reality the Old.

THE ABRAHAMIC COVENANT

The Abrahamic Covenant is described in Gen 15:1–21. In 15:5, God invites and promises Abraham: "'Look toward heaven, and number the stars, if you are able to number them.' Then he said to him, 'So shall your offspring be.'" Abraham responds by pointing out that he is childless. God in turn tells Abraham to perform a covenantal ritual: "Bring me a heifer three years old, a female goat three years old, a ram three years old, a turtledove, and a young pigeon" (15:9).

Abraham brings these animals and cuts them in half, except for the birds. As the sun is going down, a great fear befalls Abraham and then the Lord appears and repeats the promise. It is not stated what causes the

---

6. Owen, *Hebrews*, 178; Pink, *An Exposition of Hebrews*, 515.
7. Blackwood, *Commentary on Jeremiah*, 225; Clements, *Jeremiah*, 191.

Israel, Covenant, Law

fear of Abraham. However, in covenant ceremonies, the sacrifice of animals was intended to indicate what would be the punishment of a covenant participant if there was a breach of the covenant.[8] Perhaps, seeing the slain animals and aware of his own shortcomings, Abraham wonders what his fate might be if he breaks the covenant.[9]

As Abraham is filled with fear something unusual happens: "When the sun had gone down and it was dark, behold, a smoking fire pot and a flaming torch passed between these pieces" (15:17). It is generally agreed that the smoking fire pot and flaming torch that passed between the slain and dismembered animals symbolize God,[10] an indication that he would take the penalty for any breach of the covenant.[11]

Genesis 16 describes the breach of the covenant by Abraham.[12] Several years have passed since the promise was given in Gen 15 (Gen 16:3). Abraham and Sarah are getting older and they both wonder how the covenant can be possibly fulfilled.[13] On Sarah's suggestion Abraham takes Hagar, Sarah's maid, and she gives birth to a son, Ishmael. This act is a breach of the covenant because Abraham has failed to believe the promise. Indeed, when God reappears in Gen 17 to remake the covenant Abraham laughs at the suggestion that he and Sarah will have a son and instead considers Ishmael the fulfilment of the promise: "Then Abraham fell on his face and laughed and said to himself, 'Shall a child be born to a man who is a hundred years

---

8. See Jer 34:18; cf. Matt 24:51; France, *The Gospel of Matthew*, 945. J. Gerald Janzen writes, "When covenanting parties pass through the halves of sacrificial animals, they bind themselves to one another in such a way that covenant disloyalty will tear each of them in two as the animals lie cut in two." Janzen, *Abraham and All the Families of the Earth*, 40.

9. K. A. Matthews opines that the gloom and fear are related to the prophesied enslavement of Abraham's descendants. This is unlikely since fear and gloom precede the prophecy. Matthews, *Genesis 11:27–50:26*, 173.

10. Hamilton notes that the fire port and flaming torch remind of the smoke and fire on Mount Sinai and adds that in the Bible, fire is often a symbol of the presence of God. He also notes similarities between the theophany of Gen 15:7 and the appearance of God and the renewing of the covenant in Exod 33–34. Hamilton, *The Book of Genesis*, 436–37.

11. LaRondelle, *Our Creator Redeemer*, 679.

12. Hamilton, *The Book of Genesis*, 443. Hamilton insightfully observes that in Gen 16:1–6, Sarah is repeatedly referred to as Abraham's wife. This probably implies a rebuke on Abraham for taking Hagar as his wife at the instigation of Sarah.

13. Haberman, "Foreskin Sacrifice," 18. Sarah "was tired of waiting for God to do what needed to be done." Ibid.

old? Shall Sarah, who is ninety years old, bear a child?' And Abraham said to God, 'Oh that Ishmael might live before you!'" (Gen 17:17–18).[14]

God reappears to Abraham in Gen 17 and remakes the covenant, despite Abraham's doubts, giving again the promise of abundant offspring (Gen 17:1). This time, God commands Abraham that all the male members in his household will have to be circumcised—"This is my covenant, which you shall keep, between me and you and your offspring after you: Every male among you shall be circumcised" (17:10). There are two things that are important at this point about circumcision. First, circumcision was not part of the original covenant of Gen 15. It was an afterthought, a response to Abraham's failure. This is evident in the way Gen 17 begins, "When Abram was ninety-nine years old the LORD appeared to Abram and said to him, 'I am God Almighty; walk before me, and be blameless, that I may make my covenant between me and you, and may multiply you greatly" (Gen 17:1–2). The command to "be blameless" probably is a recognition that Abraham had not been. Moreover, the phrase "that I may make my covenant," which implies a cause/effect relationship, suggests that something new is in place in Gen 17 compared to Gen 15 because of what has transpired in Gen 16.

Second, there is a parallel, unfortunately not usually noticed, between the cutting of the animals in two in Gen 15 as a symbol of the punishment befitting the one who will breach the covenant and Abraham cutting himself in two, so to speak, through circumcision. As the one who has broken the covenant, Abraham should have been cut into two—like the animals of Gen 15—or at least slain, like the birds of Gen 15. But it was God, in the symbol of the smoking fire pot and flaming torch, who passed between the slain animals so Abraham escapes. By asking Abraham to circumcise his foreskin, God asks Abraham to cut in a sense himself in two both as a reminder of his failure and more importantly, as a reminder that God would be the one who would take ultimate responsibility for the breach of the covenant. Circumcision is then a type of sacrifice,[15] and was so viewed by

---

14. Gordon J. Wenham writes, "The narrative makes Abraham's astonishment very clear in three ways. First, 'Abraham fell on his face,' a gesture of awe, amazement, and gratitude (cf. v 3) . . . 'And laughed,' his second astonished response, indicates . . . he is not simply laughing with joy . . . [but] unbelief. . . . Third, he is so overcome by the announcement that he can hardly think straight. The way he frames his doubt, 'Can a man . . . give birth?'" combines two different constructions for a double-barreled question (see n. 17.c.)." Wenham, *Genesis 16–50*, 25–26.

15. Wenham calls circumcision a ritual act and notes the fact that it was to be

later rabbis and Christian commentators alike. I will develop this thought further when we discuss circumcision in Galatians in Chapter 5.

The incident of the near sacrifice of Isaac is also connected to the covenant though the word "covenant" does not appear in the narrative.[16] Genesis 22 where the story appears follows Gen 21:1–8 which outlines the birth of Isaac—the beginning of the fulfilment of the Abrahamic Covenant—and the family problems between Sarah and Hagar because of jealousy, culminating in the eviction of Hagar and Ishmael from the household (21:9–21). The story of the near sacrifice of Isaac is introduced with the words, "after these things God tested Abraham" (Gen 22:1). The test is therefore a response to the events of Gen 21, primarily the ejection of Hagar and Ishmael, which in turn are the product of Abraham's failure in Gen 16.[17] After Abraham proves faithful in Gen 22 by following faithfully the command of God, God repeats the promise of the covenant for an abundant offspring, this time with an oath: "'By myself I have sworn, declares the LORD, because you have done this and have not withheld your son, your only son, I will surely bless you, and I will surely multiply your offspring as the stars of heaven and as the sand that is on the seashore. And your offspring shall possess the gate of his enemies, and in your offspring shall all the nations of the earth be blessed, because you have obeyed my voice" (Gen 22:16–18). This reiteration of the covenant promise appears hand in hand with another: "So Abraham called the name of that place, 'The LORD will provide;' as it is said to this day, 'On the mount of the LORD it shall be provided'" (Gen 22:14). According to rabbinic tradition, it was on the mountain where Isaac was nearly sacrificed that later the temple with its offertory system was built.[18]

---

performed on the eight day, a timeframe common in Leviticus for other ritual acts. Ibid. Haberman writes, "Circumcision is one enduring remnant of the act of sacrifice unsupplanted by gentler forms of service such as prayer." Haberman, "Foreskin Sacrifice," 18.

16. Matthews observes, "There are many allusions in this chapter to the promises issued in previous events (e.g., 12:2–3; 13:14–16; 15:4–5; 16:10; 17:2, 5–6, 16, 20; 18:18; 21:18). By such a preponderance of back references, the author effectively brings forward all that has preceded. The impact is the elevation of this single event so as to make all of the past promises hang on Moriah's test." Matthews, *Genesis 11:27–50:26*, 283.

17. George W. Coats notes a parallel between the near sacrifice of Isaac and the "sacrifice" of Ishmael who is sent away with his mother and adds that "this unit follows the report of the birth of Isaac and the corresponding expulsion of Hagar and Ishmael." Coats, *Genesis*, 158.

18. Skinner, *Commentary on Genesis*, 328.

There is a question whether the Abrahamic Covenant had any legal code. None is mentioned in Gen 15 or 17. Conversely, Gen 26:4–5 states, "I will multiply your offspring as the stars of heaven and will give to your offspring all these lands. And in your offspring all the nations of the earth shall be blessed, because Abraham obeyed my voice and kept my charge, my commandments, my statutes, and my laws."[19] Here the covenant promise is reiterated and related to obedience on the part of Abraham to charge, commandments, statutes, and laws. The text does not elaborate the point and neither will we.[20] For the purposes of this study, this issue is of secondary importance.

THE SINAI COVENANT

The Sinai Covenant is often studied in juxtaposition to the Abrahamic, one being considered unconditional, the other dependent on obedience. Whatever the apparent or real differences between the two, it is important to keep two things in mind. First, the liberation of Israel from Egypt and the ensuing Sinai Covenant were seen as a consequence and by-product of the Abrahamic Covenant (Exod 2:24; 6:4–5). Second, among the Jews the two covenants were equally considered the inheritance of Israel. As such, they were complimentary not antagonistic. We will see later that the same is the case with Paul (e.g., Rom 9:4; Eph 2:11–13). With these introductory thoughts, we can briefly review the Sinai Covenant.

After Israel's departure from Egypt, on the third month since the exodus, Israel camps at the foot of Mount Sinai (Exod 19:1–2).[21] There God speaks to Israel through Moses and invites her to become his possession.

---

19. Hamilton writes, "Yahweh's evaluation of Abraham's life is that the patriarch obeyed me, keeping my mandate . . . which is broken down into three constituent parts: my commandments, my laws, my instructions. Both the verb and the nouns following the verb are close to the sequence one finds in passages like Deut. 11:1 and the Deuteronomistic 1 K. 2:3. In living by Torah, Abraham models the quality of response to God that should characterize the people Israel." Hamilton, *The Book of Genesis*, 194.

20. The idea that Abraham lived by the Torah is not uncommon in Jewish thinking. Cf. Moberly, "The Earliest Commentary on the Akedah," n. 16; and Kugel, *In Potiphar's House*, p. 121, n. 12.

21. Their stay at the foot of the mountain lasts about a year (compare Exod 19:1 and Num 10:11–12). Hamilton contrasts Israel's stay by Sinai with the time of the ten plagues in Egypt, the duration of which he also estimates to have been about one year. Hamilton, *Exodus*, 299.

Israel, Covenant, Law

Before inviting Israel to enter into the covenant, God reminds them of the mighty acts he has performed on their behalf to liberate them from the Egyptian bond (Exod 19:4–5), as a proof of his faithfulness and good disposition towards them.[22] If Israel accedes to his invitation they will become his treasured possession, a kingdom of priests and a holy people (Exod 19:5–6). Once Israel displays an initial positive response to God's invitation, God proceeds to outline the stipulations by which Israel will have to abide once they enter the covenant. They fall in two parts, the "Words" of the covenant better known as the Ten Commandments, and the Book of the Law (Exod 20:2–17 and 20:23–23:33). The difference between the two has been repeatedly noted.[23] The following is the summary:

1. The Ten Commandments were spoken audibly by God in the presence of the people in a powerful theophany (Exod 20:18–19);[24] the latter were communicated to Moses (Exod 20:21–22).[25]

2. The Ten Commandments are apodictic in that they consist of authoritative statements declaring the divine will;[26] the Book of the Law is mostly casuistic and functions as an interpretation of the apodictic statements into practical applications befitting the situation of Israel when she was in the wilderness and beyond.[27] Indeed, the Book of the Law is later expanded to incorporate further injunctions relevant to the people (Deut 31:24).

3. The Ten Commandments were possibly written on tablets of sapphire-like stone (Exod 24:12; 31:18);[28] the Book in a book (Exod 24:7).

---

22. Douglas K. Stuart notes that the last clause of Exod 19:6 is a command to "be sure that the Israelites heard Yahweh's call to covenant relationship." Stuart, *Exodus*, 424. Clear communication is foundational in a relationship between God and His people. While Moses informs the elders of Israel (19:7) about what God has said, it is the whole people who respond affirmatively (19:8), "suggesting that the elders brought Moses' words throughout the congregation of Israel, required a response from everyone, and then brought the unanimously positive response back to Moses, who then brought it back up the mountain to God." Ibid.

23. Larsson, *Bound for Freedom*, 156–83.

24. Sarna, *Exploring Exodus*, 131.

25. Meyer, *Devotional Commentary on Exodus*, 244.

26. Fretheim, *Exodus*, 220–38.

27. Ibid., 239–54.

28. Meyers, *Exodus*, 261; See also Paul, "Heavenly Tablets," 346; Hammer, *The Classic Midrash*, 256; cf. *Ned 38a*. In Exod 24:10, the elders of Israel see the throne of God and there "was under his feet as it were a pavement of sapphire stone, like the very heaven

Paul and the Covenant

4. The Ten Commandments were written by the finger of God (Exod 31:18; 32:16); the Book was written by Moses (Exod 24:4).

5. The Ten Commandments were eventually placed in the Ark of the Covenant (Deut 10:1–2); indeed, the Ark was designed specifically as a receptacle for the tablets of stone (Exod 25:16); by contrast, an expanded Book of the Law was eventually placed by the side of the Ark of the Covenant (Deut 31:26).[29]

The inauguration of the covenant is described in Exod 24:1–11 and consists of three major parts. First, Israel having already expressed a willingness to abide by the will of God even before the Ten Commandments and the Book of the Law have been pronounced (Exod 19:8), now twice reaffirms her vow of obedience (Exod 24:3, 7). Second, between the two reaffirmations, Moses orders sacrifices of burnt offerings and peace offerings of oxen (ESV) or young bulls (NIV)[30] pouring some of the blood against the altar (24:6). After Israel's final affirmation that they will abide by the laws of the covenants, Moses sprinkles the people with the remaining blood, declaring at the same time the covenant formula: "Behold the blood of the covenant that the LORD has made with you in accordance with all these words" (Exod 24:8). The sacrifice of animals, young bulls in this case, was a common part of covenant making and as with the Abrahamic Covenant, indicated the fate that would befall the party that breached the covenant.[31]

---

for clearness." Rabbis understood the "stone" of 24:12 to be anaphoric referring back to the sapphire-like stone at the base of the throne of God. Some rabbis also contended that the second set of stones prepared after Moses broke the first set were also made from sapphire stone which God revealed that it existed under Moses's tent (e.g., rabbi Rashi on Exod 34:1, in Silber, *Pentateuch With Targum Onkelos and Rashi's Commentary*) since the second set was to be "like the first" (Exod 34:1).

29. Stuart notes that "the ark symbolized God's presence, his purity, his superiority, and his covenant blessing." Stuart, *Exodus*, 569. Hamilton compares the ark of the Sinai Covenant to the cross of the new covenant, without which the respective covenants cannot stand. Hamilton, *Exodus*, 459. Hamilton is mistaken in that he compares the Ark of the Covenant which contained the Ten Commandment, with the cross where the grace of God was manifested in its greatest and most brilliant form. The comparison should rather be between the Mercy Seat which covered the Ark and where blood was spilled, with the cross, grace with grace. Be that as it may, the location of the Ten Commandments within the box indicates their significance and the location of the Book of the Law outside the Ark, its secondary importance.

30. Cassuto, *A Commentary on the Book of Exodus*, 311.

31. Stuart writes, "That worship involved the slaughtering and cooking of meat on the principle of substitutionary atonement (stated simply: 'for me to live, something

Third, once the people have been sprinkled with the blood, their leaders ascend the mountain and there partake of a meal in the presence of God, and though they "see" God, they do not die (24:11), an indication that they are now accepted into the covenant relationship. As the inauguration ceremony nears completion, Moses ascends further into the mountain and receives the tables of the Ten Commandments on the "seventh" day (24:16).[32]

It is important to note the two distinct parts of the covenant. On the one hand are the legal requirements; on the other, the ritual, sacrifice of animals, and sprinkling of the blood. Consent to the former signifies Israel's desire to belong to God; the sacrifice and sprinkling of the blood qualify them to stand before a holy God. It is only once they have been sprinkled with the blood that they can appear in his presence and dine with him. Had either of the two parts been absent, the covenant could not have been put into place.

It is perhaps surprising that at this point, there is no mechanism in place to deal with breaches of the covenant. In Exod 25:1–31:18 are the directions for the construction of the sanctuary. The purpose of the sanctuary is stated in 25:8: "And let them make me a sanctuary, that I may dwell in their midst." Now that Israel is God's people, it is understandable that he would want to dwell in their midst. The sanctuary is to be constructed after a heavenly "pattern" (Exod 25:9).[33] The function of the priesthood is also outlined. The role of the priests will be to serve God there (28:1, 3, 4, 41; 29:1, 44). While the altar of burnt offerings is mentioned (Exod 27:1–9), its purpose is to facilitate the sacrifices for the inaugural ceremony of the priesthood (29:10–21) or for food (30:20) and peace offerings (20:24; 30:28; 31:9). The only sin offering mentioned is for the inaugural ceremony of the priests (29:14, 36) and for annual atonement on behalf of the people (Exod 30:10).[34] Indeed, the penalty for serious breaches of the covenant is

---

must die in my place')." Stuart, *Exodus*, 553–54.

32. "His traveling six days outside the cloud and then entering it may in some manner recall Yahweh's role as the six-day Creator of Genesis 1." Stuart, *Exodus*, 560.

33. On the earthly sanctuary as a copy of a heavenly archetype, see Poniatowski, "Interactions Between Heaven and Earth," 31–42.

34. Stuart writes, "The sacrifice of the bull in this instance appears to have constituted a sort of preparatory 'sin offering,' designed to atone for any unforgiven sin the priests may have previously committed and, as it were, brought with them into their ordination ceremony, as well as any uncleanness or holiness that might have somehow defiled the altar of the tabernacle." Stuart, *Exodus*, 622.

death (Exod 21:12, 14, 15, 16, 17, 23, 29; 22:19, 24) especially for offenses against God (Exod 22:20; 28:35, 43; 30:20, 21).

Soon after the establishment of the covenant, and while Moses is absent, the people make and worship, possibly in immorality,[35] a golden calf in clear and gross breach of the covenant (Exod 32:1–35). As with Abraham, the establishment of the covenant is followed by a breach, much sooner and in a horribly more offensive way this time.[36] In response, three things happen that indicate that the covenant has been rendered invalid. First, God no longer addresses Israel as his people; now, they are Moses's people (32:7, 10; 33:1).[37] God declares their rejection and offers instead to make Moses a great nation (32:10).[38] The focal relational aspect of the covenant that Israel would be God's people is no longer a reality. Second, God announces that Israel deserves the death penalty (32:10, 27, 33, 34–35; 33:5), in harmony with the covenant stipulations, and the sacrifices offered therein. Three thousand die (32:28) but God refrains from further destruction. Third, Moses breaks the tables of stone (32:19) indicating that the covenant is no longer in force. The sum total of Israel's experience with the Sinai Covenant is that she has promptly failed to live up to her promises. This is a point Bible writers repeatedly revisit later.

Despite Israel's failure and after Moses's mediation, God decides to re-establish the covenant and does so in Exod 34. When God remakes the covenant, he does so with a view to Israel's potential future failings. He declares himself to be "merciful and gracious, slow to anger" (34:6), "forgiving iniquity and transgression and sin" (34:7). To Moses's pleading for mercy on behalf of Israel, God promises an unparalleled work of mercy, "an awesome thing" that he will do (34:10), foreshadowing in these words—in

---

35. It is very likely that immorality was involved in the worship of the calf. There is linguistic connection to Gen 26:8 and 39:17 both of which involve sexual activity. Propp notes that "Exod 34:15–16; Deut 7:2–4 and a host of other passages associate apostasy with intermarriage, simultaneously describing cultic infidelity as 'whoring.' ... The defining episode of the fornicaton = apostasy equation is Baal Peor (Numbers 25)." Propp, *Exodus* 19–40, 553.

36. Propp observes that "the people's activities parody the Covenant ratification in chap. 24, which also featured sacrifices and a sacred meal before a visible Deity." Ibid.

37. Hamilton, *Exodus*, 537.

38. Hamilton underlines the severity of the lapse of Israel by noting that this is one of only two occasions when God "is moved to wipe out that entire first generation." Hamilton, *Exodus*, 528. Psalm 106:23 reflects back on this incident and Moses' role as an intercessor: "Therefore he said he would destroy them—had not Moses, his chosen one, stood in the breach before him, to turn away his wrath from destroying them."

Christian interpretation at least—the work of mercy that would be revealed in the sacrifice of Jesus.[39] This text played an important role in Paul's theological outlook and we will revisit it in Chapter 5.

While the covenant of Exod 34 is a remaking of the covenant of Exod 24, there are some differences.[40] First, the new tables of stone are now cut by Moses not God, though they are still inscribed by the finger of God. Second, now it is only Moses who sees God, not the elders of Israel. Indeed, through his time with God, the face of Moses attains a glow to the point where he needs to cover it with a veil when talking to the people (Exod 34:29–35). Third, an elaborate system of sacrifices is set into place so that subsequent breaches of the covenant can be dealt with in a way that will not jeopardize the standing of Israel before God (e.g., Lev 4:2, 3, 13, 27; 5:1, 15, 17; 6:2).

This system of sacrifices is outlined in Lev 1:1—7:38. Five types of offerings are mentioned—burnt, meal, peace, sin, and trespass. Sacrificial offerings were offered from the earliest of times. And indeed the first three offerings were known before.[41] However, Lev 1:1—7:38 is the first time they appear in such a systematic arrangement and their function explained in detail. Moreover, of the five types of offerings, sin offering is not mentioned before Sinai and is only mentioned before the incident of the golden calf in relation to the appointment of priests and Aaron's service in the sanctuary. The trespass offering is not mentioned before the incident of the golden calf.[42] Keil and Delitzsch comment, "The sacrifices treated in chap. i.-iii. are introduced by their names, as though already known, for the purpose of giving them a legal sanction. But in chap. iv. and v. sacrifices are appointed for different offences, which receive their names for the first time from the objects to which they apply . . . a clear proof that the sin and debt

---

39. Frethein, *Exodus*, 307, 308.

40. That is not to say that the remaking of the covenant is half-hearted or incomplete. James K. Bruckner speaks of a "complete resolution to the crisis and a return to the harmony between the Lord's intention and the people's actions." Bruckner, *Exodus*, 3145.

41. E.g., Gen 22:2, 3, 6, 7, 8, 13; Exod 18:12.

42. Alfred Edersheim described the sin and trespass offerings as follows: "*The sin-offering.—* is the most important of all sacrifices. It made atonement for the *person* of the offender, whereas the trespass-offering only atoned for one special offence. Hence sin-offerings were brought on festive occasions for the whole people, but never trespass-offerings (comp. Num 28, 29). In fact, the trespass-offering may be regarded as representing ransom for a special wrong, while the sin-offering symbolised general redemption." Edersheim, *The Temple*, 100–1.

[trespass] offerings were introduced at the same time as the Mosaic law."[43] Keil and Delitzsch are correct in connecting the last two types of offerings with Sinai, but miss the short chronological but important theological gap between the giving of the legal requirements at Sinai before the establishment of the covenant, and the giving of the sacrificial offerings some weeks later after the incident of the golden calf.

Bringing the discussion together, we see a legal and ritual dimension to the Sinai Covenant. The legal is encapsulated in the Ten Commandments and the Book of the Law; the ritual in the initial sacrifice of bulls to establish the covenant and in the elaborate description of the different offerings, part of their purpose being to deal with breaches of the covenant.

THE PROMISE OF A NEW COVENANT

The Sinai Covenant became a defining point in Israel's self-understanding and identity. However, in some of the darker moments of the kingdom prophets looked forward to a time when a new everlasting covenant would be made,[44] associated with the coming of the Messiah.[45] Foremost among such texts stands Jer 31:31–34: "Behold, the days are coming, declares the LORD, when I will make a new covenant with the house of Israel and the house of Judah, not like the covenant that I made with their fathers on the day when I took them by the hand to bring them out of the land of Egypt, my covenant that they broke, though I was their husband, declares the LORD. But this is the covenant that I will make with the house of Israel after those days, declares the LORD: I will put my law within them, and I will write it on their hearts. And I will be their God, and they shall be my people. And no longer shall each one teach his neighbor and each his brother, saying, 'Know the LORD,' for they shall all know me, from the least of them to the greatest, declares the LORD. For I will forgive their iniquity, and I will remember their sin no more."[46] The new covenant promise is quoted twice in the NT (Heb 8:7–12; 10:16–17) and alluded to at least four

---

43. Keil and Delitzsch, *Biblical Commentary on the Old Testament*, 302.

44. See Jer 32:36–41; Ezek 37:19–28; Isa 55:31; 61:8; Ezek 11:19, 28; 36:26, 27.

45. Isaiah 42:6; 49:8.

46. Bruggemann calls this "the best known and most relied upon of all of Jeremiah's promises," while for J. A. Thompson, "one of the deepest insights in the whole OT." Bruggemann, *A Commentary on Jeremiah*, 291; Thompson, *Book of Jeremiah*, 580.

times (Rom 11:27; 2 Cor 3:1–18; Heb 9:15; 12:24), indicating that it played a formative role in the covenantal self-understanding of the early church.[47]

Four points need to be highlighted about this promised new covenant. First, it would be made with the "house of Israel and the house of Judah" (31:31).[48] This affirms what we discussed in the previous chapter, namely, that those who enter the new covenant, covenantly speaking, belong to Israel irrespective of national background. Second, the promised new covenant did not envisage any change to the legal codes of the covenant, apart from a change in location. It would now be written on the hearts of those who enter it (31:33). This is not a new idea. The concept of having the law in the heart is common in the OT (Deut 32:46; Josh 22:5; 2 Kgs 10:31; 2 Chron 31:21; Pss 37:31; 40:8; 119:34; Isa 51:7), though Jeremiah considers that this was not the reality for Israel in his time.[49]

Third, God promised to forgive Israel's iniquity and remember their sin no more (31:34). The incident of the golden calf is alluded to specifically (31:32). Were not sins forgiven under the Sinai Covenant, especially the sin of the golden calf? We cannot be clear on what Jeremiah had in mind when he promised a future forgiveness for sins committed centuries earlier.[50] But we do know how Christians understood this promise. Hebrews declares that the sins of the Old (Sinai) Covenant, including presumably the sin of the golden calf, were forgiven not under the system of sacrifices

---

47. Thompson notes that it was not only foundational in the covenantal understanding of the early church but also of the Essenes. Thompson, *Book of Jeremiah*, 580.

48. Ibid. The fact that the covenant was to be made with both Israel and Judah is peculiar. At the time of Jeremiah, Israel had already been in captivity for a number of centuries and from this captivity she never really returned. Thompson suggests that Jeremiah anticipated the restoration of both Israel and Judah. More likely, Israel and Judah stands for the totality of God's people and should not be understood simply in ethnic terms. Ibid., 578. L. Allen compares with the 31:33 occurrence which he terms, "theocratic term" with a "wider sense." L. Allen, *Jeremiah*, 356.

49. In Jeremiah, the writing of the law on the heart contrasts with the writing of sin on the heart (Jer 17:1) which seemed to have been Israel's experience (see L. Allen, *Jeremiah*, 356). The changing of the heart from one in which sin is written to one in which the law of God is written is nothing short of "miraculous transformation" (L. Allen, *Jeremiah*, 356), and a promise that will reach absolute fulfillment in the age to come.

50. Jack R. Lundbom, rather surprisingly in my view, holds that "forgiveness of sins is not what undergirded the Sinai covenant; in fact, it played no part at all in that covenant's earliest formulation or in the formulation of Deuteronomy (Exod 32:32–34; Deut 31:16–29);" though Lundobom seems to operate on historical critical considerations overlooking Moses's intervention and God's self-declaration as a merciful God which he probably considers secondary. Lundbom, *Jeremiah 21–36*, 470–71.

of the Sinai Covenant but through the sacrifice of Jesus: "For it is impossible for the blood of bulls and goats to take away sins" (Heb 10:4; cf. 10:11); "Therefore he [Jesus] is the mediator of a new covenant . . . since a death has occurred that redeems them from the transgressions committed under the first covenant" (Heb 9:15). While the importance of Hebrews might be secondary in understanding Jeremiah, it is foundational in understanding early Christian theology.

Fourth, the reason why a new covenant was necessary was because Israel broke the first covenant (Jer 31:32; cf. Heb 8:8). If humanity had the capacity to remain faithful to the covenant, there would have been no sin and no need for sacrifice. It is sinful human nature that produces sinful acts and necessitates sacrifice; the sacrifices of animals in the case of the Sinai Covenant. Paul touches on this point in Galatians, as we will see in Chapter 5.

PAUL AND THE COVENANTS

Having discussed the concept of covenant in the OT, we now come to the NT and more specifically to Paul. The most detailed and clearest exposition of the new covenant appears in Hebrews. But since its authorship is not confirmed Pauline, we will not go into it at length. It will be, nonetheless, insightful to highlight some of the main points of Hebrews as it helps establish a background, a theological context that existed in early Christian thought. In Chapter 4, we will return to Hebrews but for different reasons.

The Sinai Covenant (a) was established with Israel, (b) on the basis of the blood of sacrifices, (c) had law, (d) had priesthood, (e) had a tabernacle, and (f) had an ark of the covenant where the tables of stone were deposited. According to Hebrews, the new covenant is likewise: (a) established with Israel (Heb 8:8); (b) on the basis of the blood of the sacrifice of Jesus (e.g., Heb 9:7, 12–25; 10:29); (c) has law (Heb 8:10; 10:16); (d) has priesthood in Jesus (Heb 5:1–10);[51] (e) has a tabernacle in heaven of which the earthly was a copy (Heb 8:2, 5; 9:11);[52] and (f) has an ark of the covenant (Heb 8:5; Rev 11:19). Indeed, the appearance of the heavenly ark of the covenant in Rev 11:19 is accompanied by signs reminiscent of the theophany at Sinai.[53]

---

51. Tholuck, *The Epistle to the Hebrews*, 294–301. Ellingworth, *The Epistle to the Hebrews*, 398–400.

52. Ellingworth, *Hebrews*, 400–3.

53. Witherington, *Revelation*, 160. George E. Ladd rather surprisingly misses the

It is immediately clear that the concepts of tabernacle/temple and their sacrificial ritual that played a prominent role in the Sinai Covenant, do so likewise in the new covenant but on a whole different level.

Paul discusses directly the Sinai Covenant and its relation to the new covenant in three passages: 1 Cor 11:25, 2 Cor 3:1–18, and Gal 4:21–31. Of the three, Gal 4:21–31 will be discussed in Chapter 5 so I will withhold comments at this stage. Paul also discusses directly the Abrahamic Covenant in Gal 3:13–17. In all these, the ritual dimension is evident. He also touches on both covenants in Rom 9:4 and Eph 2:11–13. Clearly the concept of covenant spans other pericopes too, but we will focus on these where the word "covenant" appears directly.

1 Corinthians 11:25

The ritual dimension is most evident in 1 Cor 11:25: "In the same way also he took the cup, after supper, saying, 'This cup is the new covenant in my blood. Do this, as often as you drink it, in remembrance of me.'"

First Corinthians 11:25 describes the inauguration of the new covenant during the Last Supper, shortly before Jesus died on the cross. The phrase "this cup is the new covenant in my blood" draws directly from Exod 24:8, the inauguration formula of the Sinai Covenant.[54] This phrase became extremely important in early Christian covenant theology as evident from the fact that it appears also in Matt 26:28, Mark 14:24, Luke 22:20, Heb 9:20, 10:29, and 13:20. Let us look at these occurrences:

"Behold the blood of the covenant" (Exod 24:8).

"For this is my blood of the covenant" (Matt 26:28).

"This is my blood of the covenant" (Mark 14:24).

"This cup that is poured out for you is the new covenant in my blood" (Luke 22:20).

"This cup is the new covenant in my blood" (1 Cor 11:25).

"This is the blood of the covenant" (Heb 9:20).

---

significance of the appearance of the heavenly temple, the ark of the covenant, and even the manifestations in nature, and sees in the depiction of Rev 11:19 simple symbolism that the way to God is now open to all people. Ladd, *A Commentary on the Revelation of John*.

54. Fitzmyer notes that Mark is the closest to Exod 24:8. Fitzmyer, *First Corinthians*, 442.

"The blood of the covenant" (Heb 10:29).

"The blood of the eternal covenant" (Heb 13:20).

The first five NT texts listed above reference the words of Jesus at the Last Supper; the last two speak of the blood of the covenant in other contexts. As can be seen Matthew, Mark, and Hebrews follow closer the wording of Exod 24:8 and lack the adjective "new." Luke and Paul contain not only the adjective but a mention of the cup.

Three points need to be highlighted here. First, and most obviously, great importance is attached to blood in the context of covenant. Blood means sacrifice. It confirms the assertion that a key dimension of covenant, whether Abrahamic, Sinai, or New, is the ritual aspect.[55] Second in the context of a Passover meal, in the presence of the disciples who are all Jews, Jesus announces the new covenant using the exact phraseology of the inaugural formula of the Sinai Covenant. Clearly, Jesus wanted to draw an immediate parallel between the Sinai Covenant and the New, else the reference to Exod 24:8 is inexplicable. Third, in Greek an articular substantive is always definite.[56] When an articular substantive is followed by a genitive phrase, "the entire expression often suggests a monadic notion."[57] Thus, the phrase τὸ αἷμα τῆς διαθήκης (Exod 24:8) is monadic. There is only one blood that can inaugurate the covenant. In Exod 24:8, the blood in question is the blood of bulls. Likewise, τὸ αἷμά μου τῆς διαθήκης (Matt 26:28 and Mark 14:24) and τὸ αἷμα τῆς διαθήκης (Heb 9:20 and 10:29) are also monadic. In Luke 22:20, 1 Cor 11:25, and Heb 13:20, the monadic use cannot be confirmed by the syntax but is probably also in view since in Christian theology the blood of Jesus is the only one that can establish the covenant.

We have a problem here. Exodus declares that the blood of bulls is the monadic blood of the covenant; Matthew, Mark, and Hebrews state that the blood of Jesus is the monadic blood of the covenant. Who is correct? Both are, of course, in their context. When the Sinai Covenant was initiated, the blood of bulls was the only blood available to initiate the covenant and therefore Moses could use a monadic expression to highlight this reality.

---

55. "Covenants are made through the shedding of blood." Garland, *First Corinthians*, 547.

56. The article in Greek is always definite. It can serve a number of functions and one is to denote a monadic, one of a kind, substantive. A monadic use is frequently in view when the substantive is followed by a genitival adjunct phrase, here, "the blood *of the covenant*." See Wallace, *Greek Grammar Beyond the Basics*, 223–24, emphasis mine.

57. Ibid., 224.

However, now that Jesus is about to be sacrificed, the blood of Jesus replaces the blood of bulls. It now stands as the only blood that can initiate the covenant. The blood of bulls has become redundant. The one monadic blood has given its place to the other.

We need to note that Matthew, Mark, and Hebrews do not refer to an alternative or different covenant. Rather they are referring to "the covenant," a definite expression referring to what had already been established at Sinai. What in essence is portrayed here is that the Sinai Covenant has now reached its fullness in Jesus Christ.[58] The blood of bulls on which it was initiated was shadowy and consequently, the covenant was shadowy. Now the real blood is about to be shed/has been shed, the blood of Jesus, in which case the covenant will also now become a reality in the fullest sense of the term. Garland observes, "The two texts [Ex 24:8 and Jer 31:31–34] are combined in Heb. 9:20 and 10:16–18 to emphasize that Jesus' sacrifice replaces the ineffective blood of bulls and goats."[59] At the cross, shadow has met reality.

There is a further link to the Sinai Covenant. The Sinai Covenant was initiated in the context of a meal where the elders of Israel saw and dined with God. In the Passover meal the disciples, elders in God's Israel (see Chapter 2), likewise see the face of God in the person of Jesus, the Son of God, and dine with Him—a sign of most intimate fellowship.[60]

Luke and Paul differ from Matthew, Mark, and Hebrews in that they include the adjective "new" when speaking of the covenant. The purpose of the adjective is not to detach the Last Supper and crucifixion of Jesus from Sinai; no, that connection is there in the adjusted repetition of the covenant formula of Exod 24:8. The inclusion of the adjective "new" aims to bring into the picture the promise of the new covenant of Jer 31:31–34. Thus, while Matthew, Mark, and Hebrews point back only to Exod 24:8, Luke and Paul accept the Exod 24:8 connection and go a step further by bringing into the picture Jer 31:31–34. Thus for them, the Sinai Covenant, the Jeremiah promise of the new covenant, and the new covenant in Jesus make up one coherent and intertwined whole.[61] What changes from one to the next is the

---

58. "The Pauline prep. phrase *en tō emō haimati*, "in my blood," expresses the mode in which the covenant is ratified." Fitzmyer, *First Corinthians*, 442.

59. Garland, *First Corinthians*, 547.

60. Green, *The Gospel of Luke*, 757–59; Garland, *First Corinthians*, 547.

61. Joel B. Green highlights the importance of the word "remembrance" used in the Last Supper, as a word that ties the past, for present and future benefit, and cites as evidence Num 5:15; 1 Kgs 17:18; Ezek 33:13–16. Green, *Luke*, 762.

blood upon which the covenant is established. No change is envisaged in the legal dimension of the covenant.

2 Corinthians 3:1–18

"And you show that you are a letter from Christ delivered by us, written not with ink but with the Spirit of the living God, not on tablets of stone but on tablets of human hearts" (2 Cor 3:3).

Second Corinthians 3:1–18 is one of the most lengthy and important discussions on the new covenant in the NT outside Hebrews. Several points can be noted. First, Paul's new covenant theology draws heavily on Jer 31:31–34. He uses the phrase, "new covenant" (2 Cor 3:6) as in Jer 31:31 (LXX 38:31); and he speaks about the writing of God's law on the heart (2 Cor 3:2, 3 cf. 3:15), as does Jer 31:33 (LXX 38:33).

Second, Paul envisages covenant law written on the heart. But which law? Paul's discussion on the covenant is initiated it seems in response to some in Corinth who were questioning Paul's authority as an apostle (2 Cor 3:1). Paul responds that the best proof of his apostleship is the changed lives of the believers in Corinth. The key text is 2 Cor 3:2–3: "You yourselves are our letter of recommendation, written on our hearts, to be known and read by all. And you show that you are a letter from Christ delivered by us, written not with ink but with the Spirit of the living God, not on tablets of stone but on tablets of human hearts." The once pagan sinners who now form the membership of the Corinth church, have experienced the transforming power of the Spirit after they believed in Jesus and have the law of God written on their hearts.

The key words that describe the law in question are "tablets of stone," "tablets of human hearts," "Spirit," and "ink." The phrase "tablets of stone" clearly points to the Ten Commandments given to Moses on Mount Sinai.[62] Paul says that what was on the tablets of stone has now been written on the "tablets of human hearts," the hearts of the believers in Corinth, demonstrating that the promise of the new covenant has become a reality. Paul then mentions ink. This harkens back to the Book of the Law, spo-

---

62. Barnett notes the obvious connection to Moses and the Decalogue, but holds that it is the opponents of Paul who evidence continuity with Moses: "By referring to their 'letters of recommendation,' which are '*written . . . in ink*' (3:1, 3), and by adding immediately '*written . . . in tablets of stone*' (3:3), Paul points to the continuity of these ministers with Moses." Barnett, *The Second Epistle to the Corinthians*, 160, emphasis in original. He fails to note that this very Decalogue is written on "tablets of human hearts."

ken by God but written by Moses. The twofold mention of ink and tablets therefore points to the twofold division of the legal pronouncements of the Sinai Covenant: The Ten Commandments and the Book of the Law. These, Paul declares, have been written on the hearts of the believers in Corinth. Paul clearly envisages a fulfilment of the new covenant promise and a continuum between the Sinai Covenant, the prophecy of Jeremiah, and the new covenant; as was the case in 1 Cor 11:25.

Third, the writing of the legal codes on the heart is specifically declared to be the work of the Holy Spirit (2 Cor 3:3, 6, 8, 17, 18; cf. Rom 8:1–5). This work of the Spirit results in a transformed life lived in conformity to the will of God (3:2), from glory to glory (3:18). It is precisely because of this ministration of the Spirit that true new covenant believers exemplify a lifestyle that is in harmony to the laws of the covenant: "But the fruit of the Spirit is love, joy, peace, patience, kindness, goodness, faithfulness, gentleness, self-control; *against such things there is no law*" (Gal 5:22–23, emphasis added). The indwelling Spirit brings freedom (1 Cor 3:17), not from the law as some have superficially suggested,[63] since the law is already written on the heart, but from the bondage of sin from lawless behavior. By contrast, those present at the institution of the Sinai Covenant did not have the law written on their hearts. As such, as soon as Moses was absent on the mountain, they broke the covenant by making the golden calf. The law, written only on tablets of stone, kills—"for the letter kills" (2 Cor 3:6); the law written on the heart through the Spirit becomes a force of life: "but the Spirit gives life" (2 Cor 3:6).

Fourth, Paul contrasts the shadowy nature of the Sinai Covenant with the permanent nature of the new covenant. The Sinai Covenant was a ministration of death (2 Cor 3:6, 7) because since it had no effective sacrifice to deal with the problem of sin, it effectively condemned transgressors to death.[64] By contrast the new covenant, established on the blood of Jesus, offers true forgiveness, a foundation for a true relation to God and therefore

---

63. Laurin, *Second Corinthians*, 68; Donker, *2 Corinthians*, 58; cf. Barnett, *Second Corinthians*, 202–3: "In our view it is a 'freedom' from 'the letter'; 'letter' is the antithesis of 'the Spirit' (v. 6). 'The letter . . . inscribed in stones'—the dispensation of law—is 'a ministry of death.'" Harris, *The Second Epistle to the Corinthians*, 312. Wright equates "freedom" with "boldness in speech." Wright, "Reflected Glory," 139–50.

64. This is a point most commentators fail to grasp. E.g., Alfred Plummer writes, By ministration of death "it means the whole dispensation of the Mosaic Law. The Apostle's main object is to show the superiority of the Christian ministration. This involves disparaging the Jewish ministration, which he does in strong language, because of the mischief done by the Judaizers." Plummer, *The Second Epistle of St. Paul to the Corinthians*, 89.

is a ministration of life (3:6). Indeed, true forgiveness can only be attained through the new covenant (Rom 11:27). The believer can now have full confidence of status before God in Christ (3:4, 12, 18). Incidentally, when Paul discusses the Sinai Covenant vis-à-vis the New in Gal 4:21–31 (to be discussed in Chapter 5), he likewise draws a contrast between the Sinai which leads to slavery (Gal 4:24–25) and the New that leads to freedom (Gal 4:26). The concept of slavery and freedom is given a geographical dimension. The former leads to slavery because it is centered in the earthly Jerusalem (Gal 4:25); the latter to freedom because it is centered in the heavenly Jerusalem (Gal 4:26). What is about these two Jerusalems connected to the covenant? The earthly temple in the earthly with its insufficient offertory ritual; the heavenly sanctuary in the heavenly where Jesus is High Priest and mediates the blood of his own once-and-for-all, all sufficient sacrifice.

Returning to 2 Cor 3:1–18, though shadowy, the Sinai Covenant was nonetheless glorious (3:7, 9, 11). Moses's face glowed so that the Israelites could not behold him (3:7, 13).[65] But this glory was to disappear when the shadow met reality, and the glory of the new covenant would far exceed that of the Sinai Covenant (3:8, 9, 10, 11). Paul makes a word play to highlight the contrast. While in the Sinai Covenant it was Moses who communed with God and was his face only that shone with glory, now every believer can behold "the glory of God" and be "transformed into the same image from one degree of glory to another" (2 Cor 3:18). Such is the impact when shadow meets reality. But alas according to Paul, Jews who read about the Sinai Covenant have a veil over their eyes (3:14) and cannot perceive its shadowy and transient nature and remain within it and therefore in their sins. It is only in Christ that this veil is removed. So just as Moses had a veil because they could not behold his glory, now they have a veil and in turn cannot behold the Christ.

Search as one may but nowhere in 2 Cor 3:1–18 does Paul intimate either the removal of the law from the covenant or its change. If anything, its importance is upgraded as it is relocated from the tablets of stone to the tablets of the heart and it is transformed from being a code that condemns to one of righteousness by the ministration of the Spirit.

This analysis of Paul's discussion of the Sinai Covenant in relation to the New indicates that Paul does not envisage any abrogation of the legal

---

65. There is a well-represented Jewish tradition that the face of Moses shone, as a reflection of the divine glory embedded in his face during the time he spent on the Mountain with God. Cf. Thrall, *The Second Epistle of the Corinthians*, 241–43.

framework of the Sinai Covenant. Rather, he only sees the ineffective ritual of the Sinai replaced by the effective ritual of the sacrifice of Jesus. The difference between the two lies in the ritual, not the law. We now turn to the one pericope where Paul addresses clearly the Abrahamic Covenant.

Galatians 3:13–18

"Christ redeemed us from the curse of the law by becoming a curse for us—for it is written, 'Cursed is everyone who is hanged on a tree'—so that in Christ Jesus the blessing of Abraham might come to the Gentiles, so that we might receive the promised Spirit through faith. To give a human example, brothers: even with a man-made covenant, no one annuls it or adds to it once it has been ratified. Now the promises were made to Abraham and to his offspring. It does not say, 'And to offsprings,' referring to many, but referring to one, 'And to your offspring,' who is Christ. This is what I mean: the law, which came 430 years afterward, does not annul a covenant previously ratified by God, so as to make the promise void. For if the inheritance comes by the law, it no longer comes by promise; but God gave it to Abraham by a promise" (Gal 3:13–18).

We will return to Gal 3 in Chapter 5, when we talk about Paul and the law. In 2 Cor 3:1–18, Paul spoke about the relationship of the new covenant to the Sinai Covenant. Here, he addresses the Abrahamic Covenant. As far as Paul is concerned, the seed promised to Abraham is none other than the Seed, Jesus Christ.[66] And not only Jesus in his gentle and ministering life but primarily in his death on the cross. It is through this death that the "blessing of Abraham" reaches maturity. It is his death on the cross that delivered believers from the "curse of the law," that is, the penalty of the law which rests upon all sinners.[67] As such, Paul can declare that the gospel was preached to Abraham (Gal 3:8) and that the reality Paul was experiencing with the Gentiles coming to faith was already ingrained in the promise to Abraham in Gen 15:22 (Gal 3:8): "And the Scripture, foreseeing that God would justify the Gentiles by faith, preached the gospel beforehand to Abra-

---

66. Fung, *The Epistle to the Galatians*, 155–56: "Paul interprets the 'issue' as a reference to Christ. He is well aware of the collective sense of *sperma* (Greek) or *zera*ʽ (Hebrew) in the Genesis passages; his identification of the 'issue' spoken of in the promise as the Christ of history is not derived from a direct exegesis of the OT texts, but rather from an interpretation of them in the light of the Christ-event." See also Bruce, *The Epistle to the Galatians*, 167.

67. Cf. Fung, *The Epistle to the Galatians*, 148.

ham, saying, 'In you shall all the nations be blessed.'" For Paul therefore, the covenant and promise to Abraham was essentially a promise of deliverance from sin through the sacrifice of Jesus.

Other NT writers also made a connection with the sacrifice of Jesus on the one hand, and the promise to Abraham in Gen 15 and the repetition of the promise in the incident of the near sacrifice of Isaac. For example, Luke 1:68–69, 72–73 notes, "Blessed be the Lord God of Israel, for he has visited and redeemed [λύτρωσιν] his people and has raised up a horn of salvation [σωτηρίας] for us in the house of his servant David . . . to show the mercy promised to our fathers and to remember his holy covenant, the oath that he swore to our father Abraham." Both λύτρωσις[68] and σωτηρία[69] and their cognates have a strong ritual dimension.

Hebrews 6:13–20 also makes a reference to the oath made to Abraham in Gen 22:16–17, and connects it to the priestly ministry of Jesus through which believers have access "into the inner place behind the curtain" (Heb 6:19), in the heavenly sanctuary/temple. In John 8:56, Jesus says that Abraham was able to see his day: "Your father Abraham rejoiced that he would see my day. He saw it and was glad." Other prophets also desired to see though they could not, at least not to the extent Abraham did: "Truly, I say to you, many prophets and righteous people longed to see what you see, and did not see it, and to hear what you hear, and did not hear it" (Matt 13:17). While Jesus does not specify what Abraham saw and what the other prophets could not quite see, the sacrificial death of Jesus on the cross and his victorious resurrection stand at the apex of his life, and the near sacrifice of Isaac is the only instance in which Abraham prophesied of the future that God would provide.[70] Therefore, what Abraham saw by faith was nothing less than the sacrifice of Jesus.[71]

We see therefore that the covenant with Abraham in Gen 15 for both Paul and other NT writers is essentially a promise that God would deal with

---

68. E.g., Luke 24:21; Acts 7:35; Titus 2:14; Heb 9:12; 1 Pet 1:18–19.

69. E.g., Matt 1:21; Mark 16:8; Luke 1:77; John 3:17; 12:47; Acts 4:12; Rom 1:16; 5:9–10; 10:9, 13; 2 Cor 2:15; Eph 1:13; Phil 1:28; 2 Tim 2:10; 3:15; Heb 2:10; 9:28; 1 Pet 1:10; Rev 7:10.

70. In Jewish thought, Abraham's foresight into the future was one of his more characteristic abilities. See for example the discussion in Morris, *The Gospel According to John*, 418; Beasley-Murray, *John*, 138–39. Leon Morris is of the opinion that this "prophecy" of Abraham referred to "the whole of Christ's work." Morris, *The Gospel According to John*, 418.

71. Bruce, *The Gospel of John*, 200–7.

the problem of human sin through the death and resurrection of Jesus. In discussing it, Paul is primarily concerned with the ritual dimension of the covenant, the role of sacrifice. The Abrahamic covenant was, as far as Paul is concerned, still valid and believers in Jesus as the heirs.

Having looked at how Paul deals with the Sinai Covenant and the Abrahamic Covenant, we now turn to two texts that deal with "covenants" in the plural.

Romans 9:4

"They are Israelites, and to them belong the adoption, the glory, the covenants, the giving of the law, the worship, and the promises" (Rom 9:4).

We now move to a text that on first sight appears to offer little but on closer scrutiny can make an important contribution to Pauline new covenant understanding. Romans 9:4 appears in the context of Paul's prolonged entreaty on behalf of his fellow Israelites (9:1–11:36). Paul is careful to highlight both the positive aspects in Judaism,[72] as well as Israel's failure to exercise faith in Jesus.[73] Romans 9:4 belongs to the former.

Three important points need to be made here. First, Paul describes Israel as the recipient of the covenants, in the plural (9:4). The obvious question is, which covenants? The use of an articular plural implies that Paul does not have one specific covenant in mind, or a select plural, but rather the totality of covenants given to Israel.[74] These covenants must still be valid in equal measure to the other substantives mentioned in the text. Furthermore, the Abrahamic and Sinai Covenants must be included in the articular plural and be of relevance to his audience, the mostly Gentile

---

72. Robinson, *Studies in Romans*. Ernst Käsemann points to the use of "Israelites" in 9:4 in contrast to "Jews" earlier, and this "establishes a link to the . . . [fathers], the patriarchs as the bearers of the promise." Käsemann, *Commentary on Romans*. Similarly, Luke Timothy Johnson considers "Jews" as an ethnic category and Israel as a religious entity. Johnson, *Reading Romans*, 155–56.

73. Sanday and Headlam, *The Epistle to the Romans*, 229–31.

74. Douglas J. Moo writes, "Paul's use of the plural 'covenants' is unusual, the singular being much more frequent in both OT and NT. He could be referring to (1) the covenants with Abraham and the other patriarchs, (2) the several ratifications of the Mosaic covenant, (3) the several covenants mentioned throughout the OT (with Noah, Abraham, the people of Israel at Sinai, and David [e.g., 2 Sam. 23:5]), or (4) all the biblical covenants, including the New Covenant (Jer. 31:31–34; cf. 11:26–27)." Moo, *The Epistle to the Romans*, 563. Moo opts for the third option, though the new covenant should not be excluded.

Paul and the Covenant

church in Rome. Also the promised new covenant. It would not help Paul's argument to point to Israel as the recipient of covenants if the covenants were now obsolete, or the covenants were irrelevant to the audience he is addressing.

While Paul is here addressing primarily historical biblical Israel whence the covenants originated, within the context of Rom 9-11 they apply to Christians. This thought is augmented by several statements that follow. In 9:6, Paul declares that not all Israel is Israel. The implication is that those who fail to exercise faith in Jesus are not Israel; but those who do exercise faith are. In 9:27, he adds that of the multitude of Israelites only a remnant will be saved. In 11:3-4, he compares those who have not believed in Jesus to the Israelites who worshipped Baal, while those who have believed to the 7,000 who had not bowed to Baal. Finally, in the parable of the olive tree (11:16-23) discussed in Chapter 2, believers in Jesus constitute the living branches of the olive tree which represents Israel. We see therefore that all the covenants find true meaning in Jesus and his community of faith, a true Israel. The Abrahamic and Sinai Covenants are not antagonistic to the New, but the shadows that have reached fulfilment. The whole package describes the totality of God's interaction with his people.

Three other words are also worth pointing out from Rom 9:4. The first is υἱοθεσία, "adoption" and it also came through Israel. This noun is only used by Paul in the NT and only appears in four other texts (Rom 8:15, 23; Gal 4:5; Eph 1:5), in all of which believers are being adopted into the family of God. Though adoption was given to Israel,[75] according to Gal 4:5 only through the sacrifice of Jesus can it become a reality. This confirms the suggestion that the sacrifice of Jesus and the covenant he established bring to the fullness rather than nullify the faith of Israel.

The second word is νομοθεσία, "legislation" or "giving of law,"[76] which also came through Israel. The word appears only here and is particularly implying a specific legal corpus, the corpus of Israel at the heart of which were the Ten Commandments. Paul ties νομοθεσία to διαθῆκαι, covenants,

---

75. Moo notes the difficulty in that Paul uses "adoption" both of Israel and of believers in Jesus. Moo, *Romans*, 293. He explores but rightly dismisses the option that "adoption" as a "national blessing that does not confer salvation," and suggests a tension between the promises to Israel and the blessings to the church. The tension disappears if we understand the church as a continuation of Israel.

76. Fitzmyer observes that "the Greek noun *nomothesia* could mean either the active giving or promulgation of the law or passively the collection of laws." Fitzmyer, *Romans*, 545-47. He is of the opinion that the second view is valid here.

and views both in a positive light. They both form part of the legacy Israel has given to the people of faith.

The third word is ἐπαγγελίαι, "the promises." Paul ties ἐπαγγελίαι to salvation in Jesus and consistently presents them as an OT concept manifested to the fathers, especially Abraham (Rom 4:13–21; 9:7–9; 15:8; Gal 3:16–22, 29; 4:23, 28). In Rom 9:4, it appears in parallel to law and covenant suggesting that rather than being antagonistic the concepts are complementary.

Bringing together the discussion on Rom 9:4, we noted that Paul ties together in a harmonious whole the concepts of covenants, giving of law, adoption, and promises and declares that they all came through Israel. They exist harmoniously and not in an antagonistic relation. Furthermore, in his discussion of Israel, we noted that Paul does not view the faith of Israel as problematic. Rather those Israelites who have failed to see in Jesus the fulfillment of their heritage have been broken off because of their unbelief. The Gentiles who believe do not depart from the faith of Israel and the covenants; they join them by faith. In light of such a context, it would be futile to speak of a radical break between the new covenant and OT precedents.

Ephesians 2:11–13

"Therefore remember that at one time you Gentiles in the flesh, called 'the uncircumcision' by what is called the circumcision, which is made in the flesh by hands—remember that you were at that time separated from Christ, alienated from the commonwealth of Israel and strangers to the covenants of promise, having no hope and without God in the world. But now in Christ Jesus you who once were far off have been brought near by the blood of Christ" (Eph 2:11–13).

In Chapter 2, we noticed who Eph 2:11–22 defined believes as citizens of Jerusalem. Now we will address the concept of covenant. Before the Ephesians came to Christ they were "strangers to the covenants of promise" because they were not Israelites, they were pagans.[77] Paul again uses the

---

77. Bruce, *The Epistles*, 293–94: "The covenants with the patriarchs, which held out the promise of great blessing for them and their posterity, did indeed make mention of 'all the nations of the earth' as somehow involved in that blessing; but not until the coming of Christ and the free proclamation of the gospel could believing Gentiles, without first becoming Jews, 'be blessed with believing Abraham' (Gal. 3:9)." Frederick F. Bruce fails to note the implication that by believing in Christ, Gentiles do become part of Israel. Markus Barth writes, "As long as the Gentiles lacked historic communion, e.g. with

plural term "covenants," this time augmenting it with the genitive "of promise." The plural, as in Rom 9:4, again probably implies all the covenants of Israel since even the Sinai Covenant entailed a promise that one day God would do a might work of forgiveness (Exod 34:10), as well as the reiteration of the promise that Israel would be God's chosen people. To these covenants, Abrahamic, Sinai, and everything else included in the covenantal framework of Israel, the pagans were strangers. "But now," νυνὶ δὲ, declares Paul, this is no longer the case. By believing in Jesus as their Savior and Lord, pagans have inherited all these covenants. And by doing so, they now have hope in the world. And all this is possible "by the blood of Christ." All covenants become a reality by the blood of Christ, highlighting the ritual dimension of covenant.

CONCLUSION

We have perused a number of texts. Several things can be said as a conclusion. First, a key element of all OT covenants was sacrifice and blood. We saw ritual in the slaying and/or cutting in two of animals in the Abrahamic Covenant of Gen 15, the sacrifice of bulls in the Sinai Covenant of Exod 24, in the system of sacrifices detailed after the re-establishment of the Sinai Covenant in Exod 34, and even in the circumcision of Gen 17. While this ritual reality is generally recognized, it is not often brought to bear on Pauline covenant theology. Second, NT writers in general and Paul in particular highlight the insufficiency of the ritual dimension of all OT covenants and present the reality that the sacrifice and blood of Jesus is the only one that can truly establish the covenants. We saw this in the new covenant formula pronounced in the Last Supper, in Paul's discussion of the new covenant in 2 Cor 3:1–18, his discussion of the Abrahamic in Gal 3:13–18, and also in Eph 2:11–13. Third, we saw that for Paul there is no dichotomy between the Abrahamic and Sinai Covenants, or between these covenants and the new covenant. The New is the fulfilment of the previous, this time on a proper ritual foundation: the blood of Jesus. The whole covenantal framework of Israel is one of harmony, no dichotomy. Believers in Jesus, who are members of a true Israel, inherit the whole framework. We saw this in Rom 9:4 and Eph 2:11–13. Fourth, at no point in any of the discussions of covenant examined is there any hint or suggestion about a change of the

---

Israel's anointed priests, kings, prophets, they were deprived of communion with the Messiah to come." Barth, *Ephesians*, 256.

legal framework of Israel, apart from the relocation from tablets of stone to tablets of the heart, something that had already been promised in the OT. Quite the contrary, 2 Cor 3:1–18 accepts the complete legal framework of Israel as God's gift to Christians through the ministry of the Holy Spirit. The only thing removed is the shadowy ritual dimension of OT covenants.

It is clear that neither the different Reformation nor the New Perspectives fully understand and acknowledge this covenant reality. Moreover, it is evident that the antinomianism of such perspectives stands on shaky ground.

4

Paul and the Law
The Ritual Dimension of Law
Part I—Establishing a Historical Context

Thesis Statement—The transition from the Biblical Hebrew faith to Christianity entailed a transition in ritual from animal sacrifices, an earthly priesthood and an earthly temple, to one without any direct earthly counterpart. This transition was neither easy nor accomplished quickly but became the source of considerable friction in the early church.

We now come to the core of this study. The key issue concerning which all perspectives on Paul hinge is his relation to biblical law. It was Luther's despondency at the inadequacy of rules and regulations to offer peace and an assurance of forgiveness that opened his eyes to the biblical truth of salvation as a free gift, and launched the Reformation. It is a different viewpoint on the kind of "law" Paul is attacking in his Epistles, namely, the boundary markers that is the driving force behind the New Perspective. And it is on this very point that I beg to differ from both schools of interpretation.

To begin to understand what is at stake, we need to remind ourselves of two things every student of the NT knows but which, very strangely, are rarely brought to bear on discussions of Pauline theology. The first concerns temple and ritual. Every ancient pagan religion (at least to my knowledge) had temples, priesthood, and ritual. This was certainly true of the Greco-Roman and Near Eastern religions that provide the milieu against which both Judaism and Christianity operated. Greco-Roman religion had the Olympian list of twelve gods with a multitude of other lesser deities, demigods, and deified heroes making up an extensive and variegated pantheon. Cities and towns had each a protector god or goddess, complete with temple, altars, priesthood, religious festivals, and rituals. Cities would also have the whole ritual gamut for other secondary deities. Characteristic is the situation Paul meets in Athens: "Now while Paul was waiting for them at Athens, his spirit was provoked within him as he saw that the city was full of idols" (Acts 17:16). When Paul addresses the Areopagus, he mentions this very point: "Men of Athens, I perceive that in every way you are very religious. For as I passed along and observed the objects of your worship, I found also an altar with this inscription, 'To the unknown god.' What therefore you worship as unknown, this I proclaim to you" (Acts 17:22–23). Evidently, the Athenians had altars and idols to many deities. Lest perchance they forget any deity, they had an altar dedicated to the "unknown god."[1] What is important here is that for the ancient Athenians, worship of a deity involved an altar and ritual offering. Pagan religious worship was based on offering, sacrifice, and ritual.[2]

Judaism stood apart from other ancient religions in that Jews believed in only one God. Judaism is also different in that whereas altars and temples to pagan deities could be built anywhere and in any number, in Judaism there was only one legitimate temple, and it could only exist in Jerusalem.[3] Sacrifice could only be offered in the Jerusalem temple.[4] While priests could

---

1. Kistemaker and Hendriksen, *New Testament Commentary*, 631: "He commends the Athenians for their thoughtfulness in constructing an altar even to a deity of whom they have no knowledge. In other words, they have expended efforts not to offend even an unknown deity." Hans Conzelmann questions the very existence of such an inscription and proposes instead, with Jerome: "In actuality, the altar inscription read 'to the unknown, foreign gods of Asia, Europe and Africa,' not 'to the unknown god.'" Conzelmann, *Acts of the Apostles*, 140–41.

2. Koester, *Introduction to the New Testament*, 156–62.

3. Friedman, "Tabernacle," 293: "During the journey from Mt. Sinai to the promised land, the Tabernacle is disassembled and transported whenever the people travel, and it is erected again whenever they stop to camp." Once in the promised land, the tabernacle is located first at Shiloh (Josh 18:1; 19:51), then at Gibeon (1 Chron 16:39), and eventually in Jerusalem.

4. History records the possibility of another temple on the small island of Elephantine,

live in other towns and villages, they could officially officiate only in Jerusalem. Even sects like the Essenes who looked upon the Jerusalem temple with ambivalence, looked forward not to another temple elsewhere, but to the restitution and cleansing of the temple in Jerusalem.[5] It was in consequence of this outlook that great multitudes thronged to Jerusalem during the three annual pilgrim feasts—Passover, Pentecost, and Tabernacles—as well as on other occasions like the Day of Atonement.[6] Not only Jews but also proselytes from other religions and nations, as well as sympathizers to Judaism, would visit Jerusalem on such occasions.[7]

---

in southern Egypt. When the Persians conquered Egypt in the sixth century BC, they established a military colony on the island of Elephantine—in the south of the country, close to the first cataract—to defend from intruders from the south. Part of the colony consisted of Jewish mercenaries, some of whose correspondence has survived on papyri. The papyri mention a Jewish temple at Elephantine. This temple, however, is not mentioned in any of the other ancient sources. Recent archaeological excavations have discovered a small building that could be the "temple" of the papyri. What exactly it was and how it functioned, and whether sacrifices and other rituals were performed there remains uncertain. Stephen R. Rosenberg notes that "no altar was found, but there is literary evidence for animal and, later, cereal sacrifice." Rosenberg, "The Jewish Temple at Elephantine," 6, 4–13. Even if the above story is accurate, it needs to be kept in mind that the Jewish community at Elephantine was very small and on the fringes of the Jewish world, and the temple, would have been of marginal significance, as evidenced by the complete lack of references in the literary sources outside papyri and probably, had it been known by authorities in Jerusalem would have been considered renegade.

5. The literary evidence is somewhat unclear and at times, contradictory. Todd S. Beall and Joan E. Taylor both maintain that the Essenes did participate in the Temple ritual but with more stringent purity rules. The evidence is not conclusive but it is clear that they considered the Jerusalem establishment corrupt. Beall, *Josephus' Description of the Essenes*, 118–19; Taylor, *The Essenes, the Scrolls, and the Dead Sea*, 98. Florentino Garcia Martinez writes, "These two statements [by Josephus that the Essenes sent their offerings to the temple but sacrificed at Qumran, and by Philo that they completely rejected sacrifices] are difficult to reconcile with each other, but they testify to the Essene rejection of the Temple and of the worship carried out there. The Qumran manuscripts show us this same rejection and also provide us with enough data to understand the reasons for this stance and to find its origins in the concept of the eschatological Temple of apocalyptic tradition." Martinez, *The People of the Dead Sea Scrolls*, 90; Green et al., *Dictionary of Jesus and the Gospels*, 815.

6. See for example, Stubbs, *Numbers*, 99–104.

7. Bruce mentions "an impressive roll call of the nations so represented." Bruce, *The Book of the Acts*, 55. Fitzmyer likewise states, "Luke uses such a list to show the wide areas from which diaspora Jews have come to Jerusalem for the feast and for the initial apostolic proclamation of the Christian gospel: from Asia, Asia Minor, and northeast Africa, but also (strangely) from Rome." Fitzmyer, *The Acts of the Apostles*, 240; Porter and Evans, *Dictionary of New Testament Background*, "Temple."

In light of this, we can say confidently that first century Judaism was a much more temple-focused religion than any of the pagan religions around it; not because it had more temples, it did not but because its one temple, by the very virtue that it was only one, held a much more pronounced position in the religious outlook of the Jews than a pagan temple would hold in the outlook of pagans. After all, if a pagan temple was desecrated or destroyed, another could be built elsewhere. Jews did not have this possibility. First century Judaism was, therefore, the temple religion *par excellence* of the ancient world. This I believe, most students of the NT are aware of.

Fast forward to Christianity. It too had a temple, of sorts. The body of believers is repeatedly referred to as a "temple" (e.g., 1 Cor 3:16–17; 6:19; 2 Cor 6:16; Eph 2:21; Heb 3:6; 1 Pet 2:5), and reference to a heavenly temple archetype is also evident (e.g., Heb 8:2, 5; 9:11; 1 Pet 4:17; Rev 7:15; 11:19; 14:15; 15:5–8; 16:1, 17).[8] But as far as physical architectural realities on earth are concerned, it is fair to say that Christianity was the first ancient religion not to have a temple or temples. The same goes for priesthood and sacrifice.[9] Christianity had both. Jesus is presented as a High Priest (e.g., Heb 2:17; 3:1; 4:14–15; 5:5–10; 6:20; 7:26–28; 8:1; 9:11; Rev 1:12–20) and his death on the cross is repeatedly presented as a sacrifice (e.g., John 1:29, 36; Acts 8:32; Rev 5:6, 8, 12, 13; 6:1, 16; 7:9, 10, 14, 17; 12:11; 13:8; 14:1, 4, 10; 15:3; 17:14; 19:7, 9; 21:9, 14, 22, 23, 27; 22:1, 3). But again, Jesus's High Priesthood is in heaven and his sacrifice was not an experiential reality repeated daily, as in the Jewish temple or at regular intervals, but a once and for all sacrifice: "Christ, having been offered once to bear the sins of many, will appear a second time, not to deal with sin but to save those who are eagerly waiting for him" (Heb 9:28). Moreover, the sacrificial dimension of the death of Jesus is a theological reality; there was nothing inherently sacrificial in death on a cross.[10] As far as ceremonial temple ritual on earth is concerned, Christianity had none.

The transition from Judaism to Christianity therefore in terms of the ritual dimension was of gargantuan proportions. It was a transition from the temple/ritual religion *par excellence* of the ancient world, to the first ever religion without a visible temple, priesthood, or ritual. Literally, the pendulum swung from the very edge of one side of the spectrum to the

---

8. See Papaioannou and Giantzaklidis, *Earthly Shadows, Heavenly Realities*.
9. Hurtado, *Destroyer of the Gods*, 291.
10. Giantzaklidis, "Introduction," 1.

very opposite end on the other. If one looks at Pauline bibliography, there is next to nothing discussing this transition. Are we to believe that this transition was smooth and painless and that all Christians, especially those of Jewish background, happily, easily, and without hesitation accepted the change and abandoned wholescale the Jerusalem temple and its ritual? Or could it be that this transition was anything but painless and easy, and that we somehow have failed to notice the pain entailed?

Would it not be strange if there was intense friction about whether Gentile converts to Christianity should be circumcised or not (e.g., Acts 15:1, 5; 21:21; 1 Cor 7:18; Gal 2:3; 5:2–3; 6:12–13; Col 2:11) or whether one should eat meat with its blood or not (e.g., Acts 15:20, 29: 21:25) but that Jewish Christians accepted the redundancy of the Jerusalem temple and all it represented nonchalantly? The very suggestion sounds absurd! Yet if one peruses current bibliography, one will find much more about circumcision, food laws, and the like and next to nothing about the transition from a temple-focused faith system to one without an earthly temple.

If the transition was painful, why has it been missed? The answer is semantics and brings us to the second thing every NT student knows, but is strangely overlooked in discussions of Pauline theology. It centers on the Greek word νόμος, "law." In English and other Indo-European languages, the word "law" denotes primarily a legal code.[11] However in the NT, the word νόμος represents primarily Torah, the Pentateuch, or by extension any of its constituent parts.[12] The Pentateuch contains not only legal codes, but also historical narrative, exhortation, and very importantly for this study, a detailed ritual system that was to be practiced in the tabernacle and eventually the temple. Which of the two meanings should we apply to the word νόμος in Pauline writings: the contextually accurate Torah or the one that is most familiar to us modern Christians, a legal code? The answer we give is extremely important in understanding Pauline theology.

---

11. For example, the *Oxford Dictionaries* online gives the following four definitions for "law": (1) "The system of rules which a particular country or community recognizes as regulating the actions of its members and which it may enforce by the imposition of penalties." (2) "A rule defining correct procedure or behaviour in a sport." (3) "A statement of fact, deduced from observation, to the effect that a particular natural or scientific phenomenon always occurs if certain conditions are present." (4) "The body of divine commandments as expressed in the Bible or other religious texts." *English: Oxford Living Dictionaries*, "Law."

12. See LSJ, s.v. νόμος.

Consider Gal 2:16 as an introductory example. Below is one of the standard English translations (ESV), and an adjusted one offered by me, giving νόμος the meaning it had in Paul's time:

"We know that a person is not justified by works of *the law* but through faith in Jesus Christ (Gal 2:16).

"We know that a person is not justified by works of *the Torah* but through faith in Jesus Christ" (Gal 2:16, adjusted translation).

It sounds very different does it not? We read it with our modern mindset and modern understanding of the word "law" and automatically conclude that Paul is referring to people who were trying to earn their salvation through obedience to a legal code. But if we read it with a first century mindset, the possibilities suddenly broaden out. Paul could have a number of things in mind when he refers to Law/Torah, and not necessary a legal code. Modern scholarship has failed to put two and two together. We read an ancient word with a very well-known and recognized ancient meaning, but when it comes to exegesis unwittingly and by the force of habit apply to it our modern understanding and voila, Paul has become an antinomian.

I believe both the Reformation and the New Perspective understandings of Paul and the law are skewed because of this semantic mishap. What I intend to do in these last two and most important chapters of this study is to attempt to set the record, if not straight, at least on the road to becoming straight. In this chapter, Chapter 4, we will endeavor to establish a historical context by demonstrating from evidence from within the NT that the transition from a temple-based religion to one without a visible earthly temple was neither easy nor quick. We will see that it caused considerable friction in the early church. Then, in the next and final chapter, Chapter 5, we will see how Paul was most likely addressing this problem in Galatians and other texts that are considered antinomian. In Chapter 4, we will begin with a study in the book of Hebrews because it is the NT that most forcefully exposes this challenge faced by early Christians. Then we will explore two incidents from the look at Acts, plus some *pericopae* from other books. Together, they paint quite a convincing picture.

RITUAL—THE EVIDENCE OF HEBREWS

The most clear and weighty piece of evidence that Christians were still struggling with adherence to the Jerusalem temple and its ritual is the book of Hebrews. The short study below has already appeared in similar format in print,[13] but I am including it here as it underscores the thesis I am endeavoring to demonstrate.

Hebrews, like other Epistles, was written to address a specific problem. What was this problem? One theory is that Hebrews was written in part "to warn Jewish Christians against apostasy to Judaism."[14] In other words, the Epistle is a polemic against falling back into the Jewish faith. Such an assertion is an oversimplification and rather vague. Christianity adopted much of its outlook from Judaism. Which aspects of the Jewish faith was the writer opposed to? The real danger addressed in Hebrews was not a vague apostasy to Judaism but a return to the temple and its sacrificial ritual. The temple had been the central focus of Israel's spiritual existence for fifteen hundred years, ever since Moses first built the tabernacle in the wilderness.

But now, for the writer of Hebrews, new realities had dawned, making such an attraction inappropriate. The death and resurrection of Jesus had called into question the need for the temple ceremonial services. Shadow had met reality, and what had seemed so foundational had now become defunct. Hebrews is not an attempt to prevent Christians from falling back into Judaism; it is an endeavor to wean them away from Israel's ritual context by highlighting the earthly temple's inadequacy[15] and drawing them to Christ's heavenly sanctuary ministry.[16] This is noted by the author himself who declares, "Now the point [κεφάλαιον] in what we are saying is this: we have such a high priest, one who is seated at the right hand of the throne of the Majesty in heaven, a minister in the holy places, in the true tent that the Lord set up, not man" (Heb 8:1–2). The Greek κεφάλαιον literally means "that which belongs to the head,"[17] and has the meaning of "main point" or

---

13. Papaioannou, *Sanctuary, Priesthood, Sacrifice, and Covenant*, 189–203.

14. Wallace, "19. Hebrews: Introduction, Argument, and Outline," under "2. Purpose," para. 1.

15. George W. Buchanan notes the centrality of "Jesus' sacrifice as an atonement offering," in the Epistle. To believers who might be tempted to offer sacrifices, "the author's response was that Jesus' sacrifice was once-for-all." Buchanan, *To the Hebrews*, 266.

16. Stegemann and Stegemann, "Does the Cultic Language?," 14. They note that "no other document of the New Testament seems to make a more comprehensive use of sacrificial metaphors with regard to the death of Jesus than Hebrews." Christian A. Eberhart has mentioned likewise: "The Epistle to the Hebrews is the only writing of the New Testament extensively employing sacrificial images and metaphors." Eberhart, "Characteristics of Sacrificial Metaphors in Hebrews," 37.

17. Buchanan, *To the Hebrews*, 132.

"summary."[18] Ray C. Stedman observes, "The terrible problem which human sin presents can be solved by one, and only one, remedy—the death of Jesus. This is the central theme of the epistle, to which the writer returns many times."[19] The main point the author is developing is the sacrificial and priestly ministry of Jesus in heaven.[20]

The Ritual Context

The inadequacy of the earthly sanctuary system and the superiority of Christ are most fully developed in the central part of Hebrews. But even in the introductory and paraenetic/concluding sections, ritual elements play a prominent role.

For example, the author begins by declaring the superiority of the Son over the prophets. One thing that entitles the Son to sit at the right of the Father is that he has made καθαρισμὸν τῶν ἁμαρτιῶν, "purification for sins" (1:3).[21] The phrase is temple centered[22] and probably draws from Exod 30:10 (cf. Job 7:21), while καθαρισμός is used primarily in ritual contexts (Exod 29:36; 30:10; Lev 14:32; 15:13; 1 Chron 23:28; Neh 12:45; Mark 1:44; Luke 2:22; 5:14; John 2:6).[23] Moreover, Christ is the ἀπαύγασμα, "radiance" or "reflection"[24] of the glory of God (Heb 1:3). The word ἀπαύγασμα is an *hapax legomenon*: it appears only once in the Bible. Δόξα, "glory," of which Christ is the radiance/reflection, is a common word to describe (1) the glory of God as it appeared in the sanctuary (Exod 29:43; 40:34, 35; Lev 9:6, 23; Num 14:10) and (2) other aspects of the sanctuary service

---

18. Cf. LSJ, s.v. κεφάλαιον.

19. Stedman, *Hebrews*, 3.

20. Eberhart, "Characteristics," 60. "This statement [Heb 10:11] prepares the exclusive claim that only Christ's sacrifice is valid." Ibid.

21. Buchanan understands the purification in view to relate to Jesus's own person: "purification for [his] sins." Buchanan, *To the Hebrews*, 8. Variant (and probably later, interpretative) readings stress that purification was for the sins of others, giving an atoning meaning to the sacrifice of Jesus, which Buchanan believes is not in the original. Buchanan is wrong. The use of the verb form *katharizō*, cognate to *katharismon*, is used in Hebrews repeatedly and consistently for the cleansing power of the blood of Jesus (9:14, 22, 23; 10:2).

22. Heil, *Hebrews, Chiastic Structures and Audience Response*, 31. John Paul Heil sees the phrase as signifying the making of expiation.

23. LSJ, s.v. καθαρισμός.

24. LSJ, s.v. ἀπαύγασμα.

(Exod 28:2, 40; 33:5). Ἀπαύγασμα then can be seen as the reflection of God's sanctuary glory.

In his discussion of the superiority of Christ over the angels, the author again uses ritual language. He uses the adjective λειτουργικὰ (1:14) and the noun λειτουργοὺς (1:7) when referring to angels. The adjective appears only here in the NT, but it also appears six times in the LXX—always in a temple-related context (Exod 31:10; 39:12; Num 4:12, 26; 7:5; 2 Chron 24:14). The evidence for the noun is less clear-cut,[25] but the ritual use is still dominant (Ezra 7:24; 10:39 [LXX 40]; Isa 61:6; Heb 8:2). Buchanan observes, "In biblical terms... the word is almost always employed in relationship to the service of the priests in the temple."[26] Hebrews 1:7 is in itself a quotation from Ps 104 (LXX 103), where the heavenly temple is not explicitly mentioned but the heavenly majesty of God is presented in language elsewhere used of the temple. In extra-biblical Jewish writings, angels were often depicted as priests serving in the heavenly realms. In biblical writings such imagery is uncommon, but the heavenly residence of God was understood to be a heavenly temple/sanctuary, making the realm's description in sanctuary and priestly terms not appear out of place.

The paraenesis and conclusion sections also abound with ritual language. The paraenesis begins with the statement, "we have the confidence to enter the holy places by the blood of Jesus" (10:19), where the "holy places" refer to the heavenly sanctuary and the blood of Jesus to his sacrificial offering on the cross. Other references to the heavenly sanctuary include: (1) the veil (10:20); (2) the house of God (10:21); (3) perhaps the heavenly city that the patriarchs awaited (11:10, 16); and (4) the contrast between the presence of God on Mount Sinai (12:18–21), which functioned as a temple of God (Exod 15:13),[27] and the heavenly Mount Zion/Jerusalem (Heb 12:22–24), which is the seat of God's throne. The throne is (1) surrounded

---

25. LSJ, s.v. λειτουργικός. It seems that in secular contexts, the noun implies secular ministry while in religious contexts, ritual ministry is more in view.

26. Buchanan, *To the Hebrews*, 19.

27. Spence-Jones, *Exodus*, 3–4: "By 'God's holy habitation' some understand Mount Sinai, others Canaan, others Mount Moriah, or even the temple there to be built ultimately." That it is a reference to the temple that was built centuries later, some understand it as a prophecy, others as *vaticinium ex eventu*, history in the guise of prophecy. Neither option seems to fit here. The description of the context seems very local with reference to the redemption from Egypt and the impact the events have had on Philistia, so a prophecy about the temple in Jerusalem would seem out of place and detached from the context. Since the presence of God makes a place holy, it would be fair to say that Sinai functioned as a temple of God for as long as God dwelt there.

by innumerable angels (12:22), (2) where the saints have been perfected (12:23), and (3) the locus for the ministration of a new and higher covenant based on the blood of Jesus (12:24).

Clearly, temple ritual not only forms the core argument of the book but also appears in the introduction and paraenesis/conclusion, enveloping the main argument into a sanctuary-ritual context. The problem the author of Hebrews addresses is not a lapse into Judaism, but how Jewish Christians once attached to the Jerusalem temple and its ritual should look away from Jerusalem and towards heaven.

In highlighting the superiority of the heavenly ministry, Hebrews expounds on a number of juxtapositions between the heavenly and earthly realities. The first we will look at is between the heavenly and earthly sanctuaries.

Earthly Sanctuary—Heavenly Sanctuary

The juxtaposition between the earthly and heavenly sanctuaries is developed mostly in Heb 8 and 9. The existence of a heavenly sanctuary is taken for granted. "We have such a high priest, one who is seated at the right hand of the throne of the Majesty in heaven, a minister in the holy places, in the true tent that the Lord set up, not man" (8:1–2).[28] "When Christ appeared as a High Priest of the good things that have come, then through the greater and more perfect tent (not made with hands, that is, not of this creation), he entered once for all into the holy places, not by means of the blood of goats and calves but by means of his own blood, thus securing an eternal redemption"[29] (9:11–12). The author expounds on this, knowing

---

28. Gordon, *Hebrews*, 109. Robert P. Gordon pointedly observes, "The assumption behind v. 2 is that the Jewish sanctuaries were the earthly counterparts of the real and permanent shrine of God in heaven. Seen in this light, the Mosaic tabernacle was only a 'sketch and shadow' of the heavenly archetype (v. 5)." Ibid.

29. Ray C. Stedman is of the opinion that the church is the "true tent" in heaven described in Hebrews. Stedman, *Hebrews*, 33, 50. He admits that this is "difficult" to grasp, and he also admits that an actual heavenly temple is depicted in texts like Rev 4–5. But Stedman affirms that in Hebrews the "true tent" is the church, going so far as to say that "what Moses saw on the mountain was the human person as we are meant to be" (p. 54). Stedman's approach is too farfetched. It is true that temple language is at times applied to the church (1 Cor 3:16–17; 6:19; 2 Cor 6:16; Eph 2:21; 2 Thess 2:4; Rev 3:12). A "temple" is the dwelling place of deity and since God dwells among his people, the church constitutes a type of temple. But such usage is only metaphorical and secondary. The Father and the Son's true dwelling place is in heaven, and their heavenly habitation is the

that his readers are aware of its existence and at least partly cognizant of its significance.

The heavenly sanctuary was not built with human hands (οὐ χειροποιήτου) but by the Lord and therefore is "not of this creation" (9:11). By contrast, the earthly was built by man (8:2; 9:24). As such, the heavenly is "greater and more perfect" (9:11).

The heavenly is called τῆς σκηνῆς τῆς ἀληθινῆς, "the true tent" (8:2).[30] When an articular noun is qualified by another articular genitive noun, the use is monadic:[31] there is only one true sanctuary—the one in heaven. This implies that the earthly was not true in the fullest sense of the word but was rather a more shadowy and transient reality. Edgar McKnight rightly observes that the contrast is not between a true and a false sanctuary but between what is true (the heavenly) and what was symbolic and imperfect (the earthly).[32]

This thought is enhanced through the use of five words to describe the earthly: ὑπόδειγμα (8:5), σκιά, (8:5), κοσμικόν (9:1), παραβολή (9:9), and ἀντίτυπα (9:24). Ὑπόδειγμα signifies a copy, type, or example. Most English translations prefer to translate it as "copy" (e.g., ESV, NAB, NASB, NIV) because it was built according to the model shown to Moses on Mount Sinai (8:5). "Example" could also serve well, indicating that its function would be of limited duration. Heil sees a negative connotation in "example," since

---

true "temple" or "sanctuary." McKnight, *Hebrews-James*. McKnight refers repeatedly to the heavenly sanctuary but then brings in Plato's dualism, which in turn influenced Philo and (indirectly) Hebrews. "A parallel exists between Philo and Hebrews," McKnight writes. He understands Philo's view (and Hebrews'?) to have been that "the ultimately real counterpart of the earthly temple is found to be a variety of spiritual and ethical realities: wisdom, virtue, the human soul, or the 'powers' of God." McKnight, *Hebrews-James*, 184. However, if the heavenly sanctuary is thus spiritualized, how about the remainder of Hebrews' ritual language—the high priestly ministry of Jesus, his sacrifice, the new covenant? Platonic thought cannot provide a valid framework for understanding the ritual context of Hebrews. Gordon is closer to the truth when he observes, "To the extent that *Hebrews* envisages an actual heavenly sanctuary with a terrestrial counterpart the comparison could be said to lean towards Platonic idealism, but the concept of a heavenly temple is so clearly present in the Old Testament that the author's dependence upon non-biblical categories would require further demonstration." Gordon, *Hebrews*, 111.

30. There seems to be a parallel here with an LXX reading of Num 24:6 where the Lord pitches tents. Gordon notes that this would highlight the heavenly sanctuary's permanence in contrast to that of the earthly. Gordon, *Hebrews*, 109.

31. Wallace, *Greek Grammar Beyond the Basics*, 223–224.

32. McKnight, *Hebrews-James*, 182.

the same word is used of the wilderness generation who failed to show faith (4:11).[33] McKnight observes that the earthly sanctuary being built on the pattern shown to Moses (Exod 25) was a positive connotation because it showed that the sanctuary did not originate in Moses's mind, but in God's. "For Hebrews, the use of Exodus 25 is pejorative. The earthly sanctuary is *only* a shadow of the real sanctuary."[34]

Σκιά signifies a "shadow" and in this context, carries two meanings. The earthly was a shadow because it replicated the heavenly original ("See that you make everything according to the pattern that was shown you on the mountain" [8:5]), just like a shadow is a reflection of a more substantial reality. But the earthly was also a shadow because it was transient.

The concept of the earthly sanctuary as a shadow is not platonic as some have wrongly assumed.[35] Plato did envisage earthly physical realities to be mere shadows of invisible, immaterial, philosophical, and intellectual realities existing in the realm of ideas. But the concept of the sanctuary and its services as shadows of something greater was common in the ancient Near East and thoroughly biblical. Whereas in platonic thought the true realities were immaterial concepts reached by the intellect, for Hebrews the heavenly realities are real and tangible.[36]

Κοσμικόν is an adjective from the noun κόσμος, "world" and signifies that which is of this world. In Titus 2:12, it is used in a negative sense: "worldly desires." In Hebrews, there is no negative moral sense but it signifies the earthly nature of the earthly sanctuary and therefore its imperfection and limitations.

Παραβολή signifies a "parable," "symbol" (e.g., NASB, NJB), "figure" (KJV), or "illustration" (NIV). Παραβολή is a compound word, which literally means "to place something next to something else"[37]—as an illustration, a comparison, or analogy[38]—or "to explain something." In that sense,

---

33. Heil, *Hebrews, Chiastic Structures*, 197: "The negativity of this earthly 'pattern' is implicitly present now as the audience hear about those who offer worship in a mere earthly 'pattern' (*hypodeigmati*) and shadow of the heavenly things (8:5a)."

34. McKnight, *Hebrews-James*, 182.

35. Ibid., 184. He writes, "The use of the term 'shadow' for elements of the material world is Platonic" and cites *The Republic* 7.515 A-B. Similarity of terminology does not imply similarity of outlook. The concept of earthly shadows versus heavenly realities can better be explained within a biblical framework and worldview.

36. See Buchanan, *To the Hebrews*, 134–35.

37. Cf. LSJ, s.v. παραβολή; BDAG, s.v. παραβολή.

38. Heil, *Hebrews, Chiastic Structures*, 223.

the heavenly sanctuary is the original and the earthly was constructed as a parallel illustration to demonstrate on earth how God operates in heaven.

Ἀντίτυπα is a copy, counterpart, or figure pointing to something[39]—a "mere" copy, as Heil puts it.[40] As such, all five words used of the earthly sanctuary highlight its shadowy and transient nature. That five different words are used indicate an effort to underline this transience: the author wants to leave no doubt in the mind of the reader.

Not only the sanctuary but also its apartments and furnishings were modeled after the heavenly. Thus in 8:5, Moses was told to "make everything according to the pattern" shown to him on the mountain (cf. Exod 25:8–27:21).[41]

Given their transient nature, the whole earthly sanctuary and its services were to be of significance only "until the time of reformation [διορθώσεως]" (9:10). They had an expiration date, so to speak. The word διορθώσεως signifies the establishment of a new order.[42] The earthly sanctuary and its services were to be significant until the new order, inaugurated by the sacrifice of Jesus, was established (cf. Dan 9:24).[43]

Earthly Priesthood—Heavenly Priesthood

Sanctuaries require a priestly ministry. Priests from the line of Levi, descendants of Aaron (Heb 5:4; 7:5, 9, 11), served in the earthly. As humans, they

---

39. BDAG, s.v. ἀντίτυπος.

40. Heil, *Hebrews, Chiastic Structures*, 251.

41. "The inclusion of the word 'everything' in the quotation from Exodus underlines the fact that in all respects the tabernacle was derivative from, and subordinate to, the heavenly exemplar." Gordon, *Hebrews*, 111.

42. Cf. BDAG, s.v. διόρθωσις.

43. Buchanan mistakenly understands the "time of reformation" or the "time of making straight" as the end of the present evil age and compares it with Acts 3:21. Buchanan, *To the Hebrews*, 146. But the context is different. Acts 3:21 speaks of Christ's ascension to heaven, where he waits for the time to "restore all the things" as prophesied by the "holy prophets long ago." Hebrews 9:9–10 speaks about the "gift and sacrifices" of the earthly temple service, which "cannot perfect the conscience of the worshipper." These were replaced by the sacrifice of Jesus who, by dying once, secured "eternal redemption" (9:12). So the time of reformation in Hebrews is not the end of the age but the point at which the sacrifice of Christ secured this redemption. Heil describes it as "the time that has now definitively arrived (9:9a) for the audience, as the time in which the old 'first' covenant is being replaced by the new covenant promised by God (8:13)." Heil, *Hebrews, Chiastic Structures*, 226.

Israel, Covenant, Law

were "beset with weakness" (5:2) since they were also sinful and required to offer sacrifices[44] for their own sins just as they did for the rest of the people (5:3). Earthly priests ministered regularly in the Holy Place (9:6), and the high priest could only minister in the Most Holy Place once a year—and not without blood (9:7), lest he die (Lev 16:2).

By contrast, in the heavenly sanctuary, the high priest is no other than Jesus Christ (Heb 2:17). He is merciful and faithful, provides true atonement for sin, and attained this exalted position through his incarnation (2:17), during which he suffered and was tempted like other humans but remained without sin (4:15; 7:26).[45] While human priests were sons of Aaron, Jesus is the Son of God (5:5). And while human high priests barely dared to go into the shadowy, typological throne of God in the earthly sanctuary, Jesus sat next to the real, heavenly throne of God (8:1).

Jesus is a high priest after the order of Melchizedek (5:6, 10; 6:20; 7:11, 15, 17). Space does not permit a full discussion of the significance of this statement, but a key thought is that the Melchizedek priesthood was different and higher than the Levitical because Levi—through his great-grandfather Abraham—paid tithe to Melchizedek, acknowledging his superiority (7:9–10).

Moreover, there is a sense of heavenly origin for this priesthood. The author declares that Melchizedek was "without father or mother or genealogy, having neither beginning of days nor end of life" (7:3). Melchizedek means "king of righteousness" or "justice,"[46] and he was the king of Salem (Gen 14:18). "Salem," depending on how it is pointed, could mean either "completed, paid in full" or "peace,"[47] with the Masoretic text opting for the former and the writer of Hebrews opting for the latter.[48] Some have understood this to mean that Melchizedek was the pre-incarnate Jesus ap-

---

44. The word for "offer," *prospherō*, is used nineteen times in Hebrews. The meaning is to "bring something" but in the LXX and NT, it is often used of gifts and sacrifices in the temple. See Buchanan, *To the Hebrews*, 93–94; Eberhart, "Characteristics," 38; Attridge, *The Epistle to the Hebrews*, 14.

45. Eberhart, "Characteristics," 56: "Hebrews 7 explores the image of Christ as the holy and blameless high priest. As such, he appears in opposition to the human high priest, who is still defiled by sin and will always be so. While the human high priest therefore needs to offer ... many sacrifices *for* himself, Christ has offered *himself* once."

46. See for example, Hamilton, *The Book of Genesis*, 409.

47. Buchanan, *To the Hebrews*, 118.

48. Gordon observes that it was common at the time to understand the place-name *Salem* as denoting "peace." Gordon, *Hebrews*, 100.

pearing to Abraham.[49] Such a theophany is not impossible given that Abraham received a theophany on another occasion when the heavenly visitors stopped by his tent on their way to destroy Sodom and Gomorra (18:1–33). The Genesis account does not provide sufficient evidence to fully identify Melchizedek but from the viewpoint of Hebrews, it is unlikely.

For Hebrews, Melchizedek seems to be a human person. First, he is described as "king of Salem," whereby Salem is more likely to be a toponym rather than a characteristic, even though the writer later renders "king of Salem" as "king of peace" (7:2). Second, Melchizedek "resembled" "the son of God" (7:3), and Jesus was priest in the "likeness" of Melchizedek (7:15). These suggest that the two individuals are not the same but that one is a symbol of the other. Third, Jesus is a priest "after the order of Melchizedek" (5:6, 10; 6:20; 7:11, 17), but he is not Melchizedek. It is not Melchizedek who was to become enthroned in heaven but Jesus as a high priest after the order of Melchizedek. There seems to be a distinction between Melchizedek as a person, and Jesus as a priest in the order of Melchizedek. The promise that a priest would come after the order of Melchizedek had already been given in Ps 110:4 and now in Jesus it finds fulfillment. The statement "without father or mother or genealogy, having neither beginning of days nor end of life" (Heb 7:3), referring to Melchizedek, should therefore not be understood to imply that Melchizedek had no father or mother but rather that he was a symbol of the divine Son who had none.

Not least is the contrast between life and death. Earthly priests are described as "mortal men" (7:8). This compares unfavorably with Christ who "lives" (7:8). The mortality of Levitical priests meant that they had to be replaced whenever they died. So there were many of them: "the former priests were many in number" (7:23; cf. 7:20). By contrast, Christ is alive and lives forever, which means that he can also be a priest forever—a point that Heb 7 repeats five times (7:3, 17, 21, 24, 28).

---

49. E.g., Templeton, *Understanding Genesis*, 210; cf. Kennard, *Messiah Jesus*, 358. In extra-biblical Jewish thinking, there was speculation as to the identity of Melchizedek, with the fragmentary Qumran 11Q13 scroll ascribing him quasi-messianic status. See Gordon, *Hebrews*, 100.

Earthly Sacrifices—
The Sacrifice of Jesus

The earthly sanctuary sacrifices of animals (5:1) were offered daily (5:3; 7:27). Sacrifices were the main task to which priests were appointed (8:3). The blood of sacrifices served also to sprinkle the book of the covenant (9:19), the people of the covenant (9:19), the sanctuary, and its vessels (9:21). Through blood, atonement was made for human sin.[50]

Earthly sacrifices had a problem. Like the sanctuary itself, they were shadowy (10:1).[51] The blood of animals cannot cleanse sin (10:4, 11), and sacrifices being constantly repeated indicated that the problem of sin had not found full resolution (10:1–3).[52] Indeed, since every defilement needs blood to be cleansed (9:22), and the blood of animals cannot cleanse sin, this indicates that earthly sacrifices were only shadows, just like the earthly sanctuary itself.

The sacrifice of Jesus is superior, was offered once, and is sufficient to deal with the problem of sin (9:12). "By a single offering he has perfected for all time those who are being sanctified" (10:14). In light of Jesus's sacrifice, God promises not to remember human sin any longer (10:17). This assurance of forgiveness offers believers the privilege of boldly approaching the throne of God (4:16).

---

50. Gese, "Die Söhne," 95–99. Eberhart pointedly observes that after the inauguration of the covenant in Exod 24, Moses and the elders saw God but did not die because they had been sprinkled with the blood of the covenant. Eberhart, "Characteristics," 41–42. By contrast, Jacob Milgrom has argued that the aim of sacrifices was to cleanse not personal sin but the defilement brought upon the sanctuary. The views are not mutually exclusive. Blood cleansed individual, corporate, and sanctuary sin in the sense that human sin defiles the sanctuary where humans entered and ministered. Milgrom, *Leviticus 1–16*, 254.

51. Gordon, *Hebrews*, 128. Gordon correctly notes a parallel with Col 2:17 (both of which share a ritual framework) but draws a wrong conclusion when he states that "the Old Testament system of law was founded on the Levitical priesthood the failure of the latter, which the writer sought to demonstrate in ch. 9, would have implications for the whole superstructure" and it is therefore a "shadow." Gordon is right in that in Hebrews, Israel's temple ritual is seen as a shadow. However, her moral, legal framework, as exemplified in the Ten Commandments, continues unaffected and indeed strengthened (Heb 8:10–11).

52. Buchanan notes that Hebrews ties the concept of perfection to sacrifices. "The law ... can never ... make perfect those who offer sacrifices" (Heb 10:1; cf. 9:9). Buchanan, *To the Hebrews*, 163.

Old (Sinai) Covenant—New Covenant

We now come to a ritual dimension not often understood clearly: the concept of covenant. Many Christians understand the old and new covenants as a juxtaposition of law and grace: the old covenant was one of law whereby a person kept the Ten Commandments and other epexegetical laws to be saved; the new covenant offers salvation freely through faith in the saving sacrifice of Jesus. This outlook is badly skewed. We discussed this issue in the last chapter, but let us revisit it here again briefly.

Law played an important part in the old covenant. The Ten Commandments defined the moral framework of God's governance, and other laws in the Pentateuch were usually a practical application of the principles outlined in the Ten Commandments in the specific *sitz im leben* of Israel in the wilderness. Before we consider this arrangement redundant on the assumption that the sacrifice of Jesus supposedly makes us immune to the need for obedience, we should hear the words of Hebrews about law and the new covenant: "I [God] will put my laws into their minds, and write them on their hearts" (8:10).

The new covenant does not envisage an abrogation or change of the law[53]—only a change of location from the tablets of stone to the heart. This is also probably reflected in 7:12, where the author speaks of νόμου μετάθεσις, literally "a change of location of the law,"[54] not "a change in the law" as the ESV and other translations infer. Paul further informs this new covenant transition by making the parallel of "tablets of stone" and "tablets of human hearts" (2 Cor 3:3), as discussed earlier, indicating that what is written in the heart under the new covenant is the Ten Commandments. The notion of the Decalogue being written on the heart is from the OT (Pss 37:31; 40:8; Isa 51:7), but it would become a reality in fullness only on the sacrifice of Jesus.

The change from the old covenant to the new is in its ritual dimensions,[55] as discussed in the previous chapter. Thus, Scott W. Hahn notes that the

---

53. Buchanan, *To the Hebrews*, 123. Buchanan understands the law in question to be "either Leviticus or, more likely, the entire Pentateuch." Ibid.

54. See LJS, s.v. μετάθεσις; BDAG, s.v. μετάθεσις.

55. Hahn, "Covenant, Cult, and the Curse-of-Death," 67. Hahn pointedly notes that ancient covenants—even those outside the Bible—had two dimensions: legal and ritual. "The two aspects of the covenant, legal and liturgical, are inextricably bound in a reciprocal relationship. On the one hand, cultic acts (i.e., sacrificial rites) establish the covenant (Heb 9:18–21, 23), and also renew it (Heb 9:7; 10:3). On the other hand, the covenantal

book of Hebrews takes more interest in the concept of covenant than does any other NT book (Hebrews contains seventeen out of the thirty-three NT occurrences of *covenant*). He observes that Hebrews places emphasis on the covenant "as a *cultic* and *liturgical* institution" (emphasis his).[56]

Hebrews 8 declares the old covenant faulty or blameworthy (8:7), not because there was anything wrong with it but because the people were sinful (8:8–9). Since the blood of the animals cannot cleanse sin (10:4, 11), the old covenant could not bring a holy God and sinful humanity into full covenant union. The problem was with human sin, not the covenant. But the old covenant could not resolve this problem and therefore was inadequate.

By contrast, as noted above, the blood of the sacrifice of Jesus does cleanse sin effectively and can establish union between God and humanity on a firm foundation. Because of this, the author makes this truly amazing statement: "Therefore he [Jesus] is the mediator of a new covenant . . . *since a death has occurred that redeems them from the transgressions committed under the first covenant*" (9:15, emphasis mine).

The author is saying that the sins committed during the old covenant were forgiven—not through the animal sacrifices but through the sacrifice of Jesus to which the sacrifices pointed. They were forgiven under the blood of the new covenant. This is why part of the promise of the new covenant was that God would not remember the sins of his people any longer (8:12; 10:17). The new covenant has replaced the ineffective blood of animals with the purifying blood of Jesus.

The difference between the old and new covenants is not grace versus law; it is the grace of the shadows versus the grace of the heavenly ritual realities (cf. John 1:16: "from his [Jesus's] fullness we have all received, grace upon grace," literally, "grace in place of grace").

---

law provides the legal framework for the cult, determining the suitable persons, materials, acts, and occasions for worship (Heb 7:11–28; 9:1–5). Thus, the liturgy mediates the covenant, while covenant law regulates the liturgy." Ibid.

56. Ibid., 65. Hahn is right in highlighting the cultic dimension of covenant but wrong in assuming that Hebrews is unique in this respect. The cultic dimension of covenant is evident from the moment it was established with Abraham (Gen 15:9–21) to the blood of the covenant sprinkled on the altar and the people in Exod 24, to the Passover cup as the "blood of the covenant" in the Gospels (Matt 26:28; Mark 14:24; Luke 22:20). Covenant and sanctuary ritual are inseparable throughout Scripture, but Hahn is correct in that Hebrews especially highlights the ritual dimension.

About to Vanish Away

The old covenant encapsulated all that was shadowy and insufficient: earthly sanctuary, earthly sinful priesthood, and earthly inadequate sacrifices. These could not provide forgiveness and salvation. To those tempted to cling to these, Hebrews offers a twofold warning.

First, to cling to the shadows means to reject the reality. After highlighting the superiority of the high priesthood of Jesus over the Levitical order (5:1–14), Hebrews offers a warning to those who "fall away" (6:6). What this falling away refers to is not spelled out. Buchanan suggests that the implication is that the sacrifice of Jesus cleanses sins only once.[57] A person who has been forgiven but then lapses back into a life of sin would therefore be beyond repentance. This is a possible reading, but it is negated by statements elsewhere in Scripture about believers who may fall and be reinstated.[58] Stedman understands the warning to be aimed primarily at Jews who have intellectually understood the gospel and have received some of the blessings of heaven, but who have not really believed. By refusing to believe and by going back to their previous Jewish life, they are placing themselves beyond repentance. But this explanation makes little sense given that the recipients of the warning clearly have experienced a saving faith in Christ (6:1–5).

Given the tone of the whole Epistle and the emphasis on the inadequacy of the Jerusalem temple system of priests and sacrifices, it seems that this temple system is in view. The recipients of the warning were believers who had accepted the sacrifice of Christ on their behalf but were lapsing into offering sacrifices in the temple. This is hinted at by the utilization of words used elsewhere in a ritual context. For example, we have τελειότητα (6:1). The cognate adjective τελειοτέρας (9:11) is used for the heavenly sanctuary, and the cognate verb τελειόω is used for the system of sacrifices and the sacrifice of Jesus (5:9; 7:19, 28; 9:9; 10:1, 14; cf. 11:40; 12:23). Likewise, the participle γευσαμένους, those who "have tasted" is used twice (6:4, 5) and it could refer to participation in the Lord's Supper, which is a symbol of the sacrifice of Jesus.[59] In 6:8 the writer warns, "But if it

---

57. Buchanan, *To the Hebrews*, 108.

58. E.g., Prov 24:16; Isa 1:26; 60:10; Jer 3:12–14; 15:19; 33:10–16; Ezek 20:44; Hos 2:14–20, 23; 11:8; Rom 9:25.

59. Hebrews 6:4–5 reads, "For it is impossible to restore again to repentance those who have once been enlightened, who have tasted the heavenly gift, and have shared in the Holy Spirit, and have tasted the goodness of the word of God and the powers of the

[the land] bears thorns and thistles, it is worthless and near to being cursed, and its end is to be burned [καῦσιν]." The noun καῦσις, which appears only here in the NT, may have a simple meaning of burning. However, it is worth pointing out that of the eight times it appears in the LXX, four have a ritual context (Exod 39:16; Lev 6:2; 2 Chron 13:11; Isa 40:16). Moreover, the word translated "fall away" is not the usual ἀφίσταμαι/ἀποστασία (from whence "apostasy") but the rare (only here) παραπίπτω. Παραπίπτω is a compound word made of the verb πίπτω, "to fall" and the preposition παρά, "next to." As such, it may not have the exact meaning of the ἀφίσταμαι/ἀποστασία family of words, to "fall away," but may have the slightly different nuance that the falling is not just a falling off a path but a falling into something parallel or cognate, "to fall next to, or back onto something parallel." It seems likely that the "falling away" here referred to Christians who had accepted the sacrifice of Christ but were lapsing back into the OT system of sacrifices—of which the sacrifice of Christ was the fulfillment. Those who fall back to the shadows of old covenant ritual "are crucifying once again the Son of God" (6:6) since in practice they are declaring his sacrifice to be insufficient. The possible ritual nature of the sin described in 6:4–8 is further supported by the writer's entreaty that his audience follows the example of Abraham. Two things are mentioned concerning him, the "promises" (Heb 6:12), which he received by divine "oath" (6:16). The promises point to the covenant of Gen 15 and 17, as well as Gen 12 and in the incident of the near sacrifice of Isaac. The oath relates to the latter incident. We noted in the previous chapter that both the covenant promise and the near sacrifice of Isaac were understood to be pointing to Jesus by early Christian writers. The admonition to not lose sight of Abraham in Heb 6:12–20, therefore, could be an admonition to look beyond the Jerusalem ritual to the sacrifice of Jesus. This understanding of Heb 6 outlined above is not conclusive, but there is enough suggestive evidence to make it very likely.

In 13:10, the author declares that believers "have an altar from which those who serve the tent have no right to eat." The altar for believers refers to the sacrifice of Jesus, commemorated in the Lord's Supper. Of that altar, "those who serve in the tent"—meaning those who still cling to the earthly sanctuary ritual—"have no right to eat." In other words, faith in the

---

age to come." The heavenly gift tasted is probably salvation offered through the sacrifice of Jesus, symbolized by participation in the Lord's Supper. Thus, while γευσάμενος is not used elsewhere clearly of the Lord's Supper, it could be in view here by implication.

sacrifice of Jesus is totally incompatible with any participation in the rituals of the sanctuary of the old covenant.

But Hebrews also offers a second warning, when it declares that the old covenant with its earthly sanctuary, priesthood, and sacrifice, was "obsolete" and "ready to vanish away" (8:13). This is no doubt a prophecy about the destruction of the Jerusalem temple and the physical end to sacrifices and priestly ministry.[60] The word translated "vanish away," ἀφανισμός, suggests not just destruction—as happened in Jerusalem—but something that disappears, possibly never to appear again (Deut 7:2; 1 Kgs 13:34; Mic 1:7). To Christians therefore who clang to old covenant ritual, Hebrews gives the warning that not only are they rejecting the sacrifice of Jesus but are about to witness the total destruction of the system they have built their faith upon and experience a painful disappointment.

EVIDENCE FROM THE REST OF THE NEW TESTAMENT

Hebrews is the NT book that best demonstrates the ritual conflict raging in the hearts of early Christians, especially those of a Jewish background. But it is by no means the only one. Numerous other NT texts also underline the fact that the temple and its sacrificial system still held a strong hold on the mind of Christians. We can briefly explore a few.

Paul and the Vow in the Temple— Acts 21:18–26

The first and one in which Paul was caught in the middle is Acts 21:18–26. As Paul returns to Jerusalem at the conclusion of his third missionary journey with an offering for believers there, and recounts the fruits of his ministry, James and "the elders" inform him that they too have experienced great success in the promulgation of the gospel: "And when they heard it, they glorified God. And they said to him, 'You see, brother, how many thousands there are among the Jews of those who have believed. They are all zealous for the law [νόμος/Torah]'" (Acts 21:20). They also inform him that there

---

60. Gordon notes that "it would be a strangely disinterested comment by an otherwise interested party if it were not also a comment on the imminent fate of the Jerusalem cultus." Gordon, *Hebrews*, 113.

Israel, Covenant, Law

are rumors that Paul is teaching Jewish believers to abandon circumcision and not walk according to Jewish customs (Acts 21:21).

The word translated "customs," ἔθος, denotes customs or common practices,[61] and interestingly for our study, is used repeatedly of the ritual system of the Jerusalem temple. Luke 1:9 speaks about the ἔθος of the priesthood in relation to Zechariah, the father of John the Baptist; Luke 2:9 about the ἔθος of the feast[62] in this case the Passover (2:8), one of the pilgrim feasts of the Jewish calendar when Jews would bring their offerings and sacrifices to the temple; Acts 6:13–14 connects ἔθος directly to the temple and both of these to the "law" highlighting the ritual dimension here of both ἔθος and law; Acts 21:21 connects ἔθος to circumcision which was a prerequisite for any male to participate in the ritual of the temple. Though the word ἔθος is absent from the OT, it does appear in connection to the temple in 2 Macc 11:25, and in connection to the priests and their customs in Bel 1:15. Word statistics might shed some light. Of the eighteen uses of the word ἔθος in the Apocrypha and NT, six times for sure and twice likely it is connected to ritual realities; five times it refers to the customs of pagans; three times it refers to non-religious customs; and two times it is indeterminate, but ritual could well be in view. This indicates that when used in a religious context and in relation to the biblical faith, the word appears predominantly in a ritual context. It might be going too far to describe ἔθος as a ritual term. It is however accurate and important to note that ἔθος has strong ritual overtones when used in a religious context, as is the case in Acts 21:21.

The accusation brought against Paul is anything but trivial. Apparently, it is causing a lot of grief to the Jerusalem believers. This is evident in the somewhat anguished words of James: "What then is to be done? They will certainly hear that you have come" (Acts 21:22).[63]

To refute the accusations against Paul and silence potential discontent before it erupts, James gives the following advice: "Do therefore what we tell you. We have four men who are under a vow; take these men and purify yourself along with them and pay their expenses, so that they may shave their heads. Thus all will know that there is nothing in what they have been

---

61. LSJ, s.v. ἔθος; BDAG 277.

62. BDAG 277.

63. Bruce calls the elders who confront Paul "well-meaning but deeply worried men." Bruce, *Acts*, 407–8.

told about you, but that you yourself also live in observance of the law" (Acts 21:23–24).

In (misjudged?)[64] compliance, Paul joins the four men under a vow and together the five men act accordingly: "Then Paul took the men, and the next day he purified himself along with them and went into the temple, giving notice when the days of purification would be fulfilled and the offering [προσφορά] presented for each one of them" (Acts 21:26). The "offering" would be in line with OT ritual practice. Fitzmyer notes, "The offering of two young pigeons or two turtledoves to the priest at the door of the tent of meeting, one as a sin offering and the other as a burnt offering, was prescribed for the Nazirites"[65] (e.g., Num 6:2–10). This was done in order that Paul could demonstrate that he was in "observance of the law [νόμος/Torah]" (21:24). So here, we have νόμος connected again directly to sacrificial offerings in the temple.

Interestingly, such action was, according to James and the elders who met Paul, required only of circumcised Jewish believers (Acts 21:25). Uncircumcised Gentile Christians did not have to do such things. The elders demonstrate this by referring to the decisions of the Jerusalem Council: "But as for the Gentiles who have believed, we have sent a letter with our judgment that they should abstain from what has been sacrificed to idols, and from blood, and from what has been strangled, and from sexual

---

64. Bruce writes, "The wisdom of Paul's complying with the elders' plan may well be doubted." Ibid. He adds, however, that Paul was operating on the principle of 1 Cor 9:20: "To the Jews I became as a Jew, in order to win Jews. To those under the law I became as one under the law (though not being myself under the law) that I might win those under the law." He therefore finds Paul without fault: "Certainly he cannot fairly be charged with compromising his own gospel principles." Richard I. Pervo and Harold W. Attridge try to get Paul out of the dilemma by suggesting that perhaps the telling of this story is historically flawed. It may have been, to use their words, "a Lukan invention." Pervo and Attridge, *Acts*, 546–47. C. K. Barrett likewise questions whether this incident happened as described, suggesting that it would constitute hypocrisy. Barrett, *The Acts of the Apostles*, 2:1012–13. John B. Polhill seems to miss the point by calling the requested action, a "symbolic act of Jewish piety." Polhill, *Acts*, 450. He thus seems to miss the ritual/sacrificial dimension of the vow (though he does admit it was a Nazirite vow) and the offering in question and so finds Paul "more than willing to participate." That it is a misjudged response can probably be confirmed by the outcome. As Paul is in the temple, Jews who had also heard the rumors about Paul, and having seen him with Trophimus the Ephesian in the city, and thinking that he may have brought him into the temple begin a riot that nearly leads to his death. However, thanks to the intervention of the Roman guard, Paul is rescued but arrested (Acts 21:27–36), imprisoned, and eventually transferred to Rome to appear before Cesar.

65. Fitzmyer, *Acts*, 697.

immorality" (21:25). So the Jerusalem Council, apparently, absolved Gentile Christians from circumcision and participation in the temple and its ritual but it was such participation that was still expected of Jews. Nonetheless, the very fact that James made a reference to the Jerusalem Council, and the freedom of the Gentiles, indicates perhaps that some overzealous or misguided Jewish Christians were putting pressure even on Gentiles to circumcise and offer sacrifice in the temple.

This incident takes place shortly before Paul's arrest and first imprisonment, possibly around AD 58, more than twenty five years after the sacrificial death of Jesus on the cross was supposed to have done away, in Christian theology, with the need for temple and sacrifice. And yet what do we see? The very leaders of the Jerusalem church and the many thousands of Jewish converts still faithful to the ritual requirements of the Torah, requiring Paul to do the same to demonstrate that he too is faithful to the temple ritual. Clearly the transition from a temple-centered faith to one without a temple was anything but smooth. In fact, for some, even among the leaders of the Jerusalem church, it just does not seem to have registered! The force of the situation is such that Paul, against his better judgment, obliges.

The Jerusalem Council—
Acts 15:1–31

Moving a step further, let us explore for a moment the Jerusalem Council which, by common consent, seems to have taken place around AD 48, ten years before the vow incident discussed above and more than fifteen years after the crucifixion. We have already noted the possibility, based on the words of James in Acts 21:26, that the Jerusalem Council dealt with ritual issues. We will explore this avenue of thought a little further. While the real issues at the Jerusalem Council are harder to pinpoint than the issue just discussed, there is still considerable corroborative evidence that ritual was at the core.

Paul is visiting Jerusalem to deliver alms, and he is suddenly confronted with a situation not unlike the one he faced again in Jerusalem ten years later: "but some men came down from Judea and were teaching the brothers, 'Unless you are circumcised according to the custom [ἔθος] of Moses, you cannot be saved'" (Acts 15:1) and "but some believers who belonged to the party of the Pharisees rose up and said, 'It is necessary to circumcise them and to order them to keep the law of Moses'" (Acts 15:5).

Two things are worth noting here. First, we meet again the word ἔθος which, as noted above, when it appears in a religious context, usually has ritual implications. Second, Acts 15:5 which functions epexegetically to verse 15:1, sets the stage for the council by declaring the issues that called for it: namely, circumcision and the Law of Moses. While the Law of Moses, or Pentateuch, encompasses many things, circumcision was the passport of entry into the impressive world of temple sacrifice and ritual. So it seems that there is a parallel between the situation Paul faced in AD 48 and that faced in AD 58, as evidenced also by the fact that the situation of AD 58 was resolved by reference to the decisions of the AD 48 Council. Ritual was at the core of the controversy.

Of interest is the way the Jerusalem Council resolves the problem of Jewish Christians requiring circumcision of Gentile Christians. It decides that Gentile Christians should abstain from four things: food offered to idols, blood, meat of strangled animals, and sexual immorality.[66] The tetrad appears three times: Acts 15:20, 29, and 21:25. There is a slight variation in the first prohibition. James recommends that Gentile believers abstain from ἀλιγησμάτων τῶν εἰδώλων, "defilement of idols" (Acts 15:20)—a statement that does not contain a direct reference to food. The Council adjusts this to εἰδωλοθύτων, "what has been sacrificed to idols" (15:29), a minor adjustment that is nonetheless useful in helping us determine the source and

---

66. There are textual critical issues. P45, the Ethiopic text and Origen, *Cels.* VIII.29 lack the reference to immorality. Werner Georg Kümmel correctly considers these readings mistaken. Kümmel, "Die ältest Form des Aposteldekrets," 87. Other manuscripts omit "strangled" and instead insert the golden rule: "And do not do to others what you do not wish others to do to you." Bruce, Conzelmann, and others correctly see this reading as secondary though, see Bowman, "Das text kritische Problem des sogenannten Aposteldekrets," 26–36; Bruce, *Acts*, 299; Conzelmann, *Acts of the Apostles*, 118. By the omission of "strangled," copyists were attempting to give a spiritual rather than ritual hue to the prohibitions: namely, idolatry, bloodshed (instead of meat eaten with blood) and immorality, crowned by the addition of the golden rule, and to do so by bringing the prohibitions into harmony with rabbinic thought which named idolatry, bloodshed, and immorality as three cardinal sins applicable to all humankind (e.g., *Seb.* 7b). Textual critical considerations confirm the validity of the text as currently appearing in the critical text and modern English translations.

reasoning of the prohibitions (Lev 17:1–9).[67] Three of the four prohibitions pertain to food and draw from the Levitical lists of prohibitions.[68]

It is unusual that the apostles decide on these four things, bypassing apparently weightier issues like the Decalogue, clean and unclean meats, and many more. Commentators often explain this on the basis that the problem was table fellowship with Gentiles (Gal 2:11–14) and that therefore food issues were bound to be prevalent.[69] The problem, as explained in Acts 15:1 and 5, was not table fellowship but what was required of Jewish and Gentile Christians. This objection aside, even if we accept table fellowship as a key problem, does not answer the question fully of why these four prohibitions because there were other food issues between Jews and Gentiles like unclean meats which the Council did not directly address. Moreover, the problem of association of Jews and Gentiles did not revolve only around food but also status; Gentiles were considered unclean (Matt 8:8; Luke 7:6; John 4:9; Acts 10:28). Gentile adherence to a sampling of food laws could not be sufficient to ensure smooth brotherly interaction.

The key to unlock this passage is to understand that the apostles were not legislating specific laws but rather assigning a theological/spiritual status to Gentiles. Commentators have long noted that the four prohibitions of Acts 15 come from Lev 17 and 18.[70] A brief overview of these two chapters is insightful. Leviticus 17:1–9 indicates that the slaying of animals, presumably for food, could only be done in the tabernacle, lest animals be offered to idols; this parallels the first prohibition of the Council and explains why the Council changed James's more general prohibition against idols to animals sacrificed to idols. Leviticus 17:10–14 (cf. 16:29) discusses animals killed without the blood being drained making their meat for-

---

67. In Lev 17:1–9, the prohibition is against sacrificing, or killing animals away from the sanctuary, presumably for consumption as food. The reason for this command is given in 17:7: "So they shall no more sacrifice their sacrifices to goat demons, after whom they whore." James's phrase, "abstain from the things polluted by idols," is more general. The Councils' final verdict to prohibit "what has been sacrificed to idols" seems to be a deliberate endeavor to follow more closely the prohibition of Lev 17:1–9.

68. Polhill notes that even immorality is ritual, possibly on the basis that πορνεία is an allusion to Levitical prohibitions. Polhill, *Acts*, 330–31. Cf. Simon, "The Apostolic Decree," 437–60; Conzelmann, *Acts of the Apostles*, 118. Morality and ritual are not always clearly distinguished. The setting of immorality within a list of three food prohibitions serves to see the triad as a group. At the same time, sexual immorality to Jews was not just an issue of ritual purity but part of their moral code.

69. Conzelmann, *Acts of the Apostles*, 118.

70. Ibid.; Jervell, *Die Apostelgeschichte*, 397.

bidden for consumption; this parallels the second prohibition. Leviticus 17:15–16 deals with animals that have died a natural death or have been torn by another animal, likewise forbidden; this parallels the third prohibition. Leviticus 18:1–30 is a prolonged list of detestable sexual relations; this parallels the fourth prohibition.

The sequence of the four prohibitions in Lev 17 and 18 is identical to Acts 15:29, the formal pronouncement of the Council and Acts 21:25, the repetition of the formal pronouncement; but not Acts 15:20, James's initial recommendation. It appears that in 15:20 James in his speech was recalling the Levitical prohibitions from memory, without attention to order, whereas the official decisions of the Council in Acts 15:29 and 21:25 ensured that the final draft of the decision followed Leviticus accurately.

The list of four Levitical prohibitions is the only collection in the Torah, outside the Decalogue, that specifically singled out foreigners as required to comply (Lev 17:8, 10, 12, 13, 15; 18:26).[71] The application of the four Levitical prohibitions to Gentile Christians possibly suggests that the Council was not so much legislating rules and laws as assigning a status. Gentile Christians were to have the same status in the church as sojourners had in ancient Israel and, one might add, Godfearers or proselytes-at-the-door had in Jewish synagogues.[72] That such was the aim of the Council

---

71. Foreigners also had to honor the Sabbath (Exod 20:10), refrain from sacrificing their children to Molech (Lev 20:2), refrain from blaspheming the name of God (Lev 24:16), keep the Sabbatical year (Lev 25:6), and refrain from high-handed sin (Num 15:30). What makes Lev 17–18 indicative is not that it exhausts what was required of foreigners but rather that is consists of a collection or corpus of prohibitions that is specifically said to apply to them; whereas other prohibitions are scattered throughout the Pentateuch. As such, Leviticus can be considered characteristic.

72. Before we dismiss this scenario, as suggesting that the Jerusalem Council was creating second class Christians, three things need to be noted. First, the most common LXX translation of the Hebrew גר, sojourner, is προσήλυτος, indicating closest association with the Israelite. Another LXX rendering πάροικος is used deliberately by Luke in Acts 7:6 and 29 of Abraham's descendants and Moses respectively to create a link between Israelite and sojourner. In other words, not only Gentile Christians but even Abraham's descendants and Moses himself were in some sense sojourners.

Second, sojourners had a very privileged legal status in ancient Israel. They were entitled to live form the land (Lev 25:6); inherit property (Ezek 47:22–23); own Israelite slaves (Lev 25:47); have access to the cities of refuge (Josh 20:9); participate in Feasts (Lev 16:29; Num 9:14; 19:10; though cf. Exod 12:48); and work in the temple (1 Chron 22:2). They had equal standing before the law (Exod 12:49; Num 15:15, 29–30; Deut 24:17; 27:19). Israel was warned specifically not to oppress sojourners (Exod 23:9; Lev 19:33; Zech 7:10). Indeed, failure to do so would bring God's judgments (Jer 7:6; Mal 3:5). Most importantly, perhaps, the sojourners were present at the renewal of the covenant

seems evident from subsequent references and allusions to it.[73] More importantly, it highlights that in contrast to Jewish Christians but in similarity to sojourners of old, Gentile Christians would not be required to either get circumcised or offer sacrifices in the temple. But Jewish Christians would, and this explains the stance of James and the elders in the incident of AD 58 discussed above, who did not bother with Gentiles but requested of Paul, a Jew, a vow and a sacrifice on the basis of the Jerusalem Council decision.

Other Passages in the New Testament

There are other telling passages that highlight the importance of the temple and its system among early Christians. In Matt 17:24–27, there is the well-known incident of the temple tax. When those collecting the tax ask Peter whether Jesus pays it, Peter is quick to answer in the affirmative. But he receives a gentle rebuke from Jesus: "What do you think, Simon? From whom do kings of the earth take toll or tax? From their sons or from others?"

---

recorded in Josh 8:33. They were to be considered in Israel equal to the native born (Lev 19:34) and be loved (Deut 10:19) because God loves them (Deut 10:18) and because Israel herself had been a sojourner (Gen 23:4; 35:27; Exod 2:22; Deut 23:7; Ps 39:12).

Third, the aim of the Council's decision was practical more than theological. It aimed to find a format, establish a modus operandi, whereby Jewish and Gentile Christians could co-exist in harmony. And this bold decision created exactly such a context.

73. That such an interpretation of the Jerusalem Council fits the evidence is further highlighted by the repeated references to covenantal civic status in the Epistles. In a possible reference to the Council's decision Peter writes, "Beloved, I urge you as sojourners [παροίκους] and exiles [παρεπιδήμους] to abstain from the passions of the flesh, which wage war against your soul" (1 Pet 2:11). He introduces his Epistle which is addressed to all believers, Jews and Gentiles alike, with the words: "Peter, an apostle of Jesus Christ, To those who are elect exiles [παρεπιδήμοις] of the dispersion" (1 Pet 1:1). It appears that, possibly as a reflection on the Jerusalem Council's decision, Peter in these two texts endeavors to equate Jews and Gentiles by stating that all believers are in a sense strangers and sojourners because their real civic rights are in heaven. Hebrews 11:13 takes a similar viewpoint. Speaking of the faithful of the Old Testament, it concludes that "having acknowledged that they were strangers [ξένοι] and exiles [παρεπίδημοί] on the earth."

More commonly, Paul wants to highlight that this piece of church polity did not make Gentiles second class Christians. So he repeatedly asserts their full covenantal civic status as part of the Israel of God (Gal 6:16) and declares, "So then you are no longer strangers [ξένοι] and aliens [πάροικοι], but you are fellow citizens with the saints and members of the household of God" (Eph 2:19). The same thought appears in Eph 2:12: "remember that you were at that time separated from Christ, alienated from the commonwealth of Israel and strangers [ξένοι] to the covenants of promise, having no hope and without God in the world" which he then contrasts with their current status [νυνὶ δὲ] as fully integrated into the body of Christ (Eph 2:13).

(17:25). When Peter replies, "from others" (17:26), Jesus makes this very important statement: "Then the sons are free" (17:27). But in order not to give offense, Jesus commands Peter to fish a fish and pay the tax with the coin he would find in the fish's mouth.

It is interesting that Jesus says the "sons" are free. Apart from casual uses, or from references to Jesus as the "Son of God," "sons" appears to have been a self-designation for early Christians and repeatedly appears as such.[74] In declaring therefore that "sons" are free from the temple tax, Jesus and Matthew are declaring that Christians are not required to pay the temple tax. However, if they come under pressure to do so or if society will frown upon them if they do not, they are allowed to pay it solely so as to not cause offense. The inclusion of this incident in the Gospel of Matthew probably suggests that at the time of the composition of the Gospel, perhaps two decades or more after the crucifixion, the Jerusalem temple was still casting a heavy shadow on the early Christian communities.

Other incidents that can be cited. The tearing of the veil of the temple at the crucifixion is mentioned by all Synoptics (Matt 27:51; Mark 15:38; Luke 23:45).[75] The veil, probably the one that separated the Holy Place from the Most Holy Place,[76] was a key part of the Jerusalem temple hiding the presence and glory of God from the casual look of the priests who ministered in the temple every day. That the veil should be torn clearly indicated that the presence of God had departed from the temple and there was no need to hide anything, any more. Perhaps it is because of this that Jesus calls

---

74. E.g., Matt 5:9, 45; 9:15; 13:38; Mark 2:19; Luke 6:35; 16:8; 20:36; John 12:36; Rom 8:14; 9:26; Gal 3:26; 4:6; 1 Thess 5:5.

75 See Morris, *The Gospel According to Matthew*, 724; Powell, *Mark's Superb Gospel*, 409–10; Pate, *Luke*, 457–58.

76. R. T. France notes, "None of the synoptic evangelists specify whether this is the great outer curtain which covered the entrance to the sanctuary as a whole, or the inner curtain which separated the Holy of Holies from the sanctuary's outer chamber." France, *The Gospel of Matthew*, 1079–80. The outer would be visible to the people outside, the inner only to the priests who ministered within the Holy Place. France considers the outer to have been more likely the one to have been torn but nonetheless notes that "the inner curtain, however, would offer a more potent symbol of cultic exclusion." Ulrich Luz and Helmut Koester likewise leave the question open but observe that "the curtain before the Holy of Holies is more in keeping with an interpretation in terms of the temple cult: the Holy of Holies, that normally no one can see, is now exposed." Luz and Koester, *Matthew 21–28*, 565–66. I would opt for the inner in the sense that the supernatural dimension implied in the description fits better the inner veil which was less accessible and more profoundly important in terms of symbolism, as France has observed.

the temple, "your house" (Matt 23:38; Luke 13:35)[77] rather than the "Father's house" (e.g., Luke 2:49; John 2:16). The depiction of the torn veil therefore functions as a confirmation that in Christ, a new ritual order has dawned. That all three Synoptics mention the veil indicates either the importance of the incidence or the need for such a confirmation in the light of the persistence of some to cling to the temple, or perhaps, both.

John does not mention the veil, but refers to Jesus as the true Lamb of God who takes away sin (John 1:29, 36):[78] clear ritual language. Moreover in John 2:18–19, we read, "So the Jews said to him, 'What sign do you show us for doing these things?' Jesus answered them, 'Destroy this temple, and in three days I will raise it up.'" The statement apparently caused a very strong impact because it was brought against Jesus both at his trial as an accusation (Matt 26:61; Mark 14:58) and was hurled at him as a taunt at the cross (Matt 27:40; Mark 15:29). The accusation at Jesus's trial is the last resort of his accusers before the High Priest takes over directly (Matt 26:60), but the accusation fails as the witnesses are divided (Mark 14:59). The accusation is brought up again at Stephen's trial (Acts 6:13–14). As with the tearing of the veil, the repetition of the replacement of the temple in Jerusalem by another ritual reality centered on Jesus is seen to be prominent among Christians and particularly offensive to Jews. It should not surprise us, therefore, that at least some Jewish Christians found the replacement of the temple and its ritual by another ritual reality hard to digest, and that the two ritual realities co-existed uneasily at least until the destruction of the temple in AD 70.

CONCLUSION

We have explored the book of Hebrews and discovered that it contrasts the earthly temple/sanctuary, priesthood, sacrifice, and covenant with the heavenly sanctuary, priesthood, sacrifice, and covenant as manifested in Jesus. This quadruple juxtaposition is enveloped in ritual language that seems to permeate the book. Hebrews is usually dated before AD 70,[79] thirty or

77. Hagner, *Matthew 14–28*, 681: "The passive verb ἀφίεται, 'left (to you),' both connotes abandonment by God and alludes to the future destruction of the temple. Very similar language occurs in Ezekiel anticipating the destruction of the first temple (e.g., Ezek 8:6, 12; 9:3, 9; 11:23; cf. Bar 4:12). The destruction of Jerusalem and the temple becomes a major subject in the discourse that follows (cf. 24:2, 15; Acts 6:14)." Hagner, *Matthew 14–28*, 681.

78. Pink, *Exposition of the Gospel of John*, 58, 59, 66.

79. Harold W. Attridge opts for a date between AD 60 and 95. Attridge, "Hebrews," 97.

more years after the crucifixion. The abundance of ritual language as well as the force of the arguments employed, and the intensity of the warnings issued, all suggest that the ritual question was a paramount issue for Hebrews, Christians of Jewish background.

We also explored the incident of the vow of Paul in Acts 21:18–26, an incident with very clear ritual overtones. Again, twenty-five years after the crucifixion we see the Jerusalem church zealous for the ritual aspects of the Law of Moses, keen to ensure that even an apostle like Paul does not depart from the ἔθος. That Paul caved in to the demand of the Jerusalem party shows the strength and intensity of the views they represented. We also explored the Jerusalem Council and though we cannot draw fool proof conclusions, the parallels with the incident in Acts 21:18–26 as well as several pointers within the text indicate that ritual realities played a dominant role. We then looked at several smaller examples that also highlight the tension between the Jerusalem-centered ritual and the new ritual realities as exemplified in Jesus.

The above examples are more than sufficient to demonstrate that the transition from a temple-focused faith system to one without a visible earthly temple was wrought with challenges and was anything but smooth and easy. While some of the early leaders like Paul, Matthew, Mark/Peter, Luke, and other apostles understood the need to move away from the temple cultus since in Jesus a new ritual reality had emerged, it seems that most Jewish Christians—especially those based in Jerusalem— did not see any friction between the death of Jesus as a sacrifice and ongoing sacrifices in the temple and were happy to continue with it as had been done for centuries. James seems to also have been caught up in this movement. Moreover, some such Jewish Christians endeavored to enforce Gentile Christians to fall within this pattern and outlook as well. We therefore have a clear historical context against which to understand Paul's objections to the "Law" as an opposition to the Law's ritual dimensions.

The *terminus ante quem* is the reference to Hebrews in 1 Clement; the *terminus post quem* is the possibility that the author heard the gospel from others (Heb 2:3) and that believers have been in the faith for quite some time (Heb 5:12). Walter A. Elwell and Philip Wesley Comfort are more confident of a date before AD 70 by virtue of the fact that the destruction of Jerusalem is not mentioned. Elwell and Comfort, "Hebrews," 585.

5

Paul and the Law
The Ritual Dimension of Law
Part II—Paul's Attacks on the Law

Thesis Statement—Paul's attacks on the "Law" especially as exemplified in Galatians, Paul's most "antinomian" Epistle, are not an attack on any legal code of behavior but rather on the temple ritual of sacrifices and offerings as described in the "Law" or Torah, the aim of which was to offer forgiveness of sin.

Having established the historical reality of the ambivalent attitudes of early Christians towards the temple and its cultus in Chapter 4, I will now endeavor to demonstrate from Paul's own words that when he writes again law in his Epistles, he is not against the legal codes of Israel, as is most commonly believed, but primarily against the system of sacrifices contained in the Law/Torah. The study cannot be exhaustive since law underlines many of Paul's writings. Exhaustiveness would require many hundreds, indeed thousands of pages. I will instead focus on specific passages. We will begin our study with Acts 13:32–41 and especially verses 38–39 in what is possibly Paul's own programmatic statement, his own summation of what his ministry and preaching was all about. Then we will spend some time in Galatians, since the Epistle appears to be the most "antinomian," in that it exemplifies the most negative attitude to law. Lastly, we will look at Colossians 2:16–17 which is also a strong candidate in antinomian rhetoric.

ACTS 13:32–41—THE RITUAL NATURE OF THE PREACHING OF PAUL

Acts 13:32–41 is part of Paul's sermon (13:16–41) in the synagogue of Antioch in Pisidia (13:14) during his first missionary journey. This is Paul's first and longest sermon recorded. It is also his only clearly evangelistic sermon to a synagogue audience.[1] Therefore, it is very important and a strong clue to help us understand what Paul's evangelistic outlook entailed. Paul begins his sermon with a brief recounting of the history of Israel (13:16–22), briefly discusses the ministry of John the Baptist (13:24–25), and focuses primarily on Jesus (13:23, 26–41), with a special emphasis on his death and resurrection.

Having recounted the historical events, he then makes his appeal, so to speak, the implication[2] of what he has just recounted—"Let it be known to you therefore, brothers, that through this man [Jesus] forgiveness of sins is proclaimed to you, and by him everyone who believes is freed [δικαιόω, "to justify"] from everything from which you could not be freed [δικαιόω] by the law of Moses" (Acts 13:38–39).[3] Forgiveness and the way it is accomplished, evidently, is the focus of Paul's message.

---

1. In addition to Paul's synagogue sermon at Pisidian Antioch, Acts records Paul's sermon at the Areopagus to a pagan audience (Acts 17:22–31); his parting speech/sermon to the believers in Ephesus (20:17–35); his defense before a crowd in Jerusalem where he recounts his conversion (22:1–21); his defense before Felix in Caesarea (24:10–21); his defense before King Agrippa (26:2–23); and his words to the Jewish leaders in Rome who come to visit him (28:17–20).

2. Bruce notes that it was customary to round off the preaching with "a direct application to the hearers" and to include forgiveness, and mentions as examples Acts 2:38; 3:19; 5:31; and 10:43. Bruce, *Acts*, 262.

3. Some question whether this sermon, or at least 13:38–39, are indeed Paul's. There seems to be a twofold problem. First, the key word ἄφεσις (15:38) is very uncharacteristic of Paul but a favorite of Luke. Second, some perceive differences between the view on justification espoused in 15:39 and the one presented by Paul in Romans and Galatians. For example, Benjamin W. Bacon states, "The language of 13:39 is claimed as Pauline because of the single word 'justify'. The doctrine is exactly that which Paul fundamentally repudiates." Bacon, *The Story of St. Paul*, 103. Cf. Vielhauer, "On the 'Paulinism' of Acts" (1950/51), 41–42. Bruce takes a softer approach on the apparent contradiction on justification and states, "One could conceivably understand the words in this sense: 'Even if you hope to enjoy a right relationship with God on the basis of Moses' law, remember

Israel, Covenant, Law

There are a number of things that can be brought out from these two verses. First, the Greek οὖν, "therefore," with which Paul introduces his programmatic statement, is an inferential conjunction that gives a "deduction, conclusion, or summary to the preceding discussion."[4] The statement therefore of verses 38–39 brings to a climax and purpose everything that has been recounted earlier in Paul's sermon.

Second is the noun ἄφεσις, here translated "forgiveness," but with a meaning that includes "release" or "cancellation."[5] It appears seventeen times in the NT. In the OT, the word is used in a variety of contexts both religious and secular. However, in the NT, it has a decidedly ritual hue. With the exception of Luke 4:18 (2x), in all other fifteen occurrences, it is connected to the forgiveness of sin. The ritual dimension is explicitly in view in seven of these (Matt 26:28; Luke 24:47; Acts 5:31; 10:43; 13:38; Eph 1:7; Heb 9:22), and eight times it is there in the context and background (Mark 1:4; 3:29; Luke 1:77; 3:3; Acts 2:38; 26:18; Col 1:14; Heb 10:18). Paul therefore, in using the word ἄφεσις, is presenting the death of Jesus as a ritual sacrificial reality that provides forgiveness of sin. This perhaps is not surprising.

What is important is the next phrase: "and by him everyone who believes is freed from everything from which you could not be freed by the law of Moses." The phrase "freed from everything" clearly points back to

---

that Moses' law does not provide for the forgiveness of sins committed with a high hand.'" Bruce, *Acts*, 262. For Bruce therefore, the contradiction is not as great. Both objections to a Pauline origin of the climax of the sermon can be answered quite easily. The use of a favorite Lukan term like ἄφεσις possibly is a case of Luke utilizing a favorite word to convey a Pauline concept. Indeed, this seems to be the case since ἄφεσις in 15:38 functions as a direct equivalent of δικαιόω, a favorite Pauline term, in 15:39. Perhaps Fitzmyer mentions the "Lukan Paul," Pauline theology perhaps in Lukan language. Fitzmyer, *Acts*, 518. As for apparent contradiction between justification in 15:39 and Romans/Galatians, it is only apparent. The problem lies in the suggestion that Jesus justifies "from everything from which you could not be freed [δικαιόω, "justified"] by the law of Moses" (Acts 13:39). It seems to suggest that the law offers some justification and for everything else, there is Jesus. But this is a skewed reading of the text. The key word is "everything." The Law/Torah could not offer justification for any sin and for this reason, for everything now believers can find justification in Jesus. Understood in this way, Acts 15:39 is in full harmony to Romans/Galatians. Polhill is correct when he states, "The next statement [about justification], which is a fuller explication of the forgiveness of sins, could hardly be more Pauline." Polhill, *Acts*, 304–5.

4. Wallace, *Greek Grammar Beyond the Basics*, 673.
5. LSJ, s.v. ἄφεσις; BDAG, s.v. ἄφεσις.

"forgiveness of sins."[6] The sacrifice of Jesus by forgiving sins brings freedom from guilt and condemnation. By contrast, the "law of Moses" cannot forgive sins and therefore cannot offer freedom.[7] In what way did the law of Moses deal with the problem of sin? As a monk, Luther perhaps may have felt that he could attain forgiveness through pilgrimages, alms, and other deeds of obedience to the rules of his faith community. Not so the first century Jew. Search one as they may, they will not find any reference in the Jewish writings where forgiveness is the result of good deeds or obedience to any legal code. Forgiveness was the result of offering sacrifices.[8] This is what the law of Moses defined, "For the life of the flesh is in the blood, and I have given it for you on the altar to make atonement for your souls, for it is the blood that makes atonement by the life" (Lev 17:11).

When Paul contrasts in Acts 13:38–39 two systems of forgiveness and freedom from condemnation, he is not contrasting the sacrifice of Jesus with rules and regulations of Israel's legal codes but the blood of Jesus with the offertory system of the OT the aim of which was to forgive sin. Paul highlights that while the blood of Jesus can cleanse sins, the offertory system cannot. The writer of Hebrews echoes the exact same negative sentiment to the OT offertory system when he declares, "For it is impossible for the blood of bulls and goats to take away sins" (Heb 10:4); and again "And every priest stands daily at his service, offering repeatedly the same sacrifices, which can never take away sins" (10:11).

Possibly relevant is also Paul's statement in 13:41: "Look, you scoffers, be astounded and perish; for I am doing a work [ἔργον] in your days, a work that you will not believe, even if one tells it to you." Paul's emphasis is on the first part, a warning to scoffers lest, in the context of his sermon, they refuse the sacrifice of Jesus for their sins. Paul's words are a quotation from Hab 1:5: "Look among the nations, and see; wonder and be astounded. For I am doing a work [ἔργον] in your days that you would not believe if told." The wording is closer in the Greek text of the NT and LXX.[9]

---

6. Conzelmann et al., *Acts of the Apostles*, 106. Polhill, *Acts*, 304.

7. Bruce, *Acts*, 202: "Moses' law does not justify; faith in Christ does."

8. See discussion below on Galatians.

9. *Habakkuk 1:5*, ἴδετε οἱ καταφρονηταί καὶ ἐπιβλέψατε καὶ θαυμάσατε θαυμάσια καὶ ἀφανίσθητε διότι ἔργον ἐγὼ ἐργάζομαι ἐν ταῖς ἡμέραις ὑμῶν ὃ οὐ μὴ πιστεύσητε ἐάν τις ἐκδιηγῆται.
Acts 13:41, ἴδετε οἱ καταφρονηταί, καὶ θαυμάσατε καὶ ἀφανίσθητε, ὅτι ἔργον ἐργάζομαι ἐγὼ ἐν ταῖς ἡμέραις ὑμῶν, ἔργον ὃ οὐ μὴ πιστεύσητε ἐάν τις ἐκδιηγῆται ὑμῖν.
Cf. *Exodus 34:10*, καὶ εἶπεν κύριος πρὸς Μωυσῆν ἰδοὺ ἐγὼ τίθημί σοι διαθήκην

The work, ἔργον, at which scoffers would be astounded is the context of Paul's sermon is nothing less than the sacrifice of Jesus. In Habakkuk, the work is a response to the sinfulness of Judah (Hab 1:1–4) and though it appears as a part of God's punitive action by bringing the Chaldeans to punish Judah (1:6–11), it is not difficult to see how Paul could apply it to Jesus whose sacrifice on the cross was also as a response, and more so, a solution to the problem of human sinfulness. Intriguing is the possibility that behind Paul's statement lies not only Hab 1:5 but also Exod 34:10, which is a response of a merciful God to the sin of the golden calf: "And he [God] said, 'Behold, I am making a covenant. Before all your people I will do marvels, such as have not been created in all the earth or in any nation. And all the people among whom you are shall see the work of the LORD, for it is an awesome thing [ἔργα] that I will do with you.'" While the word agreement in the Greek between Acts 13:41 and Hab 1:5 on the one hand, and Exod 34:10 on the other is not very high, the conceptual and contextual parallels are strong. That Exod 34:10 could have been in Paul's mind is supported by Paul's introduction to the quotation from Hab 1:5, as described in Acts 13:40: "Beware, therefore, lest what is said in the Prophets should come about." Though Paul uses a plural word, "prophets," he quotes only one prophet: Habakkuk. This could suggest that in speaking of "prophets" Paul has in mind the second division of the Hebrew scriptures, the "Prophets" or it could be that though he quotes only Habakkuk, he had other similar statements in mind like Exod 34:10. We cannot of course know with certainty what was in Paul's mind. If, however, Exod 34:10 forms indeed a background to Paul's argumentation, it would underscore quite dramatically the ritual (rather than legal) inadequacy of the law of Moses and the Sinai Covenant, contrasted with the absolute efficacy of the sacrifice of Jesus to cleanse sin.

In light of the above, I consider Paul's programmatic statement in Acts 13:38–39 a summation of what his preaching and ministry was all about because it stands at the apex and as a conclusion to his first recorded evangelistic sermon in a Jewish context. As such, it can serve as a guide and a benchmark against which we can understand other, more detailed, and convoluted theological discussions in his Epistles.

ἐνώπιον παντὸς τοῦ λαοῦ σου ποιήσω ἔνδοξα ἃ οὐ γέγονεν ἐν πάσῃ τῇ γῇ καὶ ἐν παντὶ ἔθνει καὶ ὄψεται πᾶς ὁ λαὸς ἐν οἷς εἶ σὺ τὰ ἔργα κυρίου ὅτι θαυμαστά ἐστιν ἃ ἐγὼ ποιήσω σοι.

Paul and the Law

THE RITUAL NATURE OF THE CONFLICT IN GALATIANS

Though Luther understood the concept of justification by grace apart from the law while teaching from Romans, Galatians is probably the one Bible book that has contributed most to Christian antinomianism. Relevant statements abound: "a person is not justified by works of the law" (Gal 2:16); "through the law I died to the law, so that I might live to God" (2:19); "O foolish Galatians! Who has bewitched you? ... Did you receive the Spirit by works of the law or by hearing with faith?" (3:1-2); "all who rely on works of the law are under a curse" (3:10); "the law is not of faith" (3:12); "if a law had been given that could give life, then righteousness would indeed be by the law" (3:21); "we were held captive under the law, imprisoned until the coming faith would be revealed" (3:23); "the law was our guardian until Christ ... we are no longer under a guardian" (3:23-24); and the law makes us slaves like Hagar, and those under the law will not inherit (4:22-31). Modern phrases like "salvation by works," "works-based religion," or simply "works" draw from Paul's "works of the law," a preferred Galatian expression (e.g., Gal 2:16 [3X]; 3:2, 5, 10; cf. Rom 3:20, 27, 28; 4:2, 6; 9:12, 32; 11:6; Eph 2:9) and are used pejoratively of Christians who are perceived as trying to earn their salvation either through obedience to the Ten Commandments, other rules and regulations, or simply through good works.

This antinomian understanding of Galatians I believe is not reflective of Paul's real intent and is based on a superficial reading of the text. We noted in the previous chapter that early Christians, primarily those from a Jewish background, had a strong attachment to the temple and its ritual and often tried to force others to conform to this outlook. We also noted above in the discussion of Acts 13:32-41 that Paul's programmatic statement and the superiority of Christ over the Law/Torah were not in legal matters but in the way the problem of sin is dealt with, the sacrifice of Jesus versus the OT offertory system. In this section, I will argue that what holds true for Acts 13:32-41 holds true for Galatians. In speaking of law, Paul is arguing against the OT offertory system enshrined in the Law/Torah.

To do this we need to understand that the traditional law versus grace understanding of Galatians, reflected in different ways in both the Reformation and the New Perspectives, popular though it might be, is based on a limited understanding of the word "law" (Greek, νόμος). "Law" today implies a legal code that prescribes proper behavior. However in the biblical context, "law" referred to the Law, the Torah, Genesis to Deuteronomy, which constituted the heart of Israel's Scriptures and contained not only a legal code like the Ten Commandments but also historical narrative, exhortation and, very importantly for our study, a detailed discussion of a system of sacrifices the aim of which was to make atonement for human sin. "Law" can refer to constituent parts of the Torah, but only in a secondary sense.

In contrast to the common paradigm of law versus grace, I want instead to propose another paradigm for understanding Galatians; namely, that Paul is not contrasting law and grace but two systems of grace—the grace offered through the sacrifice of Jesus versus the grace offered in the Law/Torah through the sacrifices of animals in the temple.

In this part of our study, we will examine seven cues from within Galatians that testify to this. Throughout, we need to keep asking the question, is Paul talking against law in the sense of obedience to a legal code or is he talking against the temple and its system of sacrifices contained in the Law/Torah.

1. "Another Gospel"

The first cue comes from Gal 1:6: "I marvel that you are turning away so soon from Him who called you in the grace of Christ, to a different [ἕτερον] gospel, which [ὅ] is not another [ἄλλο]; but there are some who trouble you and want to pervert the gospel of Christ" (NKJV). The Greek for "gospel," εὐαγγέλιον, means "an announcement of good news,"[10] a declaration that something good has happened. Within the context of Paul, it means the forgiveness of sins attained through the sacrifice of Jesus.[11]

This other gospel though "different" is "not another"[12] (Gal 1:6–7, NKJV); that is, in some ways, it is the same as the gospel of Jesus but in

10. LSJ, s.v. εὐαγγέλιον; BDAG, s.v. εὐαγγέλιον.

11. E.g., Easton, "Gospel." Cf. Acts 20:24; Rom 1:1, 9, 16; 1 Cor 9:12; Gal 1:7.

12. There is an issue here with translation of the two adjectives and the pronoun noted in Greek in the text. The first adjective, ἕτερον, in Greek signifies the other in a pair of two. It can also designate something that is different, of a different kind (LSJ, s.v. ἕτερον). The second adjective, ἄλλο, has the meaning of "another." As J. Louis Martyn notes, one can consider here the two adjectives as synonymous. Martyn, *Galatians*, 110. Rather problematic is the tendency of many commentators to overlook the relative pronoun ὅ, and simply read οὐκ ἔστιν ἄλλο, "there is no other [gospel]." Daniel Wallace notes that this definite relative pronoun "is used routinely to link a noun or other substantive to the relative clause, which either describes, clarifies, or restricts the meaning of the noun." Wallace, *Greek Grammar Beyond the Basics*, 336. Here the neuter ὅ refers back to the neuter (different) gospel, and the clause that follows the pronoun describes the

some way it is different. Through this other gospel, the opponents of Paul in Galatia were trying to "distort" (ESV, NAS) or "pervert" (NIV, NKJV) the gospel of Jesus (1:7). The Greek verb in question is μεταστρέψαι and it literally means "to turn around" or "to turn about."[13]

How does a law code, for example the Ten Commandments, fit the above points? A law code is not a gospel because it is not an announcement that something good has happened; does not provide forgiveness but simply defines appropriate behavior; and is not in any way a parallel reality to the sacrifice of Jesus. Moreover, trying to earn salvation through obedience to a law code is not a "turning back" since in the Jewish mind, forgiveness was never to be earned through obedience but through the temple offertory system, as noted above.

By contrast, the system of sacrifices fits perfectly. It was a type of "gospel" since it announced forgiveness of sin; was similar to the sacrifice of Jesus of which it was a shadow (Heb 10:1); yet different in that animal sacrifices could not cleanse sin (Acts 13:38; Heb 10:4, 11) while the blood of Jesus can (Acts 13:38); opponents who practiced temple sacrifices, were "turning back" from the reality of Jesus's sacrifice to the shadow of animal sacrifices. We therefore have a perfect fit in the sacrificial system being the "other gospel" Paul's opponents were espousing.

Paul continues by saying that the one who promotes this "other" gospel: "let him be accursed [ἀνάθεμα]" (Gal 1:9, ESV, NKJV). The English translation is awkward. The verbal phrase "let him be," which in English is passive, translates the Greek verb ἔστω which is active imperative. While the English says what a person should become ("accursed"), the Greek designates what a person should do with him, "go and make himself an anathema." The translation of ἀνάθεμα is also problematic. Ἀνάθεμα is a compound word of the preposition ἀνὰ, "upon"[14] and the noun θέμα, "a deposit" or "something placed before someone"[15] from the verb τίθημι, "to lay down" or "place something."[16] So, for example, the meaning of the compound cognate verb ἀνατίθημι has the meaning to place something upon

---

noun. Therefore, the best translation is to give the pronoun its due weight and the see the clause that follows as descriptive: "A different gospel which is not another." This is why, in this instance, I believe the NKJV offers a better translation.

13. LSJ, s.v. μεταστρέφω.

14. LSJ, s.v. ἀνὰ; Wallace notes that when used in composition with a verb, it indicates upward motion. Wallace, *Greek Grammar Beyond the Basics*, 364.

15. LSJ, s.v. θέμα.

16. LSJ, s.v. τίθημι.

something else.¹⁷ Ἀνάθεμα could thus literally be translated "that which is placed before." In the LXX, Apocrypha, and NT both the noun and verb are used in two related ways. First, of things devoted to God. An example is, "But no devoted thing [ἀνάθεμα] that a man devotes [ἀνατίθημι] to the LORD, of anything that he has, whether man or beast, or of his inherited field, shall be sold or redeemed; every devoted thing [ἀνάθεμα] is most holy to the LORD" (Lev 27:28).¹⁸ In 2 Macc 9:16, ἀνάθεμα is used in parallel to sacrifices and holy temple vessels: "and the holy sanctuary, which he had formerly plundered, he would adorn with the finest offerings [ἀνάθεμα]; and the holy vessels he would give back, all of them, many times over; and the expenses incurred for the sacrifices he would provide from his own revenues." In Num 18:14 we read, "Every devoted [ἀνατίθημι] thing in Israel shall be yours" (Num 18:14). The devoted things in question would be the food offerings and sacrifices Israelites would bring to the sanctuary (Num 18:8–14).

Second, it is used of things again devoted to God but this time through destruction. An example is, "And the city and all that is within it shall be devoted [ἀνάθεμα] to the LORD for destruction. Only Rahab the prostitute and all who are with her in her house shall live, because she hid the messengers whom we sent" (Josh 6:17). This is the more common usage, especially for the verb.¹⁹

An interesting case is Ezra 10:8: "If anyone did not come within three days, by order of the officials and the elders all his property should be forfeited [ἀνατίθημι], and he himself banned from the congregation of the exiles." The context is Israel taking foreign wives and Ezra summoning the people to Jerusalem to resolve the problem. It is not clear what "forfeited" implies in this case. It could mean that the property would be destroyed or, more likely, that perhaps it would become a gift to the temple.

---

17. See LSJ, s.v. ἀνατίθημι.

18. See also Jdt 16:19: "Judith also dedicated to God all the vessels of Holofernes, which the people had given her; and the canopy which she took for herself from his bedchamber she gave as a votive offering [ἀνάθεμα] to the Lord"; 2 Macc 2:13: "The same things are reported in the records and in the memoirs of Nehemiah, and also that he founded a library and collected the books about the kings and prophets, and the writings of David, and letters of kings about votive offerings [ἀνάθεμα]."

19. See also Num 21:3; Deut 7:26; 13:16, 18; 20:17; Josh 6:18, 21; 7:1, 11, 12, 13; 22:20; Judg 1:17; 21:11; 1 Sam 15:3; 2 Kgs 19:11; 1 Chron 2:7; 4:41; Zech 14:11.

While Henry George Liddell and Robert Scott do give "cursed" as a translation,[20] the texts we perused give a substantially different picture. Ἀνάθεμα is something devoted to God either as a gift, sacrifice, or as something devoted to destruction. With these thoughts in mind, we can look at Paul's use.

In addition to Galatians, Paul uses ἀνάθεμα in Rom 9:3: "For I could wish that I myself were accursed [ἀνάθεμα] and cut off from Christ for the sake of my brothers, my kinsmen according to the flesh." Was Paul really willing to become accursed and lose his eternal salvation for the sake of his fellow Jews, as the ESV and other translations of this text suggest? Absolutely not! He himself declared, "But I discipline my body and keep it under control, lest after preaching to others I myself should be disqualified" (1 Cor 9:27). Paul wanted to make it clear that in his endeavors to win many for Jesus, he by no means wanted to risk his own salvation. Indeed, to do so would make him unfit for the kingdom, since Jesus declared, "Whoever loves father or mother [or fellow countrymen] more than me is not worthy of me, and whoever loves son or daughter more than me is not worthy of me" (Matt 10:37). In willing to become ἀνάθεμα for his Jewish brethren, Paul was not offering to become accursed in the sense of losing his salvation but rather to give his life unto death to God on their behalf.

In 1 Cor 12:3, no one can call Jesus ἀνάθεμα when guided by the Spirit. Here probably Paul is responding to detractors of the gospel who were perhaps mocking the Christian belief in the sacrificial death of Jesus, saying that Jesus had become ἀνάθεμα, an offering to God by destruction.

If we understand ἀνάθεμα in this way, Paul's warning in Gal 1:9 to anyone clinging to temple sacrifices could be translated as follows: "if anyone preaches any other gospel to you than what you have received, he should offer himself as a sacrificial offering [ἀνάθεμα]." The statement is both sarcastic and contains an element of foreboding. The persons who want to attain forgiveness through the sacrifices of animals, the "other gospel," would do well to offer themselves instead as a sacrifice, since the sacrifices of animals offered on their behalf under the OT ritual system are ineffective. Sarcasm. Since they cannot attain to forgiveness through animal sacrifices, on the Day of Judgment they will literally become ἀνάθεμα, destroyed in the holy flames of God for their sins. Foreboding. Interestingly, Paul makes a similar point in 1 Cor 16:22: "If anyone has no love for the Lord, let him *offer himself as* ἀνάθεμα" (section in italics is my rendering).

20. LSJ, s.v. ἀνάθεμα.

2. The Verb "to Justify"—δικαιόω

The verb δικαιόω, "to justify," appears thirty nine times in the NT of which eight are in Galatians. Only Romans has more occurrences (fifteen) but proportionately, it is more common in Galatians. The verb is a legal term and refers to acquittal from wrongdoing. It also appears in Paul's programmatic statement in Acts 13:32–41, as discussed above. In a religious context, it refers to the forgiveness of sin which allows a person to stand clean before God.[21] In Galatians, Paul is contrasting two systems of δικαιόω: the sacrifice of Jesus and through the νόμος, Law/Torah. Here are a few relevant texts with emphasis provided.

"We know that a person is not *justified* by works of the *law* [Law/Torah] but through *faith in Jesus Christ*, so we also have believed in *Christ Jesus*, in order to be *justified* by faith in *Christ* and not by works of the *law* [Law/Torah], because by works of the *law* [Law/Torah] no one will be *justified*" (Gal 2:16).

"But if, in our endeavor to be *justified* in *Christ*, we too were found to be sinners, is Christ then a servant of sin? Certainly not!" (Gal 2:17).

"And the Scripture, foreseeing that God would *justify* the Gentiles by *faith* [in the atoning sacrifice of Jesus], preached the gospel beforehand to Abraham, saying, 'In you shall all the nations be blessed'" (Gal 3:8).

"Now it is evident that no one is *justified* before God by the *law* [Law/Torah], for 'The righteous shall live by faith'" (Gal 3:11).

"So then, the *law* [Law/Torah] was our guardian until Christ came, in order that we might be *justified* by faith [in the atoning sacrifice of Jesus]" (Gal 3:24).

"You are severed from Christ, you who would be *justified* by the *law* [Law/Torah]; you have fallen away from grace" (Gal 5:4).

No amount of keeping of a legal code can forgive the sinner since legal codes prescribe proper behavior, not a solution to breaches of the code. By contrast, every Jew—even the worst of legalists—knew that in the Torah, forgiveness could be sought through the system of sacrifices. Michael L. Rodkinson, editor and translator of the Babylonian Talmud, states in his introductory remarks to the tractate *b. Shabbath*: "Wherever throughout the Mishna the expression guilty, culpable (Hayabh), or free (Patur)

---

21. Fitzmyer, *Acts*, 518: "The image behind 'justification' is drawn from a judicial setting, in which sinful human beings find themselves standing before the tribunal of the divine Judge. Paul thus proclaims here what he advocated in Gal 2:16 and Rom 3:28: 'We maintain that a human being is justified by faith apart from deeds prescribed by the law.'"

is used, the meaning of the former (guilty) is that the transgressor acting unintentionally must bring the sin-offering prescribed in the law; of the second expression (free), that the accused is absolved from punishment." And again: "The penalty for the first class of infractions was simply the sacrificing of a sin-offering, which, however, involved a great many hardships, as the culprit had to bring the sin-offering to the temple in Jerusalem in person, and was frequently compelled to travel quite a distance in order to do so, besides sustaining the loss of the value of the offering."[22] References in the Talmud and in other rabbinic sources to sacrifices for even minor infractions abound.[23]

It is evident that in speaking of being "justified by the law," Paul is specifically addressing the means through which forgiveness is attained—the sacrifice of Jesus versus the sacrifices prescribed in the "law of Moses." The former can justify, the latter cannot.

3. The Works of the Law/Torah

In speaking of those who wanted to attain to justification through the Law/Torah, Paul uses the expressions "works of the law." This phrase appears a total of six times in Galatians (Gal 2:16 [3x]; 3:2, 5, 10). In Reformation theology, they are nearly universally understood to refer to works of obedience to the law of God, the aim of which is to win the favor of God, or even salvation; law-keeping or more extremely, legalism.[24] In the New

---

22. Rodkinson, *The Babylonian Talmud*, xxii, xxvi.

23. E.g., *b.Yebamoth* 3b; 7a; *b.Shabbath* 3b; 6a; 12b; 35b; 48a; 58a; 62a; 62b; *b.Pesachim* 23b; *b.Yoma* 2a; 15b; 17b.

24. E.g., Ronald Y. K. Fung translates "works of the law" as "doing what the law demands." Fung, *The Epistle to the Galatians*, 115. Bruce, *The Epistle to the Galatians*, 137: "They are not deprecated in themselves, for the law of God is 'holy and just and good' (Rom. 7:12)—even if Paul's attitude to the law is more radical in Galatians than in Romans, this statement is as valid for Galatians as for Romans (cf. Gal. 5:14). What is deprecated is the performing of them in a spirit of legalism, or with the idea that their performance will win acceptance before God; cf. 3:2, 5, 10; also Rom. 3:20, 28." J. Louis Martyn renders "works of the law" as "by observance of the law." Martyn, *Galatians*, 250. Hans D. Betz maintains that the Pharisaic doctrine is that justification can "be obtained by doing." Betz, *Galatians*, 116. On one approach to justification in Pharisaism, see Strack and Billerbeck, *The New Testament From the Talmud and Midrash*, 3:160–64; as the question: "And the principal question here is: Is Paul's polemic directed against the law itself or against a particular attitude toward the law that sees the law as a means of winning favor with God (i.e., 'legalism')?" His own answer is stated as follows: "My own understanding of Paul at this point is that Paul directs his attack not just against legalism,

Perspective, they are usually thought to refer to the boundary markers, the distinguishing characteristics of Judaism the aim of which was to set them apart from Gentiles.[25]

Both the Reformation and New Perspective approaches fail to understand the phrase in its context. If "law" refers to the Law/Torah, the Pentateuch, the "works of the law" must be works described in the Torah. What kind of works does the Torah describe the aim of which was to justify? A simple word study will provide the answer.

The word ἔργα, "works" appears 149 times in the Torah and is used of three kinds of works: (a) secular works of men (about 70x); (b) mighty acts of God in history (9x); and (c) the works of the sanctuary, its construction and service (about 70x). Clearly, only the third category has anything to do with the justification of sinners. Indeed, "works" is used of priestly/Levite ministry (Num 3:7; 4:3), the care of the furnishings (Num 3:26, 31), incense (Num 4:16), sacrifices, and everything else associated with the sanctuary (4:23, 30). The totality of sanctuary ministry is called τὰ ἔργα τῆς σκηνῆς, "the works of the tabernacle" (Num 3:7). So the word "works" in the Law/Torah can refer to the totality of the service of the sanctuary; nowhere is it related to obedience to any legal code.

A modern commentator reads "works of the law" and influenced by the modern meaning of words as well as a long tradition of interpretation immediately thinks of works of obedience to a legal code and concludes that Paul is against them. Paul's Greek-speaking contemporaries in Galatia would read "works of the law" and would think of the Torah. Being conversant with it, they would immediately understand that the only works in

---

which the Old Testament prophets and a number of rabbis of Judaism denounced as well, but against even the Mosaic religious system, for he saw all of that as preparatory for and superseded by the relationship of being 'in Christ.'" Longenecker, *Galatians*, 85–86. Ernest de Witt Burton takes the opposite view stating that law is "here evidently used qualitatively, and in its legalistic sense, denoting divine law viewed as a purely legalistic system made up of statutes, on the basis of obedience or disobedience to which men are approved or condemned as a matter of debt without grace." Burton, *The Epistle to the Galatians*, 120. Timothy George is one of few who admit a ceremonial dimension: "The 'works of the law,' then, refer to the commandments given by God in the Mosaic legislation in both its ceremonial and moral aspects, precepts commanded by God and thus holy and good in themselves." George, *Galatians*, 194–95.

25. E.g., J. D. G. Dunn considers "works of the law" as "particular observances of the law like circumcision and the food laws" that were meant to set Israel apart. Dunn, "The New Perspective on Paul," 107.

the Torah, the purpose of which was to cleanse sin, was the works of the sanctuary. Such works, Paul affirms, cannot justify.

4. Circumcision

Circumcision is a key issue in Galatians, the NT book most interested in the topic.[26] Paul's opponents were insisting that Gentile believers undergo circumcision (Gal 6:12). Why this preoccupation with circumcision? If legalism or obedience to legal codes was the key issue, the emphasis on circumcision seems redundant; a Gentile believer could be fully law abiding and even an extreme legalist without circumcision. However, if participation in the sacrificial system was the problem, insistence on circumcision becomes much easier to understand. To determine how, we need to return to our discussion of the Abrahamic Covenant as well as the Sinai Covenant in Chapter 3 where we saw a parallel between the two covenants.

In Gen 15, God first makes a covenant with Abraham on the basis of the blood of cut-in-two animals and slain birds. In Gen 16, Abraham breaches the covenant. In Gen 17, the covenant is remade and circumcision is added, where Abraham cuts himself in two, so to speak, to parallel what had been done to the animals in Gen 15.

In Exod 24, God makes a covenant with Israel on the basis of the blood of bulls. In Exod 32, Israel breaks the covenant through the incident of the golden calf. In Exod 34, the covenant is remade and a detailed offertory system is outlined to deal with potential further breaches. There is thus a parallel between the two covenants, and between the offertory system of the Sinai Covenant and circumcision. Circumcision was thus a type of sacrifice.

In Jewish thought there was a very close connection between circumcision and sacrifice. In Exod 24:8, the phrase "blood of the covenant" is used of the blood of bulls sacrificed to initiate the covenant. In rabbinic writings, this phrase is used on several occasions to refer to the blood of circumcision. For example, in the Babylonian Talmud, tractate *Sabbath* folio 137b we read, "He who pronounces the benediction recites, '. . . Who

---

26. The noun περιτομή is used thirty-six times in the NT of which seven are in Galatians. The numbers for the verb περιτέμνω are seventeen in the NT and six in Galatians. Only Romans has more uses, fifteen for the noun and zero for the verb but proportionately, the noun and verb are more common in Galatians which is a considerably shorter book than Romans.

hast sanctified us with Thy commandments and hast commanded us to circumcise proselytes and to cause the drops of the blood of the covenant to flow from them, since but for the blood of the covenant Heaven and earth would not endure."[27] Some recensions of the *m. Nedarim* 31 have the following reading: "Great is circumcision, for it counterbalances all other precepts put together, as it is written, behold the blood of the covenant, which the Lord hath made with you concerning all these words (Ex. XXIV, 8)."[28] The connection of the blood of circumcision to the blood of the sacrifices of Exod 24:8 is clearly seen.[29] In *b. Sabbath* 135a: "Beth Shammai maintain: One must cause a few drops of the covenant blood to flow from him, while Beth Hillel rule: It is unnecessary;" and "Beth Shammai and Beth Hillel did not differ concerning him who is born circumcised that you must cause a few drops of the covenant blood to flow from him, because it is a suppressed foreskin."[30] In *b. Yebamoth* 71a:

> But In truth [the text referred to] includes a proselyte who had been circumcised but did not perform the prescribed ritual immersion, and a child who was born circumcised, he holding that it is necessary to provide for a few drops of the blood of the covenant to flow; while R. Eliezer follows his own view, he having stated that 'A proselyte who has been circumcised, though he has not performed his ritual immersion, is regarded as a proper proselyte.' And he is also of the opinion that it is not necessary to provide for any drops of the blood of the covenant to flow where a child was born circumcised.[31]

In the Tanhuma God announces, "If I reveal myself to bless him who offered whole-burnt sacrifices and peace offerings, how much the more to Abraham who sacrificed himself before me!"[32] Shaye J. D. Cohen observes

---

27. Epstein, *Babylonian Talmud (Soncino)*.

28. Soncino *m.Nedarim* 31.

29. Midrash *Gen. Rab.* XLVL.5 makes the interesting observation that if circumcision had been in any other part of the body than the foreskin, it would disqualify the circumcised from being a priest because priests were not allowed to be maimed in any way.

30. Soncino *b.Sabbath* 135a.

31. Soncino *b. Yebamoth* 71a.

32. Text referenced in Cohen, "Jewish Circumcision Blood," 38. An alternative recension reads, "If I come to bless him who slaughters an ox or lamb, and spills a little blood ... all the more so must I bless Abraham, from whose house a river of blood goes forth on account of circumcision."

that among rabbis, the "blood of the covenant" of Zech 9:11, instead of the blood of bulls was understood to refer to the blood of circumcision.[33]

A statement attributed to Rabbi Eliezer is especially interesting:

> Know then that on the Day of Atonement Abraham our father was circumcised. Every year the Holy One, blessed be He, sees the blood of our father Abraham's circumcision, and He forgives all the sins of Israel, as it is said, 'For on this day shall atonement be made for you, to cleanse you' (Lev. xvi. 30). In that place where Abraham was circumcised and his blood remained, there the altar was built, and therefore, 'And all the blood thereof shall he pour out at the base of the altar.' (It says also), 'I said unto thee. In thy blood, live; yea, I said unto thee, In thy blood, live' (Ezek. xvi. 6).[34]

Eliezer here connects circumcision to the Day of Atonement, forgiveness, atonement, spiritual cleansing, and life. And another:

> The sailors saw all the signs, the miracles, and the great wonders which the Holy One, blessed be He, did unto Jonah, and they stood and they cast away every one his God, as it is said, 'They that regard lying vanities forsake their own shame.' They returned to Joppa and went up to Jerusalem and circumcised the flesh of their foreskins, as it is said, 'And the men feared the Lord exceedingly; and they offered a sacrifice unto the Lord.' Did they offer sacrifice? But this (sacrifice) refers to the blood of the covenant of circumcision, which is like the blood of a sacrifice. And they made vows every one to bring his children and all belonging to him to the God of Jonah; and they made vows and performed them.[35]

Fascinating is a tradition, without historical basis, but indicative nonetheless of the way some rabbis thought that the blood of circumcision was placed on the door posts and lintel of the house of the Israelites in Egypt together with the blood of the paschal lamb: "But the Holy One, blessed be He, said: By the merit of the blood of the covenant of circumcision and the blood of the Paschal lamb ye shall be redeemed from Egypt."[36] And "the Israelites took the blood of the covenant of circumcision, and they put (it)—upon the lintel of their houses, and when the Holy One, blessed be He, passed over to plague the Egyptians, He saw the blood of the covenant

---

33. Cohen, "Jewish Circumcision Blood," 36.
34. Pirqe R. El. XXIX in Friedlander, *Pirke de Rabbi Eliezer*, 204.
35. Pirqe R. El. XI in ibid., 72.
36. Pirqe R. El. XXIX in ibid., 210.

of circumcision upon the lintel of their houses and the blood of the Paschal lamb."[37] Cohen notes, "Rabbinic exegetes understood the twofold blood of Ezekiel 16:6 to represent the sacrifice of the Paschal lamb by the Israelites in Egypt, and the observance of circumcision by the Israelites in anticipation of that sacrifice."[38]

The sacrificial and indeed salvific nature of circumcision is also evident in Zipporah's act to circumcise her son (Exod 4:24–26). The name Zipporah comes from the word צִפֹּר which means, "bird." Midrashic exegesis played on this meaning to present Zipporah as a woman who "purified her father's house,"[39] since the sacrifice of birds was often used in cleansing ceremonies; and that "sacrificial imagery and blood are affiliated with Zipporah's life."[40] When the Lord meets Moses and Zipporah on their way to Egypt, he seeks "to put him [Moses or the boy?] to death" (Exod 4:24). Zipporah takes a flint, cuts off the son's foreskin, and throws it at his feet. English translations assume it is Moses's feet, but the text is indeterminate.[41] "It was then that she said, 'A bridegroom of blood,' because of the circumcision" (4:26). The act of circumcision covers the child and protects him from divine wrath. The Targum Jonathan comments, "How precious is the blood of this circumcision that saved the bridegroom from the hands of the Destroying Angel." Cohen observes, "Many modern scholars have suggested that the function of Exodus 4:24–26 within its redactional context is to have the redemption of Zipporah's firstborn adumbrate the redemption of the Israelite firstborns, and indeed of Israel itself, God's firstborn (Exod. 4:22)."[42] Other sources could be cited but the above suffice to make the point.

The ritual nature of circumcision and its connection to sacrifice is also evident in a number of NT texts. In Rom 4:11 we read, "He [Abraham] received the sign of circumcision as a seal of the righteousness that he had

---

37. Ibid.
38. Cohen, "Jewish Circumcision Blood," 34–35.
39. Haberman, "Foreskin Sacrifice," 23.
40. Ibid., 24.
41. Cohen, "Jewish Circumcision Blood," 37.
42. There is some debate on the dating of the rabbinic traditions that equate circumcision with sacrifice. Cohen believes it is a rather late development, even medieval. Ibid., 32. Lawrence A. Hoffman maintains that it can be found throughout the time span of rabbinic sayings. Dating rabbinic traditions is never easy. Hoffman, *Covenant of Blood*. The fact that even Cohen admits that her dating is based on an argument of the silence of certain sources should caution against opting for a late development.

by faith while he was still uncircumcised." Paul here declares three things. First, Abraham received the promise while he was still uncircumcised. Second, after his failure, he received circumcision as a sign and a seal of the righteousness of Gen 15. Third, since according to Paul, the original promise to Abraham before circumcision was a promise of deliverance from sin through the sacrifice of Christ (see discussion in Chapter 3 and Gal 3:13–16), the righteousness in question is just that. Circumcision therefore was a sign pointing to the promise of Jesus. It was a ritual reality. Now that Christ had been sacrificed, circumcision meant nothing. This is why Paul can declare that now Abraham can be father to both the circumcised and the uncircumcised (Rom 4:12).

In Gal 4:11, circumcision is juxtaposed to the cross: "But if I, brothers, still preach circumcision, why am I still being persecuted? In that case the offense of the cross has been removed"; as is also the case in Gal 6:14–15: "But far be it from me to boast except in the cross of our Lord Jesus Christ, by which the world has been crucified to me, and I to the world. For neither circumcision counts for anything, nor uncircumcision, but a new creation"; and Col 2:11–12: "In him also you were circumcised with a circumcision made without hands, by putting off the body of the flesh, by the circumcision of Christ, having been buried with him in baptism, in which you were also raised with him through faith in the powerful working of God, who raised him from the dead."

In Acts 15:1, 5, circumcision is the entry point for participation in the Jerusalem cultus, as discussed above: "But some men came down from Judea and were teaching the brothers, 'Unless you are circumcised according to the custom of Moses, you cannot be saved.' . . . It is necessary to circumcise them and to order them to keep the law of Moses"; as is the case in Acts 21:21: "They have been told about you that you teach all the Jews who are among the Gentiles to forsake Moses, telling them not to circumcise their children or walk according to our customs [ἔθος]."

Circumcision was a prerequisite for sacrifices to be offered at the temple since no uncircumcised person could enter its precincts. On the door of the temple was a sign clearly warning the uncircumcised that if they went beyond it, they would be responsible for their death which would follow.[43] One of the reasons Jews wanted to kill Paul was because they thought

---

43. Bruce, *Acts*, 409, cites Josephus, *BJ* 5.194; 6.12–25; *Ant.* 15.417; *Ap.* 2.103–4; Philo, *Embassy to Gaius* 212 and notes, "The Roman authorities were so conciliatory of Jewish religious scruples in this regard that they authorized the death sentence for this trespass even when the offenders were Roman citizens." Two such notices have been

he had brought uncircumcised Greeks into the temple (Acts 21:28–30). By contrast, circumcision was not a prerequisite for keeping the Ten Commandments, other biblical laws, or indeed the multitudinous rabbinic traditions.

With this background in mind it is easy to understand why Judaizers insisted on circumcision for Gentile believers. It was intimately involved with the concept of sacrifice and only through it that they could partake in any temple ritual. It is also easy to understand why Paul opposed it. While the act of circumcision was neutral (e.g., Rom 3:30; 4:12; 1 Cor 7:19; Gal 5:6; 6:15), the attempts of his opponents to enforce it was strongly objectionable because it was intended to push believers in Christ back to the now redundant system of temple sacrifice.

5. The Law Added Because of Transgressions

We now come to the core of the argument of Paul as outlined in Gal 3. Paul begins with a very forceful statement: "O foolish Galatians! Who has bewitched you? It was before your eyes that Jesus Christ was publicly portrayed as crucified. Let me ask you only this: Did you receive the Spirit by works of the law or by hearing with faith" (Gal 3:1–2). He opens the discussion with the defining ritual reality for Christians, the crucifixion of Jesus, and contrasts it with the "works of the law" which, as discussed above, represent the system of sacrifices centered on the temple. It is this contrast that he develops in the rest of chapter 3.

Then in Gal 3:6–13 Paul contrasts the system of justification, through the Law/Torah and through Christ. Abraham believed in the promise of the coming Savior, the Seed, and he was considered righteous (3:6). Those who like Abraham believe in the Seed can likewise be considered righteous (3:7) without having experienced the righteousness that comes from the Torah, the sacrificial system. By contrast, those who want to be justified through the Torah, have only one option, perfect obedience (3:10). Anything less brings a curse, the curse of failure (3:10) which the sacrificial system cannot cleanse. Therefore those who try to be justified by the Torah ultimately find themselves unforgiven and therefore under the penalty of sin, which is death. But Jesus has redeemed believers from the curse entailed in the

---

discovered in Greek and read, "No foreigner may enter within the barricade which surrounds the temple and enclosure. Any one who is caught trespassing will bear personal responsibility for his ensuing death." See Iliffe, "The ΘΑΝΑΤΟΣ Inscription," 1–3.

Torah by becoming himself a curse for fallen humanity, that is, by dying on the cross for human sin. Therefore through him, Gentiles and Jews can both be saved.

Paul then addresses in more detail the issue of those who still cling to the sacrificial system. In 3:15, he explains that "no one annuls it [human covenants] or adds to it once it has been ratified." Since the promise of the Seed to Abraham was given in Gen 15, everything added afterwards is secondary. In Gal 3:19a, Paul explains that there is indeed something that was "added," 430 years after Abraham (3:17), that is, at Sinai. What was added? Paul answers, "law." This is one of the instances in which Paul uses νόμος, "law," not of the whole Torah but of one of its constituent parts. This is evident in the fact that (a) the Torah as a whole was not added at Sinai and (b) the promise of the Seed to Abraham is itself part of the Torah. So here, Paul cannot be speaking of the whole Torah. Rather, he hones on the one aspect of the Torah that is the focus of controversy in Galatians, the sacrifices.

Where the sacrifices "added" at Sinai? Absolutely! Let us refresh our discussion of the Sinai Covenant from Chapter 3 of this study. At Sinai, God first gives the Ten Commandments (Exod 20:1–17) and then the Book of the Law (Exod 20:22–23:33). This concludes the legal aspect of the covenant which is established in Exod 24. It would be hard to see how these could be "added" to something since as far as the exodus is concerned and the establishment of Israel as God's covenant people, the Ten commandments is the first "law" given and the Book of the Law follows immediately afterwards, almost epexegetically.

After the sin of the golden calf in Exod 32 and the re-establishment of the covenant in Exod 34, God gives the detailed list of sacrifices to deal with potential future breaches of the covenant. So it could be said that the system of sacrifices was "added" to the legal code of Israel: the Ten commandments and the Book of the Law. Moreover, when Paul speaks about a law added "because of transgressions," he clearly cannot be referring either to the Ten Commandments or the Book of the Law because these two legal codes define what a transgression is. First comes the definition of transgression and then the transgression itself. You cannot have a transgression if there is no legal code defining appropriate behavior. So when Paul speaks of law "added because of transgressions," he clearly is speaking about the system of sacrifices added to deal with breaches of the Ten Commandments and Book of the Law.

Also interesting in Gal 3:19 is the phrase "because of," the law was added "because of" transgressions (Gal 3:19). The Greek is χάριν. It comes from the noun χάρις, "grace."[44] Χάριν can function either as a noun, "grace" or as a preposition, "because." In the latter case, it nearly always conveys advantage (e.g., Luke 7:47; Eph 3:1, 14; Titus 1:5, 11), a usage it has retained until today. So when a writer uses χάριν as a preposition, the meaning is not so much "because of" but more "for the sake/benefit of" something or someone. It implies an act of grace or undeserved kindness from the subject of the verb. So the phrase "added because of transgressions," τῶν παραβάσεων χάριν προσετέθη, could be more accurately translated as "added for the sake/benefit of transgressions." But it is hard to see how something could be done for the "sake/benefit of" transgressions. It might be better to see more of the meaning of the noun embedded in the preposition here: "Why then the law? It was added as grace for transgressions."

We can take our thought a step further. Biblical Greek did not use punctuation marks. They were added centuries later. There are at least three different ways to punctuate and read Gal 3:19a and I list them below with the relevant translation:

Usual Punctuation: Τί οὖν ὁ νόμος; τῶν παραβάσεων χάριν προσετέθη. "Why then the law? It was added because of/as grace for transgressions."
Alternative A: Τί οὖν ὁ νόμος τῶν παραβάσεων; χάριν προσετέθη.[45] "Why then the law of transgressions? It was added by/as grace."
Alternative B; Τί οὖν; ὁ νόμος τῶν παραβάσεων χάριν προσετέθη. "What then? The law of transgressions was added as grace."[46]

Both alternatives offer two exegetical insights. First, they have the phrase ὁ νόμος τῶν παραβάσεων, "the law of transgressions." While there is no exact equivalent elsewhere in the Bible, we have very close semantic parallels in the phrases ὁ νόμος τῆς ἁμαρτίας, "the law of sin [offering]" (LXX

---

44. LSJ, s.v. χάριν.

45 There is a strong manuscript tradition of placing the question mark after the genitive substantive, as suggested in my alternative punctuation A, though the substantive is not always the same. Examples are Papyrus P46, an extremely important early witness dated by Kim, "Palaeographical Dating of P46 to the Later First Century," 248, as early as AD 80, and by others in the late second or third century; the uncials Codex Augiensis from the ninth century and Codex Boernerianus from the ninth to tenth centuries; the majority of Old Latin witnesses; Irenaeus's Latin translation (fourth century); Ambrosiaster (fourth century); and Speculum Pseudo-Augustine.

46. With this two alternative punctuation options, we would probably need to consider an ellipsis of a preposition like κατά and see χάριν purely as a noun, κατά χάριν προσετέθη, "It was added by/as grace."

Lev 6:18); τῆς πλημμελείας νόμος, "the law of offence" (Lev 7:7; cf. 7:1), and ὁ νόμος τῆς ἀκαθαρσίας, "the law of impurity" (Lev 15:3).[47] Of interest is Lev 7:37: ὁ νόμος τῶν ὁλοκαυτωμάτων καὶ θυσίας καὶ περὶ ἁμαρτίας καὶ τῆς πλημμελείας καὶ τῆς τελειώσεως καὶ τῆς θυσίας τοῦ σωτηρίου, "the law of whole-burnt-offerings, and of sacrifice, and of sin [offering], and of [offering for] transgression, and [of the sacrifice] of consecration, and of the sacrifice of peace-offering."[48] The words I have put in brackets are not in the Greek text but have been supplied by the translator and are indeed implied in the text.[49] What we see therefore is a string of expressions semantically similar to "the law of transgressions," all with a ritual meaning and stated or implied connections to sacrifice. Second, both alternative translations put more emphasis on the semantic nuance of the noun form of χάριν.

Whichever way we punctuate Gal 3:19a, two things are clear: (a) there is a cause and effect relationship whereby transgressions bring into operation a law the aim of which is to deal with the problem of sin; and (b) the giving of this law revolves around the concept of grace as manifested in the word χάριν. The only law that was added because of sin, and offered grace to sinners was the system of sacrifices. This is the "law" Paul speaks against.

From the discussion on Gal 3 so far, we have a strong accumulation of evidence that Paul has the sacrificial system in mind: the introduction where he juxtaposes the sacrifice of Jesus with the "works of the Law/Torah," seen to be the works of the sanctuary; his presentation of Jesus and his sacrifice as the Seed promised to Abraham in Gen 15 and the juxtaposition with the Torah which cannot lift the curse of sin; the mention of something added to the Sinai Covenant because of transgressions; the grace dimension of the word χάριν; and the different possible ways to punctuate Gal 3:19a.

Paul then makes this amazing statement: "And this I say, that the law which was [added] four hundred and thirty years later, cannot annul the covenant that was confirmed before by God in Christ, that it should make the promise of no effect" (Gal 3:17). Paul here uses a not uncommon argument of chronological priority where the older takes precedent over the

---

47. Cf. "the law of whole-burnt-offering" (LXX Lev 6:2); "the law of sacrifice" (LXX Lev 6:7); "the law of the ram for the trespass [offering]" (Lev 7:1); "the law of the sacrifice of peace offering" (Lev 7:11); "the law of him that has vowed" (Num 6:13; cf. 6:21); "they shall sacrifice it according to the ordinance [law] of the passover" (Num 9:12; cf. 9:14).

48. The translation utilized is that of Sir Lancelot Charles Lee Brenton. Brenton, *The Septuagint Version of the Old Testament*.

49. Cf. e.g., ESV, NIV, NKJV.

newer.⁵⁰ Paul states here that the law of sin offerings added at Sinai cannot "make the promise of no effect" since it is subsequent. Which promise? The promise given to Abraham in Gen 15, namely, that he would have a son, the seed. Only in the context of Gal 3, the seed in question is not Isaac but Jesus Christ, the Seed (Gal 3:16).

According to Paul therefore, the promise that the Seed would solve the problem of human sin was offered to Abraham in Gen 15. Circumcision for Abraham and the law of sacrifices for Israel were added because of human sinfulness and were stop-gap solutions until the Seed would come. They were reminders of their hapless state. They cannot negate the original promise. Now that the Seed has at last come, it is needless to offer sacrifices or circumcise, for it would be like annulling the promised Seed! Profound theology!

6. The Παιδαγωγὸς or Tutor

In Gal 3:24–25 Paul continues by declaring that the law that was added became a παιδαγωγός, a "tutor" to Christ until a time: "So then, the law was [γέγονεν, "became"] our guardian [or tutor] until Christ came, in order that we might be justified by faith. But now that faith has come, we are no longer under a guardian" (Gal 3:24–25). If what was discussed above is correct, then Paul is referring to the Torah and, more specifically, the law of sacrifices in the Torah. It is this law that became a tutor.

We first note that the law "became" a tutor, that is, something prompted this change of function. This is a reminder of Gal 3:19 where the law was "added" because of the transgressions of Israel. In essence, Gal 3:24–25 continues in the same line of thought as Gal 3:19.

Commentators often consider ancient tutors as glum and oppressive individuals and assume such a relation between God's law and the human being. Bruce, for example, writes, "The παιδαγωγός, who, for all his disciplinary function, might establish a bond of close affection for his charge, was not an instructor, not a 'pedagogue' in the modern sense."⁵¹ He adds, "For while today we think of pedagogues as teachers, in antiquity a paidagōgos

---

50. E.g., Gen 25:25–31; 1 Tim 2:13. See the discussion of Marshall and Towner, *The Pastoral Epistles*, 462.
51. Bruce, *Galatians*, 182.

was distinguished from a didaskalos ("teacher") and had custodial and disciplinary functions rather than educative or instructional ones."[52]

This negative outlook is amiss[53] and is negated by Paul's only other use of the term: "For though you have countless guides [παιδαγωγός] in Christ, you do not have many fathers. For I became your father in Christ Jesus through the gospel" (1 Cor 4:15). Here, Paul compares himself to other gospel teachers whom he calls παιδαγωγός. While he wants to stress that he is closer to the Corinthian believers than them by virtue of the things he has suffered in proclaiming the gospel (1 Cor 4:9-13), he is by no means disparaging the other teachers.[54]

Παιδαγωγὸς is a compound word from παιδίον, "child"[55] and ἄγω, "lead, bring, go."[56] Liddell and Scott say the word refers to a "slave who went with a boy from home to school and back again."[57] The mention of a slave appears to give handle for a negative hue, but the idea of leading a child to school and back is positive and requires an element of trust. Liddell and Scott also connect the word with "leader" and "teacher,"[58] a connection commentators seem to miss. BDAG define it as "one who has responsibility for someone who needs guidance, guardian, leader, guide."[59] G. W. H. Lampe uses the words "instructor, teacher, elementary instructor, preparatory trainer."[60] Emmanuil Kriaras, commenting on later Byzantine Greek usage, also connects παιδαγωγός with "teacher," as well as with a "trustee" who oversees an underage child.[61] In modern Greek, it has a totally positive

---

52. Ibid. Cf. Fung, *The Epistle to the Galatians*, 168-69: "The custodian (*paidagōgos*, literally 'boy-leader') was usually the slave who conducted the freeborn youth to and from school and who superintended his conduct generally—a function clearly differentiated from that of the teacher or 'pedagogue' in the modern sense." Longenecker, *Galatians*, 146.

53. For an informative discussion of the positive aspects of the term, see George, *Galatians*, 265.

54. Fee, *The First Epistle to the Corinthians*, 185: "This is not intended to be a put-down of their other teachers."

55. BDAG, s.v. παιδίον.

56. BDAG, s.v. ἄγω.

57. LSJ, s.v. παιδαγωγός.

58. Ibid.

59. BDAG, s.v. παιδαγωγός.

60. Lampe, *A Patristic Greek Lexicon*, s.v. παιδαγωγός.

61. Kriaras, *Epitomē tou Lexikou tēs Mesaionikēs Hellēnikēs Dēmodous Grammateias 1100-1669*, s.v. "παιδαγωγός."

sense.⁶² Selecting a negative hue to the word therefore is a very limited understanding of the term that does not do justice to it. I prefer the positive. Tutoring can be ennobling.

Of the tutors of antiquity, the most famous was Aristotle, tutor to Alexander the Great. Of him Alexander declared, "I am indebted to my father for living, but to my teacher for living well."⁶³ Noble Romans habitually hired or bought Greek tutors. A slave or hireling could hardly be oppressive to his master's son, else his head could roll. Moreover, Romans accepted the superiority of Greek culture and language and preferred Greek tutors for training their sons in the finer aspects of culture and life. Tutors were good and tutoring, ennobling.

Coming to Paul's description, we note that the law of sin offerings became a tutor "to Christ," that is, to his perfect life and atoning sacrifice. Before Christ, "we were held captive under the law, imprisoned until the coming faith would be revealed" (3:23). This translation is highly problematic. How can God give anything that holds his people captive and imprisons them? A positive outlook makes much better sense both etymologically and theologically. The phrase "imprisoned" translates the Greek συγκλειόμενοι, compound of the verb κλείω, "to close" and the preposition σύν, "together." Though sometimes translated as "confine" or "enclose,"⁶⁴ it literally implies "something attached closely to something else," in this case humans to the "faith [that] would be revealed" (Gal 3:23). The faith to be revealed is nothing less than the sacrifice of Jesus. Something in the Torah aimed to attach the faithful to, connect them with, and point forward to the sacrifice of Jesus. This is the force of Paul's statement.

Moreover, believers were "held captive" (3:23) by this something until the appearance of Jesus. The Greek verb φρουρέω, "to guard"⁶⁵ and the cognate noun φρουρά designates a guard.⁶⁶ Most translators/commentators prefer to give a negative hew to the verb here: "held captive" (ESV), "kept under" (NKJV), "held prisoners" (NIV), or "confined under" (RSV).⁶⁷ However, a positive nuance is more fitting. Notice the only other

---

62. Triantafyllidis, *Lexiko tēs Koinēs Neoellēnikēs*, s.v. "παιδαγωγός."
63. See Esar, *20,000 Quips & Quotes*, 484.
64. E.g., LSJ, s.v. συγκλείω; BDAG, s.v. συγκλείω.
65. BDAG, s.v. φρουρέω.
66. BDAG, s.v. φρουρά.
67. See Fung, *The Epistle to the Galatians*, 169–170. Fung writes, "His meaning is rather that the law brought mankind into, and kept mankind under, an objectively

instance Paul uses the word: "And the peace of God, which surpasses all understanding, will guard [φρουρέω] your hearts and your minds in Christ Jesus" (Phil 4:7).

Taking συγκλείω and φρουρέω positively, we now have a clear picture. The law of sacrifices was not there to oppress and imprison individuals but to direct or lead them to Christ, and keep them attached and guarded safely to "the faith which would . . . be revealed" (3:23). It is precisely because of this positive function that Paul can declare that this law is in no way contrary to the sacrifice of Jesus: "Is the law then contrary to the promises of God? Certainly not!" (3:21). It is not contrary; it is the shadow of the sacrifice of Jesus that has now met the reality and is thus redundant.

7. Freedom and Slavery, Sarah and Hagar

In Gal 5:1 Paul declares, "For freedom Christ has set us free; stand firm therefore, and do not submit again to a yoke of slavery." What is the freedom and the slavery Paul has in mind? Moreover in 4:21–31, Paul contrasts Sarah, the "free woman," and Hagar, the "slave woman." He declares that believers are children of the free woman while the slave woman and her children will not inherit the promise.

Commentators often assume that "liberty" refers to freedom from God's legal codes and slavery to enslavement to laws and commandments.[68] Such an outlook is amiss. I already pointed out earlier Rodkinson's quote that in rabbinic thought "freedom" indicated freedom from punishment. [69]For Paul, likewise, true slavery is the slavery to sin and true freedom is freedom from sin (Rom 6:20). The blood of animals cannot cleanse sin (Heb 10:4) but the blood of Jesus does. Therefore, when Paul contrasts a person who has been set free with a person who is enslaved, he is comparing one who has had sin forgiven through the sacrifice of Christ, with one who still clings to the shadows of the sacrificial system and has therefore not received freedom from sin.

---

desperate situation, from which there was no escape until the revelation of faith as a new possibility." Ibid.

68. E.g., Arichen and Nida, *Paul's Letter to the Galatians*, 119: "Freedom here should be understood as freedom from the Law, and the pronoun *us* is inclusive, referring to both Paul and his readers."

69. Rodkinson, *The Babylonian Talmud*, xxii.

This is evident by the examples of Sarah and Hagar which immediately precede the statement on freedom and slavery (Gal 4:22–31). Sarah was Abraham's lawful wife and the one through which the promised Seed of Gen 15 would come. In Gen 15 God promised that he would solve the problem of sin, when he passed between the animals that had been cut in two. Now the Seed has come and the true Sacrifice for sin has been offered. Therefore, Sarah's true offspring, the Seed Jesus and those who believe in him, are free from sin. Sarah is the mother of those who have received forgiveness through faith in the sacrifice of Jesus.

Hagar was the slave woman through which Abraham fathered a child in Gen 16. Paul furthermore mentions Sinai, and the earthly Jerusalem. The connection of the triad Hagar, Sinai, and earthly Jerusalem is not accidental. Abraham's breach of the covenant with Hagar in Gen 16 prompts the establishment of the ritual of circumcision, a type of sacrifice as we saw above; at Sinai, Israel breaches the covenant through the golden calf prompting God to introduce, or "add," the system of sin offerings; and in earthly Jerusalem, the rituals established in Gen 17 and Lev 1–7 were replicated on a daily basis. The triad Hagar, Sinai, earthly Jerusalem therefore, reflect the offertory sacrificial ritual. By contrast, Sarah represents "the Jerusalem above" (4:26) which is the mother of all believers. Why the Jerusalem above? Because , that is where the heavenly sanctuary/temple is located, just as the earthly one was in the earthly Jerusalem. And in the heavenly temple, Jesus is the High Priest ministering the merits of his sacrifice. Sarah, therefore, represents faith in the atoning sacrifice of Jesus, and Hagar represents a desire to attain to justification through the temple and its ritual.

Paul explains, "Now you, brothers, like Isaac, are children of promise" (4:28). By contrast, those who stick to the offertory system of the temple are the children of Hagar clinging to circumcision and sacrifices and persecuting believers in Jesus: "But just as at that time he who was born according to the flesh persecuted him who was born according to the Spirit, so also it is now" (4:29). The contrast again is not law versus no law but rather of two sacrificial systems, of two systems to salvation, the shadow versus the reality.

Paul and the Law

TEMPLE RITUAL AND COLOSSIANS 2:16-17

"Therefore let no one pass judgment on you in questions of food and drink, or with regard to a festival or a new moon or a Sabbath. These are a shadow of the things to come, but the substance belongs to Christ" (Col 2:16-17).

Having tackled Galatians, we now move to a text, Col 2:16-17, that, like Galatians, is often understood to have strong antinomian connotations. Apart from the reference to food and drink, there is the calendric triplet—festival, new moon, Sabbaths—for which there are three main interpretations. (1) Paul is addressing festal practices that were not biblical but influenced by syncretistic ascetic tendencies, a dangerous mixture of Judaism and paganism.[70] As such, the text does not impact the validity of the feasts but only malpractices related to them. The problem with this view is that is hard to see how syncretistic practices could be viewed as a shadow of the body of Christ.[71] (2) The calendric triplet refers to the Jewish festal calendar, whereby "festival" represents the annual feasts, "new moon" the monthly new moon feast, and "Sabbaths" the weekly Sabbath.[72] This is by far the most prevalent view. In the few words of these two verses, Paul allegedly does away not only with Israel's food laws, but also the yearly and monthly festivals, and the Sabbath. (3) The calendric triplet deals only with the yearly and monthly feasts of Israel. The word "Sabbaths" refers to annual feasts that were also called Sabbaths, not the weekly Sabbath.[73] The problem with this view is that the word σάββατον refers almost exclusively (67 of 68 times) to the weekly Sabbath.[74] Consistency would suggest, but not require, that the same Sabbath is in view here.

It is not my purpose here to defend or negate the validity either of food laws or of the calendric triplet. My intention is rather to demonstrate that another apparently antinomian text is primarily concerned with temple

---

70. O'Brien, *Colossians, Philemon*, xxxv–xxxvi.

71. That is of Christ's provision and possession. Eadie, *The Epistle of Paul to the Colossians*, 179.

72. Clarke, *Adam Clarke's Commentary*, 1200; Vaughan, "Colossians," 11:203; Lohse, *Colossians and Philemon*, 115–16.

73. E.g., Preez, *Judging the Sabbath*, 2008.

74. Nine times (Matt 28:1; Mark 16:2, 9; Luke 18:12; 24:1; John 20:1, 19; Acts 20:7; 1 Cor 16:2) the noun σάββατον is used together with other days of the week leading translators to translate it as "week." However, the Greek for week is ἑβδομάς. The use of the word σάββατον therefore does not mean "week" but rather signifies the Sabbath as the apex of the week to which other days of the week point to.

ritual.⁷⁵ And I intend to do this with strength and conviction because, as stated in my Introduction to this book, this is the very passage that started me on the road to questioning established paradigms for understanding Paul, and endeavoring to discover a new.⁷⁶ To build the thesis, I will pursue five lines of evidence beginning with a fresh look at the Greek as well as some inter-biblical context.

1. The Phrase "With Regard"

Paul declares, "Therefore let no one pass judgment on you in questions of food and drink, or with regard to a festival or a new moon or a Sabbath. These are a shadow of the things to come, but the substance belongs to Christ" (Col 2:16–17). The phrase "with regard" translates the Greek ἐν μέρει, a preposition followed by the dative of the noun μέρος, which in turn is qualified by the genitive substantives ἑορτῆς, νεομηνίας, and σαββάτων, "festival," "new moon," and "Sabbaths."

Is this a correct translation? The primary lexical nuance of μέρος is one "part" of a whole.⁷⁷ This means that lexically, the noun has a partitive function to distinguish one part from others. The translation "with regards" has some support in the use of ἐν μέρει in 2 Cor 3:10 and 9:3. In the former, the phrase ἐν τούτῳ τῷ μέρει is translated as "in this case"⁷⁸ or "in this respect."⁷⁹ In the latter, ἐν τῷ μέρει τούτῳ is translated as "in this matter,"⁸⁰ "case,"⁸¹ or "respect."⁸² However, two cautions need to be sounded about 2 Cor 3:10 and 9:3. First, μέρος in both verses retains a partitive function in the sense that Paul singles out one μέρος he will be addressing from others he will not, as highlighted by the pronoun τούτῳ, "this." This partitive nu-

---

75. Cf. Gane, "Sabbath and the New Covenant," 321–22. Giem, "Sabbatōn in Col. 2:16," 195–210.

76. See Sokupa, "*Skia Tōn Mellontōn* in Col 2:16, 17." Mxolisi Michael Sokupa's dissertation, as explained in the Introduction, was a key motivator that helped me begin the journey of theological discovery that culminates in this book.

77. BDAG, s.v. μέρος.

78. ESV, NAS, RSV.

79. ASV, KJV, NAB, NKJV, YLT, GNV, "in this point."

80. ESV, NIV.

81. NAB, NAS, RSV.

82. ASV, NJB, NKJV, YLT. Thayer, *Greek-English Lexicon of the New Testament*, s.v. μέρος; Abbott-Smith, *A Manual Greek Lexicon of the New Testament*, s.v. μέρος.

ance has somehow been blunted in English translations. Second and more importantly, 2 Cor 3:10 and 9:3 entail different syntactical constructions to Col 2:16. While in the former two, the dative of μέρος is accompanied by the pronoun in the dative τούτῳ, in Col 2:16 it is followed by three genitive nouns.

To get a clear meaning of μέρος in Col 2:16, we should review identical or very similar constructions elsewhere and see how these are translated. Such a review indicates that in such cases, μέρος should be translated according to its primary lexical nuance, "one part of." In the biblical text, there are three other examples where the singular dative ἐν μέρει is followed by a noun in the genitive: Gen 23:9 ἐν μέρει τοῦ ἀγροῦ, "in one part of the field";[83] Judg (A) 7:19 ἐν μέρει τῆς παρεμβολῆς, "in one part of the camp";[84] and Isa 18:7 ἐν μέρει ποταμοῦ, "in a part of the river."[85] Three identical constructions to Col 2:16 and in all three, the genitive noun forms the whole out of which ἐν μέρει designates a part. Similar constructions with identical force abound in non-biblical Greek.[86]

Furthermore, in the Greek NT and the LXX, there are 24 examples of the singular μέρος in the nominative or accusative cases followed by a noun in the genitive.[87] In every single instance, the noun in the genitive like-

---

83. Brenton, *The Septuagint Version of the OT and Apocrypha*.

84. Ibid.

85. Ibid.

86. E.g., Thucydides, *Historiae*, 1.1.2.2; 6.2.1.2; 6.62.2.3; 8.105.3.1; Plutarch, *Agis et Cleomenes*, 27.3.5; Demosthenes, 21.3.2; Dion, 3.5.1; Athenaeus Soph., *Deipnosophistae*, 2.53.6; 10.46.4; Isocrates, *Panegyricus*, 164.6; Demosthenes, *Philippica 1*, 44.2; *Contra Aphobum*, 9.6; *Contra Leocharem*, 8.7; Isaeus, *De Dicaeogene*, 6.6; Philo Judaeus, *Legumallegoriarum*, 1.24.6; 1.40.3; *De cherubim*, 86.7; *De specialibuslegibus*, 2.104.4; 3.21.6; 3.126.7; *De virtutibus*, 3.3; 187.6; *De vita contemplativa*, 67.5; *De aeternitate mundi*, 82.3; *In Flaccum*, 1.5; *Legatio ad Gaium*, 158.2; 184.4; 228.1; Aristophanes, *Aves*, 1228; Aeschines, *In Ctesiphontem*, 4.6; Dinarchus, *Fragmenta*, 60.3.5; Xenophon, *Hellenica*, 7.1.14.2; Galen, *In PlatonisTimaeum*, 2.68; *De constitutione*, 1.267.14; *Arsmedica*, 1.380.8; 1.394.6; *De anatomicisadministrationibuslibri ix*, 2.306.13; 2.333.14; 2.647.5; *De venarumarteriarumquedissectione*, 2.791.18; *De nervorumdissectione*, 2.839.11; 2.853.4; Plato, *Politicus*, Stephanus 265.c.7; *Respublica*, Stephanus 370.a.1; 460.c.2; 484.d.7; 559.e.5; 577.c.3; *Timaeus*, Stephanus 36.a.4; 71.b.5; *Leges*, Stephanus 680.a.5; Diodorus Siculus, *Bibliotheca historica*, 4.37.3.8; 11.11.3.2; 11.12.6.7; 13.7.5.4; 13.110.3.2; Pseudo-Lucianus, *Demosthenis encomium*, 21.11; Lucianus, *Juppiterconfutatus*, 2.1; *De saltatione*, 23.17; Flavius Arrianus, *Alexandri anabasis*, 4.16.1.1; 4.28.7.3; Anon. *Periplus Ponti Euxini*, 87.9; Dionysius of Halicarnassus, *Antiquitates Romanae*, 2.16.1.9; 5.65.3.11; 6.24.2.7; *De compositioneverborum*, 22.208; Apollonius Dyscolus, *De pronominibus*, 2.1.72.15; *De adverbiis*, 2.1.177.13; 2.1.205.12; Aristotle, *Analyticapriora et posteriora*, Bekker 29b.22.

87. See Exod 16:35; Num 11:1; 22:41; 33:6; Josh 2:18; 3:15; 12:2; 18:19; Judg (A) 7:11;

wise forms the whole out of which μέρος in the nominative or accusative designates a part. The same holds true when the genitive singular is followed by a genitive substantive with few exceptions.[88] The evidence is too consistent to dismiss.

In light of the above, Paul's words should be translated, "Let no one judge you in food and drink, or in a/one part of a festival, or new moon, or Sabbaths." "These are a shadow of the things that were to come." Paul is not interested in the festivals themselves but only in one part or aspect of the festal calendar. What we need to determine is what this aspect is. To this task we now turn.

This is confirmed by further syntactical considerations. The verb κρινέτω, "judge" is followed by three datives: βρώσει, "food"; πόσει, "drink"; and μέρει, "a part." The third dative μέρει is then qualified by three genitives: "festival, new moon, or Sabbaths." Syntax would suggest that what was being judged were the three datives. The three genitives, by contrast, serve to explain the third dative. Paul's issue, therefore, is not the festivals, new moon, and Sabbath as such but food, drink, and one part or aspect only of the festivals, new moon, and Sabbath.

2. The "Body of Christ"

Colossians 2:17 reads, "These are a shadow of the things to come, but the substance belongs to Christ." The second part of the verse in Greek lacks a verb. It literally reads, "but the body of Christ." This ellipsis compounds the problem of interpretation. Most translations assume ἐστίν and translate it "*is* of Christ" (e.g., KJV, NKJV, NAB) or "*belongs* to Christ" (e.g., NAS, ESV, NRS). Moreover, scholars who follow traditional interpretations understand the phrase "body of Christ" figuratively.[89] This is evident in some modern Bible translations which avoid altogether any reference to a body.[90]

---

1 Sam 9:27; 1 Kgs 6:24; 12:31; 2 Kgs 7:5; 2 Chron 36:7; Jer 32:31, 33; Ezek 47:20; 48:1; Dan 1:2; 2:33, 41, 42; Luke 15:12; 24:42.

88. Genitive with genitive with μέρους designating a part of the whole: Exod 26:5, 26, 35 (2x); Num 20:16; 22:36; 34:3; Josh 3:8; 13:27; 15:2, 5, 8; 18:15, 16 (2x); 1 Sam 23:26 (2x); 2 Sam 13:34; 1 Kgs 6:24; 13:33; 2 Kgs 7:8; Neh 7:70; Isa 7:18; 37:24; Jer 32:33; Dan 5:7, 16, 29. Genitive with genitive with μέρους designating the part in view: Josh 3:16; 18:20; Acts 23:9.

89. Ellis, "Colossians," 1341.

90. NIV, "the reality is found in Christ"; ESV/RSV, "the substance belongs to Christ:" NKJV, "the substance is of Christ."

But there is no reason to be figurative. The "body of Christ" makes sense as it is.

In Colossians, Paul uses the term "body" of Christ to designate one of two things: the church[91] or the physical body of Christ.[92] If we understand the reference in Col 2:17 as pointing to the church, one wonders which aspect of food, drink, or part of a festival, new moon, or Sabbath is a shadow of the church.

I will tentatively suggest that instead, "body of Christ" should be understood as a reference to the literal body of Christ that was sacrificed on the cross. Throughout the Epistle, Paul places a strong emphasis on the physical body of Jesus. In Col 1:22, he describes how Christ reconciled us "in the body of his flesh through death" (NKJV). In 2:9, the fullness of deity dwells in Christ "bodily." In 2:12, he explains how through baptism we participate in the death, burial, and resurrection of Jesus. And in 2:14, he makes reference to the physical cross where Jesus died bodily. In light of such texts it is natural and contextually accurate to translate the "body of Christ" in Col 2:17 as a reference to the literal, physical body of Jesus. My suggestion is tentative but will be corroborated with further evidence below.

Moreover, the ellipsis is not simply of a verb. There is a conceptual contrast between Col 2:17a and 2:17b, that is, between the listed things that were a shadow and the body of Christ, which must be the reality. As such, the NJB seems to better capture the essence of the verse when it translates it: "These are only a shadow of what was coming: the reality is the body of Christ." The sacrifices offered during the festal calendar of Israel, would be a fitting shadow of the body of Jesus sacrificed on the cross for the forgiveness of human sin. "What was coming," would then be the sacrifice of Jesus on the cross.

3. Old Testament Parallels

Scholars agree that in mentioning festival, new moon, and Sabbaths, Paul alludes to any or all of the following OT passages: Num 28:1—29:40; 1 Chron 23:31; 2 Chron 2:4; 8:12–13; 31:3; Neh 10:33; Ezek 45:17; and Hos 2:11. These are the only OT texts that contain lists of festivals similar to

---

91. Barth and Blanke, *Colossians*, 340–42. For further discussions, see also O'Brien, *Colossians, Philemon*, 140–41.

92. Lenski, *The Interpretation of St. Paul's Epistles*, 125–27.

Col 2:16. Even a casual reading of these texts shows that in every single instance, except Hos 2:11, the emphasis is not the festivals themselves but the *sacrifices and burnt offerings* offered during those festivals, additional to the morning and evening sacrifices offered daily.[93]

The lengthiest of these texts is Num 28:1–29:40, which is a list of the different meat, grain, and drink offerings to be offered through the festal calendar of Israel.[94] Space does not permit us to quote the full two chapters. Suffice it to say that the focus is not the festal calendar of Israel as such, but the offerings offered during the festal calendar. All other texts seem to derive from this text. I have added emphasis to the texts to underline the point.

1 Chronicles 23:31: "And whenever *burnt offerings* were offered to the LORD on Sabbaths, new moons and feast days, according to the number required of them, regularly before the LORD."

2 Chronicles 2:4: "Behold, I am about to build a house for the name of the LORD my God and dedicate it to him for the burning of incense of sweet spices before him, and for the regular arrangement of the showbread, and for *burnt offerings* morning and evening, on the Sabbaths and the new moons and the appointed feasts of the LORD our God, as ordained forever for Israel."

2 Chronicles 8:12–13: "Then Solomon offered up *burnt offerings* to the LORD on the altar of the LORD that he had built before the vestibule, as the duty of each day required, offering according to the commandment of Moses for the Sabbaths, the new moons, and the three annual feasts—the Feast of Unleavened Bread, the Feast of Weeks, and the Feast of Booths."

2 Chronicles 31:3: "The contribution of the king from his own possessions was for the *burnt offerings*: the burnt offerings of morning and evening, and the burnt offerings for the Sabbaths, the new moons, and the appointed feasts, as it is written in the Law of the LORD."

---

93. For a fuller discussion of this scriptural background and some extra-biblical parallels, see Giem, "Sabbatōn in Col. 2:16," 195–210. Cf. Cole, "The Sacred Times Prescribed in the Pentateuch."

94. R. Brown, *The Message of Numbers*, 29. Harrison comments as follows: "Numbers 28 introduces a series of instructions dealing with ritual materials. The material can be analyzed as follows: 2) daily offerings (vv. 1–8); 2) weekly offering (vv. 9–10); 3) monthly offerings (vv. 11–15); 4) Passover and unleavened Bread (vv. 16–25); 5) first fruits (vv. 26–31).... Chapter 29 continues the priestly concerns of its predecessor and can be divided into three compounds: 1) blowing trumpets (vv. 1–6); 2) Day of Atonement (vv. 7–11); 3) feast of Tabernacles (vv. 12–40)." Harrison, *Numbers*, 361–75.

Nehemiah 10:32–33: "We also take on ourselves the obligation to give yearly a third part of a shekel for the service of the house of our God: for *the showbread, the regular grain offering, the regular burnt offering*, the Sabbaths, the new moons, the appointed feasts, the holy things, and the sin offerings to make atonement for Israel, and for all the work of the house of our God."

Ezekiel 45:17: "It shall be the prince"s duty to furnish *the burnt offerings, grain offerings, and drink offerings*, at the feasts, the new moons, and the Sabbaths, all the appointed feasts of the house of Israel: he shall provide the *sin offerings, grain offerings, burnt offerings, and peace offerings*, to make atonement on behalf of the house of Israel.

Even in Hos 2:11 where sacrifices and offerings are not directly mentioned they are implied. In Hos 2:13, God laments that Israel kept the feasts of other gods and offered burnt offerings to them.[95] Therefore, God will cease the relevant burnt offerings (Hos 2:11; 3:4).

If all the OT passages that parallel the calendric triplet festival, new moon, and Sabbaths of Col 2:16 deal primarily with the sacrifices and burnt offerings offered therein rather than the feasts themselves, it can be assumed that the parallel text of Col 2:16—which is only interested with one aspect of the festal calendar likewise—deals with the same issues. Obviously, Paul is using the triplet as a catchphrase to direct attention to the relevant calendric OT texts and their offertory lists.[96] However, to strengthen his case, Paul provides further evidence still.

4. "Food and Drink"

Further confirmation for our suggestion comes from the phrase "food and drink"[97] which are also a "shadow" of the body of Christ. Some casually observe that this phrase refers to clean and unclean foods and conclude that OT food prohibitions are no longer valid.[98] Others note that while the OT did have several food prohibitions, it did not contain drink prohibitions with the exception of the use of wine by priests when they ministered in

---

95. Stuart, *Hosea-Jonah*, 51.

96. Giem, "Sabbatōn in Col. 2:16," 19 –210.

97. Note that βρώσει and πόσει relate more to the substance, food and drink, rather than the act of eating and drinking.

98. Earle, *Adam Clarke's Commentary on the Bible*, 1200; Gorday, *Colossians, 1–2 Thessalonians, 1–2 Timothy, Titus, Philemon*, 38–39.

Israel, Covenant, Law

the temple (Lev 10:9).[99] That is not to say that the OT condones the use of alcoholic beverages. Quite the contrary, it warns clearly against the dangers of drink.[100] But there was no specific law forbidding it.

So, Paul's words most likely do not refer to OT food prohibitions. What do they refer to? Failing to see OT food prohibitions, some assume that Paul condemns the practice of ascetic syncretists who tried to impose their own food and drink regulations on Colossian believers.[101] But this approach is hardly any more palatable because syncretistic ascetic practices could in no way be a shadow of the body of Christ.

An alternative makes better sense. The OT offertory system included food and drink offerings. Indeed, most sacrifices included a food and drink element (Num 15:1–21). Food and drink offerings are mentioned in Neh 10:33 and Ezek 45:17, two of the calendric texts quoted above and which scholars agree stand behind Col 2:16. More importantly, food and drink offerings are repeatedly mentioned in Num 28:1–29:40, the lengthy passage that forms the background to all OT calendric texts. Given that Paul is drawing from these OT calendric texts, it makes best sense that he has in mind the food and drink offerings mentioned therein.[102]

Summarizing this section, Paul's reference to "food and drink" fits neither OT food prohibitions nor supposed ascetic practices. But it fits perfectly our suggestion that in view is Israel's offertory and sacrificial system.[103]

---

99. Kings were also warned strongly against the use of wine (Prov 31:4) though it is unclear if this was a law or a strong advice.

100. See Lev 10:8–10; Deut 32:33; Prov 23:32.

101. O'Brien, *Colossians, Philemon*, 138–39; Vaughan, "Colossians," 203–4; Lohse, *Colossians and Philemon*, 115.

102. Note that βρῶσις and πόσις appear twice again together in the NT (Rom 14:17; John 6:55). In the latter case, a ritual meaning is clearly evident in Jesus's words: "For my flesh is true food, and my blood is true drink." The cognate terms βρῶμα and πόμα are also used of OT food and drink offerings: "According to this arrangement, gifts and sacrifices are offered that cannot perfect the conscience of the worshiper, but deal only with food and drink and various washings, regulations for the body imposed until the time of reformation" (Heb 9:9–10).

103. The βρώσει of 2:16 should not be confused or be seen as parallel to the μηδὲ γεύσῃ of 2:21. Whereas the former is connected to the OT God-instituted calendric triplet—of feast, new moon, and Sabbath—and is part of the elements that were a shadow of the body of Christ, the latter is connected to non-biblical ascetic practices together with "do not handle" and "do not touch" (2:20) that were "human precepts and teachings" (2:22).

5. Hebrews 10:1–10

The last piece of evidence is Heb 10:1–10. This passage bears a very close thematic and linguistic parallel to Col 2:16–17. It (a) mentions the physical "body of Christ" (Heb 10:10);[104] (b) makes reference to the festal calendar of Israel (Heb 10:1, 3) and the Law in which the calendar was described (Heb 10:1, 8); (c) contains (with Heb 8:5) the only other typological use in the NT of the word "shadow" (Heb 10:1); (d) contains the exact same expression as in Col 2:16 "shadow . . . of things that were to come" (Heb 10:1);[105] and (e) just as in Col 2:16 where only part (ἐν μέρει) of the festal calendar is in view, likewise in Heb 10:1 only aspects of the Law of Moses ("the law has" as opposed to "the law is") are a shadow.[106] Given such impressive parallels, Heb 10:1–10 is an invaluable benchmark against which to test any interpretation of Col 2:16–17. What does Heb 10:1–10 present?

Hebrews 10:1–10 is a prolonged contrast between the sacrificial system of the OT and the physical body of Christ.[107] The writer asserts two things: (a) the sacrifices where a "shadow" of the sacrifice of Jesus[108] and (b) the sacrifice of Jesus "abolishes" the OT sacrificial system (Heb 10:9).[109] It therefore tallies completely with our view that in Col 2:16–17 are in view offerings and sacrifices, not the festal calendar as such.

The Context

How does the above analysis fit the broader context of the Epistle? Aspects of Colossians were written to counter false theology that was invading the church in Colossae. The nature of this false theology is hard to pinpoint.

---

104. Philip E. Hughes comments, "The incarnate Son abolishes the first, namely, the sacrifices associated with the Mosaic law, in order to establish the second, namely, the will of God involving the offering of himself as the one sacrifice for sins forever." Hughes, *The Epistle to the Hebrews*, 399.

105. Hughes, *Epistle to the Hebrews*, 389.

106. Kenneth S. Wuest comments, "The explanation consists in this that the law had only a shadow of good things that were to be, not the vary image of the things." Wuest, *Hebrews in the Greek New Testament*, 171. See also MacArthur, *Hebrew*, 247.

107. Wiley, *The Epistle to the Hebrews*, 281.

108. Westcott, *The Epistle to the Hebrews*, 304.

109. The verb ἀναιρεῖ in Heb 10:9 can mean to "take away" or "abolish." "Thus the old System of sacrifices (10:8) was abolished in the establishing of the new in the coming of Christ as Jesus of Nazareth." Hobbs, *Hebrews*, 99.

However, it is very clear that Jewish elements also played a part. Several elements are supportive of this.

First in Col 2:11, Paul addresses the question of circumcision declaring that believers have received "a circumcision made without hands" and therefore are in no need for circumcision of the flesh. Circumcision was a prerequisite for participation in ritual activities, sacrifice, and entry into the temple beyond the court of the Gentiles. Moreover in Col 2:13 and 14, he declares the sacrifice of Jesus adequate to remove sin, something which the temple and its services could not achieve, as discussed above. Indeed, Jesus cancelled the "record of debt" that stood against believers.

Conversely, references to "philosophy" (Col 2:8), "rulers and authorities" (Col 2:15), and asceticism and the worship of angels (Col 2:18) are harder to pinpoint and may suggest either a syncretistic attack on the Colossian church that involved both a return to temple ritual and other non-directly related practices, or different attacks by different false teachers promoting different false theologies. What is clear, however, is that the repeated references to circumcision and the emphasis on Christ as the only one who can forgive sins provides an adequate background to the issues discussed above.

CONCLUSION

We have done a number of things in this chapter. First, we looked at Paul's programmatic statement in Acts 13:13–42. Then, we looked at seven arguments from within Galatians. Then we explored Col 2:16–17 at some depth. Some of the arguments presented carry more weight, some may be considered tenuous by the reader who reads them for the first time. Taken together, I believe, they create a fairly powerful picture that the issue Paul faced repeatedly and addressed was the attachment of Jewish Christians to the Jerusalem temple and its ritual, and the attempt of some of them to enforce this outlook on other believers.

Another related question is that if Paul's concern was mainly the sacrificial ritual of Judaism, why did Paul not spell it out in clearer terms as, for example, Hebrews does? Two answers fit here. First, his message would have been much clearer to his original readers than it is to us. I already pointed out the differences in meaning of the word "law." Other things would have come into play. Today we live nearly 2,000 years after the destruction of the temple and the end of sacrifices and ritual offerings. The world of first century Judaism is far detached from our worldview. Therefore, it is hard to connect the language of Paul to concepts that are rather distant from us. For Paul's original audience, it would have been easy to connect his words with their everyday experiences and challenges.

Second, when Paul wrote Galatians (between AD 48 and 56),[110] Jewish believers were probably still the majority and the temple was deeply engrained in their mindset. He had to be very careful in his argumentation so as to make his point without overtly offending Jewish sensitivities, else he could run into troubles with them, as indeed happened in Acts 21. By contrast, when Hebrews was written nearly 20 years later, the breach between Christianity and the synagogue was beginning to take full shape. The temple was on its final days, with the coming destruction of AD 70 looming on the horizon. As such, the writer could afford to be more forthright, indeed, circumstances demanded as much so as to prepare those who clung to the temple for the disappointment awaiting them.

If we understand the contrast in Galatians as one between the grace of Jesus versus the grace of the Law/Torah, instead of grace versus law, it opens whole new windows of insight into Paul's thought. The perceived conflict of law and grace disappears and the two can now be seen as complementary, as two sides of the one harmonious character of God. Divine law in the shape of the Ten Commandments and other regulations can then be appreciated in its intended beauty, as the standard of behavior for all the believers today.

---

110. The date of Galatians depends on the destination of the Epistle. If the north Galatian theory is accepted, then a date of composition around AD 56 during the third missionary journey is likely. If the south Galatian theory is accepted, then a date even before AD 50 is possible. See for example, Elwell and Comfort, "Hebrews," 508.

Synopsis and Synthesis

SYNOPSIS

The research presented in this volume has been a beautiful journey of discovery, at least for me. We began in Chapter 1 with discussing some of the weaknesses of Reformation and New Perspectives on Paul as they relate to biblical law. While Reformation outlooks are not by definition antinomian, and neither Luther nor Calvin were, the denigration of any human effort, indeed ability, to gain favor from God contains within it the seed of antinomianism and has produced countless antinomian statements and indeed theologies within the Protestant world. New Perspectives ostensibly take a more favorable view of both law and human good works. However, the notion of boundary markers, aspects of biblical law that purportedly where put in place to socially segregate Israel from other nations, is nebulous, indeterminate, and even arbitrary and leaves the readers with a big question mark as to what was/is and was/is not required of believers in Jesus.

The remaining four chapters of the book were an attempt to build an alternative Third Perspective. In Chapter 2, we saw that for Paul, the nascent Christian church was not a break from biblical Israel; not a new different, spiritual Israel, neither an alternative parallel reality but a continuation of biblical Israel. This was not a novel approach unique to Paul, a new theology. Not by any means. Quite the contrary, in the mosaic of theologies and approaches that was first century Judaism, many groups considered themselves as the true heirs of the biblical faith of Israel.

In Chapter 3, we explored the concept of covenant: namely, the Abrahamic, especially the Sinai (Old) Covenant, and the new covenant. I argued that the transition from old to new does not envisage a change in the legal framework of the old covenant as exemplified primarily in the Ten Commandments and secondarily in the Book of the Law, but in the covenant ritual. The ineffective blood of sacrifices has been replaced by the effective blood of the effective sacrifice of Jesus on the cross. In that sense, the relation of old to new is that of shadow to reality, whereby the shadow is a replica of the reality and the reality, the full and complete realization of the shadow.

The last two chapters endeavored to explain Paul's attacks on the law. In Chapter 4, we studied the historical framework and noticed that early Christians from a Jewish background continued to frequent the temple and even participate in its rituals through ritual offerings and sacrifices. We saw clear evidence of this in Hebrews, the incident of the vow in Acts 21, possibly in the Jerusalem Council of Acts 15, and in other NT passages. Such Jewish Christians apparently saw no contradiction between the ritual, new covenant sacrificial reality of the death of Jesus on the one hand, and the sacrificial realities of the old covenant on the other, and felt the two could happily co-exist side by side. For the writer of Hebrews, however, as well as other apostles, the two were incompatible and to believe in Jesus and at the same time continue with old covenant ritual in practice constituted a rejection of Jesus. Ritual therefore was a key issue in the early church.

Then in the last and most important chapter, Chapter 5, I argued that Paul's attacks on the law in Galatians are not attacks on biblical law as such but on the system of sacrifices outlined in the Law, the Torah, the aim of which was to establish covenant and forgive sins. We noted that ritual language and descriptions abound from the "other gospel," to the concept of "anathema," the discussion of circumcision, the emphasis on justification, and the inability of the works of the Torah to provide this, to the "law" added to provide grace for sins and the aim of which was actually to point to the sacrifice of Jesus which is the only one that provides true grace for human sin, to the contrast between the old and new covenants the former based in the temple in Jerusalem and the later in the heavenly Jerusalem, the former leading to slavery (since it cannot truly forgive sin), and the later to true freedom from sin. Similarly, in the presumed antinomian Col 2:16–17 I argued, with considerable justification I believe, that again the issue was sacrifices and offerings.

Synthesis

Can the above discussion help us streamline current soteriological models in a way that does not detract from the principal reality of salvation by grace, and yet at the same time safeguards the sanctity of biblical law? I believe yes. While justification by grace as a judicial act that absolves the sinner from sin is a valid model for understanding salvation, it needs to be seen in tandem with other biblical models, chief of which is the concept of covenant. Old Testament covenants had two parts, a legal code that defined appropriate behavior, and the sacrificial, ritual element which enabled sinners to enter into and remain within a covenant relation with a holy God.

These two realities, a legal framework and grace through sacrifice, were not antagonistic but parallel, perhaps even complementary realities. The legal framework defines how the governance of God operates and what he expects of humans who want to live in close connection to him. Given the human inability and repeated failure to live within the framework defined by divine law, grace kicks in. It first enables sinners to enter into the covenant relationship by offering abundant forgiveness: "For by grace you have been saved through faith. And this is not your own doing; it is the gift of God" (Eph 2:8). And then, once within the covenant, it covers human failure: "My little children, I am writing these things to you so that you may not sin. But if anyone does sin, we have an advocate with the Father, Jesus Christ the righteous" (1 John 2:1). Grace is what brings a sinner to Christ and enables him to remain within a covenant relationship. It is the determining factor from beginning to end.

Nonetheless, for a human being to desire to and decide to enter into a covenant relationship with God is to acknowledge that the covenant operates within a legal framework. A conscious consent and commitment to conform to the covenantal framework is integral to a desire to be in a covenant relationship just as in the purely human sphere of things, a commitment to the stipulations of a human agreement or contract is expected of anyone entering any contractual agreement/relationship. Failure to keep to a contractual agreement might be forgiven but only on the prerogative of the wronged party. God is consistently willing to forgive his erring children. Jesus's admonition to Peter clearly reflects a divine characteristic: "Then Peter came up and said to him, 'Lord, how often will my brother sin against me, and I forgive him? As many as seven times?' Jesus said to him, 'I do not say to you seven times, but seventy times seven'" (Matt 18:21–22). Yet this willingness to forgive in no way detracts from the sanctity of God's

Synopsis and Synthesis

law. Indeed, it is the very sanctity of God's law that makes divine forgiveness so wonderful. If God's law was of little or no consequence, forgiveness for breaches would correspondingly be trivial or even unnecessary.

The ultimate aim of the covenant is for God's law to be written on the human heart whereby once sinners come to the point where obedience and compliance to the demand standard becomes natural to sanctified human nature: "But this is the covenant that I will make with the house of Israel after those days, declares the LORD: I will put my law within them, and I will write it on their hearts. And I will be their God, and they shall be my people. And no longer shall each one teach his neighbor and each his brother, saying, 'Know the LORD,' for they shall all know me, from the least of them to the greatest, declares the LORD. For I will forgive their iniquity, and I will remember their sin no more" (Jer 31:33–34). The knowing of the Lord goes hand in hand with his law being written on the heart. Sins will not be remembered any longer not only because they have been forgiven but also because they henceforth belong to the past. While this aspect of the covenant—the law fully written on the heart leading to full conformity to the divine will—may not be fully realized this side of eternity, it is the goal to which covenant aims. Any soteriological system which downplays this divine goal has taken a wrong turn and needs a reality check.

Biblical law defines the goal of God for the life of the believer; grace provides the framework in which humans can still be close to God despite human failure. To see these two dimensions as parallel and complementary is to more fully realize God's will for humanity.

Bibliography

Abbott-Smith, G. *A Manual Greek Lexicon of the New Testament*. 3rd ed. Edinburgh: T. & T. Clark, 1981.
Achtemeier, Paul J. *Romans*. Interpretation. Atlanta: John Knox, 1985.
Allen, Leslie C. *Jeremiah: A Commentary*. The Old Testament Library. Louisville: Westminster John Knox, 2008.
Allen, Willoughby C. *A Critical and Exegetical Commentary on the Gospel According to S. Matthew*. International Critical Commentary. New York: Scribner, 1907.
Arichen, Daniel C., and Eugene A. Nida. *A Handbook on Paul's Letter to the Galatians*. New York: United Bible Societies, 1993.
Attridge, Harold W. *The Epistle to the Hebrews: A Commentary on the Epistle to the Hebrews*. Hermeneia. Philadelphia: Fortress, 1989.
———. "Hebrews." In *The Anchor Yale Bible Dictionary*. Edited by David Noel Freedman. New York: Doubleday, 1996. 3:97.
Bacon, Benjamin W. *The Story of St. Paul*. New York: Houghton, Mifflin, 1904.
Barnett, Paul. *The Second Epistle to the Corinthians*. The New International Commentary on the New Testament. Grand Rapids: Eerdmans, 1997.
Barrett, C. K. *A Critical and Exegetical Commentary on the Acts of the Apostles*. International Critical Commentary. London: T. & T. Clark, 2004.
Barth, Markus, and Helmut Blanke. *Colossians*. Anchor Bible 34B. New York: Doubleday, 1994.
Barth, Markus. *Ephesians: Introduction, Translation, and Commentary on Chapters 1–3*. New Haven: Yale University Press, 2008.
Batten, Loring W. *A Critical and Exegetical Commentary on the Books of Ezra and Nehemiah*. International Critical Commentary. Edinburgh: T. & T. Clark, 1980.
Bauer, Walter. *A Greek-English Lexicon of the New Testament and Other Early Christian Literature*. 3rd ed. Rev. and edited by Frederick William Danker. Chicago: University of Chicago Press, 2000.
Baxter, A. G., and John A. Ziesler. "Paul and the Arboriculture: Romans 11:17–24." *Journal for the Study of the New Testament* 24 (1985) 25–32.
Beall, Todd S. *Josephus' Description of the Essenes Illustrated by the Dead Sea Scrolls*. Cambridge: Cambridge University Press, 1988.
Beasley-Murray, George R. *John*. Word Biblical Commentary 36. Dallas: Word, 2002.
Beck, Charles. *On the Roman Calendar*. Boston: Little & Brown, 1838.

Bibliography

Bernard, John H., and A. H. McNeile. *A Critical and Exegetical Commentary on the Gospel According to St. John*. International Critical Commentary. Edinburgh: T. & T. Clark, 1985.

Betz, Hans D. *Galatians: A Commentary on Paul's Letter to the Churches in Galatia*. Hermeneia. Philadelphia: Fortress, 1979.

Blackwood, Andrew W. *Commentary on Jeremiah*. Waco: Word, 1977.

Bowman, Thorleif. "Das text kritische Problem des sogenannten Aposteldekrets." *NovT* 7 (1964–65) 26–36.

Brenton, Lancelot Charles Lee. *The Septuagint Version of the Old Testament*. London: Samuel Baxter, 1844.

———. *The Septuagint Version of the Old Testament and Apocrypha: With an English Translation and with Various Readings and Critical Notes*. London: Samuel Bagster, 1851.

Brown, Colin, ed. *The New International Dictionary of New Testament Theology*. Vol. 2. Grand Rapids: Zondervan, 1986.

Brown, Francis, et al. *The Enhanced Brown-Driver-Briggs Hebrew and English Lexicon*. Oak Harbor, WA: Logos Research Systems, 2000.

Brown, Raymond. *The Message of Numbers: Journey to the Promised Land*. The Bible Speaks Today. England: Inter-Varsity, 2002.

Bruce, Frederick F. *The Book of the Acts*. The New International Commentary on the New Testament. Grand Rapids: Eerdmans, 1988.

———. *The Epistle to the Galatians*. The New International Greek Testament Commentary. Grand Rapids: Eerdmans, 1982.

———. *The Epistles to the Colossians, to Philemon, and to the Ephesians*. The New International Commentary on the New Testament. Grand Rapids: Eerdmans, 1984.

———. *The Gospel of John*. Grand Rapids: Eerdmans, 1994.

Bruckner, James K. *Exodus*. New International Biblical Commentary 2. Peabody: Hendrickson, 2008.

Bruder, Edith. *The Black Jews of Africa–History, Religion, Identity*. Oxford: Oxford University Press, 2008.

Bruggemann, Walter. *A Commentary on Jeremiah: Exile and Homecoming*. Grand Rapids: Eerdmans, 1998.

———. *Genesis*. Interpretation. Atlanta: John Knox, 1982.

Buchanan, George W. *To the Hebrews*. Anchor Bible 36. Garden City: Doubleday, 1972.

Burton, Ernest de Witt. *A Critical and Exegetical Commentary on the Epistle to the Galatians*. New York: Scribner, 1920.

Cassuto, Umberto. *A Commentary on the Book of Exodus*. Jerusalem: Magnus, 1967.

Clarke, Adam. *Adam Clarke's Commentary*. Vol. 1. Grand Rapids: Baker, 1967.

Clements, R. E. *Jeremiah*. Interpretation. Atlanta: John Knox, 1988.

Coats, George W. *Genesis: With an Introduction to Narrative Literature*. Vol. 1. Grand Rapids: Eerdmans, 1983.

Cohen, Shaye J. D. "A Brief History of Jewish Circumcision Blood." In *The Covenant of Circumcision: New Perspectives on an Ancient Jewish Rite*, edited by Elizabeth W. Mark, 30–42. Hanover: Brandeis University Press, 2003.

Cole, H. Ross. "The Sacred Times Prescribed in the Pentateuch: Old Testament Indicators of the Extent of Their Applicability." PhD diss., Andrews University, 1996.

Conzelmann, Hans, et al. *Acts of the Apostles: A Commentary on the Acts of the Apostles*. Hermeneia. Philadelphia: Fortress Press, 1987.

Bibliography

Cranfield, C. E. B. *The Epistle to the Romans: Romans 9–16; A Critical and Exegetical Commentary*. International Critical Commentary. New York: T. & T. Clark, 2004.

Danker, Frederick W., et al. *Greek-English Lexicon of the New Testament and Other Early Christian Literatur*. 3rd ed. Chicago: University of Chicago Press, 2000.

DeWitt, Dale S. *Dispensational Theology in America during the Twentieth Century: Theological Development and Cultural Context*. Grand Rapids: Grace Bible College, 2002.

Diprose, Ronald E. *Israel and the Church: The Origin and Effects of Replacement Theology*. Waynesboro, GA: Authentic Media, 2000.

Donker, Frederick W. *2 Corinthians*. Minneapolis: Augsburg, 1989.

Douglas, J. D., ed. *New Commentary on the Whole Bible*. Wheaton: Tyndale, 1990.

Dunn, James D. G. *The Epistle to the Galatians*. Grand Rapids: Baker Academic, 2011.

Dunn, James D. G. "The New Perspective on Paul." *Bulletin of the John Rylands Library* 65 (1983) 95–122.

———. *The New Perspective on Paul*. Grand Rapids: Eerdmans, 2008.

———. *Romans 9–16*. Word Biblical Commentary 38B. Waco: Word, 1988.

du Preez, Ron. *Judging the Sabbath*. Berrien Springs: Andrews University Press, 2008.

Durham, John I. *Exodus*. Word Biblical Commentary 3. Dallas: Word, 2002.

Eadie, John. *Commentary on the Epistle of Paul to the Colossians*. Minneapolis: James & Klock, 1977.

Earle, Ralph. *Adam Clarke's Commentary on the Bible*. Grand Rapids: Baker, 1967.

Easton, M. G. *Easton's Bible Dictionary*. Oak Harbor, WA: Logos Research Systems, 1996.

Eberhart, Christian A. "Characteristics of Sacrificial Metaphors in Hebrews." In *Hebrews: Contemporary Methods—New Insights*, edited by Gabriella Gelardini, 37–64. Leiden: Brill, 2005.

Edersheim, Alfred. *The Temple: Its Ministry and Services, as They Were at the Time of Jesus Christ*. London: The Religious Tract Society, 1874.

Ellingworth, Paul. *The Epistle to the Hebrews: A Commentary on the Greek Text*. Grand Rapids: Eerdmans, 1993.

Ellingworth, Paul, et al. *A Handbook on Paul's First Letter to the Corinthians*. UBS Handbook Series. New York: United Bible Societies, 1995.

Ellis, E. Earle. "Colossians." *The Wycliffe Bible Commentary*. Edited by Charles Pfeiffer and Everett F. Harrion. Chicago: Moody, 1990.

Elwell, Walter A., and Philip W. Comfort. *Tyndale Bible Dictionary*. Tyndale Reference Library. Wheaton IL: Tyndale, 2001.

English: Oxford Living Dictionaries. "Law." https://en.oxforddictionaries.com/definition/law.

Epstein, Isidore, trans. *Babylonian Talmud (Soncino)*. London: Soncino, 1961.

Esar, Evan. *20,000 Quips & Quotes*. New York: Barnes & Noble, 1968.

Fee, Gordon D. *The First Epistle to the Corinthians*. The New International Commentary on the New Testament. Grand Rapids: Eerdmans, 1987.

Fensham, Frank Charles. *The Books of Ezra and Nehemiah*. New International Commentary on the Old Testament. Grand Rapids: Eerdmans, 2007.

Fitzmyer, Joseph A. *First Corinthians: A New Translation with Introduction and Commentary*. New Haven: Yale University Press, 2008.

Fitzmyer, Joseph A. *Romans: A New Translation with Introduction and Commentary*. The Anchor Yale Bible 33. New Haven: Yale University Press, 2008.

Bibliography

France, R. T. *The Gospel of Matthew*. The New International Commentary on the New Testament. Grand Rapids: Eerdmans, 2007.
Freedman, David Noel. *The Anchor Yale Bible Dictionary*. Vol. 3. New York: Doubleday, 1996.
Frethein, Terrence E. *Exodus: A Bible Commentary for Teaching and Preaching*. Interpretation. Louisville: John Knox, 1991.
Friedlander, Gerald, trans. *Pirke de Rabbi Eliezer*. New York: Bloch, 1916.
Friedman, Richard Elliott. "Tabernacle." In *The Anchor Yale Bible Dictionary*. Edited by David Noel Freedman. New York: Doubleday, 1996. 6:293.
Fung, Ronald Y. K. *The Epistle to the Galatians*. The New International Commentary on the New Testament. Grand Rapids: Eerdmans, 1988.
Gane, Roy E. "Sabbath and the New Covenant." *Journal of the Adventist Theological Society* 10/1–2 (1999) 311–332.
Garland, David E. *First Corinthians*. Grand Rapids: Baker Academic, 2003.
George, Timothy. *Galatians*. New American Commentary 30. Nashville: Broadman & Holman, 2001.
Gese, Hartmut. "Die Sóhne." *Zur biblischen Theologie: Alttestamentliche Vortrôge*. Tübingen: Mohr Siebeck, 1983.
Giantzaklidis, Ioannis. "Introduction." In *Earthly Shadows, Heavenly Realities: Temple/Sanctuary Cosmology in Ancient Near Eastern, Biblical, and Early Jewish Literature*, edited by Kim Papaioannou and Ioannis Giantzaklidis, 1–8. Berrien Springs: Andrews University Press, 2017.
Giem, Paul. "Sabbatōn in Col. 2:16." *Andrews University Seminary Studies* 19/3 (1981) 195–210.
Good, Robert M. *The Sheep of His Pasture: A Study of the Hebrew Noun ☒Am(m) and Its Semitic Cognates*. Harvard Semitic Monographs 29. Chico: Scholars, 1983.
Goodman, Martin. *Judaism in the Roman World: Collected Essays*. Ancient Judaism and Early Christianity 66. Leiden: Brill, 2007.
Gorday, Peter. *Colossians, 1–2 Thessalonians, 1–2 Timothy, Titus, Philemon*. Ancient Christian Commentary on Scripture 9. Edited by Thomas C. Oden. Downers Grove: InterVarsity.
Gordon, Robert P. *Hebrews*. Sheffield: Sheffield Phoenix, 2008.
Gottheil, Richard, and M. Seligsohn. "Helena." In *Jewish Encyclopedia*. Edited by Isidore Singer. New York: Funk & Wagnalls, 1904. 6:334.
Green, Joel B. *The Gospel of Luke*. Grand Rapids: Eerdmans, 1997.
Green, Joel B., et al., eds. *Dictionary of Jesus and the Gospels*. Downers Grove: InterVarsity, 1992.
Haberman, Bonna D. "Foreskin Sacrifice Zipporah's Ritual and the Bloody Bridegroom." In *The Covenant of Circumcision: New Perspectives on an Ancient Jewish Rite*, edited by Elizabeth W. Mark, 18–29. Hanove: Brandeis University Press, 2003.
Hagner, Donald A. *Matthew 14–28*. Word Biblical Commentary 33B. Dallas: Word, 2002.
Hahn, Scott W. "Covenant, Cult, and the Curse-of-Death: Διαθήκη in Heb 9:15–22." In *Hebrews: Contemporary Methods—New Insights*, edited by Gabriella Gelardini, 65–88. Leiden: Brill, 2005.
Hall, Robert G. "Circumcision." In *The Anchor Yale Bible Dictionary*. Edited by David Noel Freedman. New York: Doubleday, 1996. 1:1025–31.
Hamilton, Victor P. *The Book of Genesis: Chapters 1–17*. The New International Commentary on the Old Testament. Grand Rapids: Eerdmans, 1990.

Bibliography

———. *Exodus: An Exegetical Commentary*. Grand Rapids: Baker Academic, 2012.
Hammer, Reuven. *The Classic Midrash: Tannaitic Commentaries on the Bible*. New York: Paulist, 1995.
Harris, Murray J. *The Second Epistle to the Corinthians: A Commentary on the Greek Text*. Grand Rapids: Eerdmans, 2005.
Harrison, R. K. *Numbers: An Exegetical Commentary*. Grand Rapids: Baker, 1992.
Hartley, John E. *Leviticus*. Word Biblical Commentary 4. Dallas: Word, 2002.
Hays, Richard B. *First Corinthians*. Interpretation. Louisville: John Knox, 1997.
Heil, John Paul. *Hebrews, Chiastic Structures and Audience Response*. The Catholic Biblical Quarterly Monograph Series 46. Washington: Catholic Biblical Association of America, 2010.
Hendriksen, William, and Simon J. Kistemaker. *Exposition of the Gospel According to John*. New Testament Commentary 1–2. Grand Rapids: Baker, 1953–2001.
Hobbs, Herschel H. *Hebrews: Challenges to Bold Discipleship*. Nashville: Broadman, 1971.
Hoffman, Lawrence A. *Covenant of Blood: Circumcision and Gender in Rabbinic Judaism*. Chicago: University of Chicago Press, 1996.
Holladay, William Lee, and Paul D. Hanson. *Jeremiah 1: A Commentary on the Book of the Prophet Jeremiah; Chapters 1–25*. Hermeneia. Philadelphia: Fortress, 1986.
Hughes, Philip E. *A Commentary on the Epistle to the Hebrews*. Grand Rapids: Eerdmans, 1977.
Hurtado, Larry W. *Destroyer of the Gods: Early Christian Distinctiveness in the Roman World*. Waco: Baylor University Press, 2017.
Hutton, Rodney R. "Declaratory Formulae: Form of Authoritative Pronouncement in Ancient Israel." PhD diss., Claremont University, 1983.
Iliffe, J. H. "The ΘΑΝΑΤΟΣ Inscription from Herod's Temple." *Quarterly of the Department of Antiquities in Palestine* 6 (1936) 1–3.
Jamieson, Robert, et al. *A Commentary, Critical and Explanatory, on the Old and New Testaments*. Oak Harbor: Logos Research Systems, 1997.
Janzen, J. Gerald. *Abraham and All the Families of the Earth: A Commentary on the Book of Genesis 12–50*. Grand Rapids: Eerdmans, 1993.
Jervell, J. *Die Apostelgeschichte*. Kritischexegetischer Kommentar über das Neue Testament 3. Göttingen: Vandenhoeck & Ruprecht, 1998.
Jewett, Robert, et al. *Romans: A Commentary*. Hermeneia. Minneapolis: Fortress, 2006.
Jobes, Karen H. *1 Peter*. Baker Exegetical Commentary on the New Testament. Grand Rapids: Baker Academic, 2005.
Johnson, Luke Timothy. *Reading Romans: A Literary and Theological Commentary*. Macon: Smyth & Helwys, 2012.
Käsemann, Ernst. *Commentary on Romans*. Translated by Geoffrey W. Bromiley. Grand Rapids: Eerdmans, 1994.
Keil, C. F., and F. Delitzsch. *Biblical Commentary on the Old Testament*. Translated by James Martin. 1968. Reprint. Grand Rapids: Eerdmans, 1900.
Kennard, Douglas W. *Messiah Jesus: Christology in His Day and Ours*. New York: Land, 2008.
Kistemaker, Simon J., and William Hendriksen. *Exposition of the Acts of the Apostles*. New Testament Commentary 17. Grand Rapids: Baker, 1991.
Koestler, Arthur. *The Thirteenth Tribe: The Khazar Empire and Its Heritage*. 1st ed. New York: Random, 1976.

Bibliography

Koester, Helmut. *Introduction to the New Testament.* 2nd ed. New York: Walter de Gruyter, 1995.
Kohler, Kaufmann, and Eduard Neumann. "Poppaea Sabine." In *Jewish Encyclopedia.* Edited by Isidore Singer. New York: Funk & Wagnalls, 1905. 10:129.
Köhler, Ludwig, et al. *The Hebrew & Aramaic Lexicon of the Old Testament.* CD-ROM ed. Leiden: Koninklijke Brill, 2000.
Kriaras, Emmanuil. *Epitomē tou Lexikou tēs Mesaionikēs Hellēnikēs Dēmodous Grammateias 1100–1669.* Thessalonikē: Kentro Ellēnikēs Glōssas, 2003.
Kugel, J. L. *In Potiphar's House.* San Francisco: Harper, 1990.
Kümmel, Werner Georg. "Die ältest Form des Aposteldekrets." *Spiritus et Veritas* [Festschrift für Karl Kundsin]. Eutin, Germany: Ozolins, 1953.
Ladd, George E. *A Commentary on the Revelation of John.* Grand Rapids: Eerdmans, 1972.
———. *A Theology of the New Testament.* Rev. ed. Grand Rapids: Eerdmans, 1993.
Lampe, G. W. H., ed. *A Patristic Greek Lexicon.* Oxford: Oxford University Press, 1969.
Lange, John Peter, et al. *A Commentary on the Holy Scriptures: Romans.* Bellingham: Logos Research Systems, 2008.
LaRondelle, Hans K. *Our Creator Redeemer: An Introduction to Biblical Covenant Theology.* Berrien Springs, MI: Andrews University Press, 2005.
Larsson, Goran. *Bound for Freedom: The Book of Exodus in Jewish and Christian Traditions.* Peabody: Hendrickson, 1999.
Laurin, Roy L. *Second Corinthians: Where Life Endures.* Grand Rapids: Kregel, 1985.
Lenski, R. C. H. *The Interpretation of St. Paul's Epistles to the Colossians, to the Thessalonians, to Timothy, to Titus and to Philemon.* Vol. 9. Columbus: Wartburg, 1946.
Liddell, Henry George, and Robert Scott. *An Intermediate Greek-English Lexicon.* Oxford, UK: Oxford University Press, 1945.
Lohse, Eduard. *Colossians and Philemon.* Hermeneia. Philadelphia: Fortress, 1971.
Longenecker, Richard N. *Galatians.* Word Biblical Commentary 41. Dallas: Word, 2002.
Lundbom, Jack R. *Jeremiah 21–36: A New Translation with Introduction and Commentary.* New Haven: Yale University Press, 2008.
Luz, Ulrich, and Helmut Koester, *Matthew 21–28: A Commentary.* Hermeneia. Minneapolis: Augsburg, 2005.
MacArthur, John F. *Hebrews: An Expository Commentary.* The MacArthur New Testament Commentary. Chicago: Moody, 1983.
Marshall, I. Howard, and Philip H. Towner. *A Critical and Exegetical Commentary on the Pastoral Epistles.* International Critical Commentary. London: T. & T. Clark, 2004.
Martinez, Florentino Garcia. *The People of the Dead Sea Scrolls: Their Writings, Beliefs and Practices.* Leiden: Brill, 1993.
Martyn, J. Louis. *Galatians: A New Translation with Introduction and Commentary.* The Anchor Bible 33A. New York: Doubleday, 1997.
Matthews, K. A. *Genesis 11:27–50:26.* Nashville: Broadman & Holman, 2007.
McKnight, Edgar. *Hebrews-James.* Smyth & Helwys Bible Commentary. Macon: Smyth & Helwys, 2004.
Meyers, Carol. *Exodus.* The New Cambridge Bible Commentary. Cambridge: Cambridge University Press, 2005.
Meyer, F. B. *Devotional Commentary on Exodus.* Grand Rapids: Kregel, 1978.
Milgrom, Jacob. *Leviticus 1–16: A New Translation with Introduction and Commentary.* The Anchor Bible 3. New York: Doubleday, 1991.

Bibliography

Moberly, R. W. L. "The Earliest Commentary on the Akedah." *Vetus Testamentum* 38 (1988) 302–323.

Moo, Douglas J. *The Epistle to the Romans*. The New International Commentary on the New Testament. Grand Rapids: Eerdmans, 1996.

———. *Romans*. The NIV Application Commentary. Grand Rapids: Zondervan, 2000.

Morris, Leon. *The Epistle to the Romans*. Grand Rapids: Eerdmans, 1988.

———. *The Gospel According to John*. The New International Commentary on the New Testament. Grand Rapids: Eerdmans, 1995.

———. *The Gospel According to Matthew*. A Pillar Commentary. Grand Rapids: Eerdmans, 1992.

Moule, Handley. *The Epistle to the Romans*. Fort Washington, PA: Christian Literature Crusade, 1975.

Mounce, Robert H. *Romans*. New American Commentary 27. Nashville: Broadman & Holman, 2001.

Myers, Jacob M. *Ezra. Nehemiah*. The Anchor Bible 14. New Haven: Yale University Press, 2010.

Newman, Barclay M., and Eugene Albert Nida. *A Handbook on Paul's Letter to the Romans*. UBS Handbook Series. New York: United Bible Societies, 1994.

Nolland, John. *The Gospel of Matthew: A Commentary on the Greek Text*. The New International Greek Testament Commentary. Grand Rapids: Eerdmans, 2005.

O'Brien, Peter T. *Colossians, Philemon*. Word Biblical Commentary 44. Waco: Word.

Odom, Robert L. *Sunday in Roman Paganism*. Brushton: TEACH, 2003.

Oswalt, John N. *The Book of Isaiah: Chapters 40–66*. The New International Commentary on the Old Testament. Grand Rapids: Eerdmans, 1998.

Owen, John. *Hebrews: The Epistle of Warning*. Grand Rapids: Kregel, 1953.

Papaioannou, Kim. "Sanctuary, Priesthood, Sacrifice, and Covenant." In *Earthly Shadows, Heavenly Realities: Temple/Sanctuary Cosmology in Ancient Near Eastern, Biblical, and Early Jewish Literature*, edited by Kim Papaioannou and Ioannis Giantzaklidis, 189–203. Berrien Springs: Andrews University Press, 2017.

Papaioannou, Kim, and Ioannis Giantzaklidis, eds. *Earthly Shadows, Heavenly Realities: Temple/Sanctuary Cosmology in Ancient Near Eastern, Biblical, and Early Jewish Literature*. Berrien Springs: Andrews University Press, 2017.

Pate, C. Marvin. *Luke*. Moody Gospel Commentary. Chicago: Moody, 1995.

Paul, Shalom M. "Heavenly Tablets." *Journal of Ancient Near East Society* 5 (1973) 345–353.

Pervo, Richard I., and Harold W. Attridge. *Acts: A Commentary on the Book of Acts*. Hermeneia. Minneapolis: Fortress, 2009.

Pinches, T. G. "Sabbath (Babylonian)." In *Encyclopedia of Religion and Ethics*. James Hastings. 12 vols. Edinburgh: T. & T. Clark, 2000.

Pink, Arthur W. *Exposition of the Gospel of John*. Grand Rapids: Zondervan, 1975.

———. *An Exposition of Hebrews*. Grand Rapids: Baker, 1954.

Plummer, Alfred. *A Critical and Exegetical Commentary on the Second Epistle of St. Paul to the Corinthians*. International Critical Commentary. New York: Scribner, 1915.

Polhill, John B. *Acts*. New American Commentary 26. Electronic ed. Nashville: Broadman & Holman, 2001.

Poniatowski, Felix. "Interactions Between Heaven and Earth: The Heavenly Temple in the Pentateuch." In *Earthly Shadows, Heavenly Realities: Temple/Sanctuary Cosmology in Ancient Near Eastern, Biblical, and Early Jewish Literature*, edited by

Bibliography

Kim Papaioannou and Ioannis Giantzaklidis, 31–42. Berrien Springs: Andrews University Press, 2017.

Porter, Stanley E., and Craig A. Evans. *Dictionary of New Testament Background: A Compendium of Contemporary Biblical Scholarship.* Electronic ed. Downers Grove: InterVarsity, 2000.

Powell, Ivor. *Mark's Superb Gospel.* Grand Rapids: Kregel, 1985.

Propp, William H. C. *Exodus 19–40: A New Translation with Introduction and Commentary.* New Haven: Yale University Press, 2008.

Räisänen, Heikki. *Paul and the Law.* 2nd ed. Tubingen: Mohr, 1987.

Robertson, Archibald, and Alfred Plummer. *A Critical and Exegetical Commentary on the First Epistle of St. Paul to the Corinthians.* New York: Scribner, 1911.

Robinson, Thomas. *Studies in Romans.* Grand Rapids: Kregel, 1982.

Rochberg-Halton, Francesca, and James C. Vanderkam. "Calendars." In David Noel Freedman, ed. *The Anchor Yale Bible Dictionary.* New York: Doubleday, 1996. 1:810–19.

Rodkinson, Michael L., ed. and trans. *The Babylonian Talmud.* 10 vols. Boston: New Talmud, 1903. 1:xxii and xxvi.

Rosenberg, Stephen G. "The Jewish Temple at Elephantine." *Near Eastern Archaeology* 67/1 (2004) 4–13.

Rosensweig, Bernard. "The Thirteenth Tribe, the Khazars and the Origins of East European Jewry." *Tradition* 17/1 (1977) 139–62.

Rüpke, Jörg, and David M. B. Richardson, trans. *The Roman Calendar from Numa to Constantine: Time, History, and the Fasti.* Chichester: Willey-Blackwell, 2011.

Sanday, William, and Arthur C. Headlam. *A Critical and Exegetical Commentary on the Epistle to the Romans.* International Critical Commentary. Edinburg: T. & T. Clark, 1902.

Sanders, E. P. *Paul and Palestinian Judaism.* Philadelphia: Fortress, 1977.

Sarna, Nahum M. *Exploring Exodus: The Heritage of Biblical Israel.* New York: Schocken, 1986.

Schreiner, Thomas R. *Romans.* Baker Exegetical Commentary on the New Testament 6. Grand Rapids: Baker, 1998.

Schürer, Emil, et al. *The History of the Jewish People in the Age of Jesus Christ: 175 B.C.-A.D. 135.* Vol. 1. London: Bloomsbury, 2015.

Schweitzer, Albert. *Die Mystik des Apostels Paulus.* Tübingen: Mohr, 1930.

Silber, M. *Pentateuch with Targum Onkelos and Rashi's Commentary: Torah-The Book of Shemot-Exodus.* Vol. 2. Thousand Oaks, CA: BN, 2007.

Simon, M. "The Apostolic Decree and Its Setting in the Ancient Church." *Bulletin of the John Rylands Library* 52 (1970) 437–460.

Skinner, John. *A Critical and Exegetical Commentary on Genesis.* International Critical Commentary. New York: Scribner, 1910.

Sokupa, Mxolisi Michael. "*Skia Tōn Mellontōn* in Col 2:16, 17: An Interpretation." PhD diss., Adventist International Institute of Advanced Studies, 2009.

Speiser, E. A. *Genesis: Introduction, Translation, and Notes.* New Haven: Yale University Press, 2008.

Spence-Jones, H. D. M., ed. *Exodus.* The Pulpit Commentary 2. Bellingham: Logos Research Systems, 2004.

Stedman, Ray C. *Hebrews.* The IVP New Testament Commentary. Downers Grove: InterVarsity, 1992.

Bibliography

Stegemann, Ekkehard W., and Wolfgang Stegemann. "Does the Cultic Language in Hebrews Represent Sacrificial Metaphors? Reflections on Some Basic Problems." In *Hebrews: Contemporary Methods—New Insights*, edited by Gabriella Gelardini, 13–23. Leiden: Brill, 2005.

Strack, Hermann, and Paul Billerbeck. *Commentary on the New Testament from the Talmud and Midrash*. 3 vols. Bellingham: Lexham, 2013. 3:160–164.

Stuart, Douglas K. *Exodus*. New American Commentary 2. Nashville: B&H, 2006.

———. *Hosea-Jonah*. Word Biblical Commentary 31. Waco: Word, 1987.

Stubbs, David L. *Numbers*. Brazos Theological Commentary on the Bible. Grand Rapids: Brazos, 2009.

Taylor, Joan E. *The Essenes, the Scrolls, and the Dead Sea*. Oxford: Oxford University Press, 2012.

Templeton, William M. *Understanding Genesis*. Maitland, FL: Xulon, 2010.

Thayer, Joseph H. *Greek-English Lexicon of the New Testament*. Grand Rapids: Baker, 1977.

Thiselton, Anthony C. *The First Epistle to the Corinthians: A Commentary on the Greek Text*. Grand Rapids: Eerdmans, 2000.

Tholuck, Friedrich August G. *A Commentary on the Epistle to the Hebrews*. Translated by J. Hamilton. Edinburgh: T. & T. Clark, 1842.

Thompson, J. A. *A Book of Jeremiah*. Grand Rapids: Eerdmans, 1980.

Thrall, Margaret E. *A Critical and Exegetical Commentary on the Second Epistle to the Corinthians*. International Critical Commentary. London: T. & T. Clark, 2004.

Triantafyllidis, Manolis. *Lexiko tēs Koinēs Neoellēnikēs*. Thessaloniki: Aristotle University of Thessaloniki, 1998.

Vaughan, Curtis. "Colossians." *The Expositor's Bible Commentary*. Edited by Frank E. Gaebelein. Grand Rapids: Zondervan, 1978. 11:203.

Vielhauer, P. "On the 'Paulinism' of Acts." In *Studies in Luke-Acts*, edited by L. E. Keck and J. L. Martyn, 33–50. Nashville: Abingdon, 1966.

Wallace, Daniel. *Greek Grammar Beyond the Basics: An Exegetical Syntax of the New Testament*. Grand Rapids: Zondervan, 1996.

———. "19. Hebrews: Introduction, Argument, and Outline." https://bible.org/seriespage/hebrews-introduction-argument-and-outline.

Ward, James M. *Hosea: A Theological Commentary*. New York: Harper & Row, 1966.

Wenham, Gordon J. *Genesis 16–50*. Word Biblical Commentary 2. Dallas: Word, 2002.

Westcott, Brooke F. *The Epistle to the Hebrews*. Grand Rapids: Eerdmans, 1955.

Wiley, H. Orton. *The Epistle to the Hebrews*. Kansas: Beacon Hill, 1984.

Williamson, Hugh G. M. *Ezra, Nehemiah*. Word Biblical Commentary 16. Waco: Word, 1985.

Witherington, Ben, III. *Revelation*. New Cambridge Bible Commentary. Cambridge, UK: Cambridge University Press, 2003.

Wright, N. T. *Justification: God's Plan and Paul's Vision*. London: SPCK, 2009.

———. "New Perspectives on Paul." http://ntwrightpage.com/2016/07/12/new-perspectives-on-paul/.

———. *Paul and His Recent Interpreters*. Minneapolis: Fortress, 2015.

Wright, N. T. "Reflected Glory: 2 Corinthians 3:18." In *The Glory of Christ in the New Testament: Studies in Christology; In Memory of George Bradford Caird*, edited by L. D. Hurst and N. T. Wright, 139–50. Eugene: Wipf & Stock, 1987.

———. *What St. Paul Really Said*. Grand Rapids: Eerdmans, 1997.

Wuest, Kenneth S. *Hebrews in the Greek New Testament*. Grand Rapids: Eerdmans, 1893.

Scripture Index

GENESIS

1	52n32
2:21	44
3:8–11	44
3:10	44
12	90
12:2–3	48n16
12:7	36
13:14–16	48n16
14:14	24
14:18	84
15	46, 47, 49, 65, 69, 90, 115, 119, 121, 123, 124, 128
15:1–21	45
15:2	24
15:4–5	48n16
15:5	45
15:9	45
15:9–21	88n56
15:10–11	44n5
15:17	46
15:18	44n5
15:22	64
16	46, 47, 115, 128
16:3	46
16:10	48n16
17	46, 47, 49, 69, 90, 115, 128
17:1	47
17:1–2	47
17:1–14	44n5
17:2	48n16
17:3	47n14
17:5–6	48n16
17:10	47
17:16	48n16
17:17–18	47
17:20	48n16
18:1–33	85
18:18	48n16
18:19	24
21	48
21:1–8	48
21:9–21	48
21:18	48n16
22	48
22:1	48
22:2	54n41
22:3	54n41
22:6	54n41
22:7	54n41
22:8	54n41
22:13	54n41
22:14	48
22:16–17	65
22:16–18	48
23:4	98n72
23:9	131
25:25–31	124n50
26:4–5	49
26:8	53n35
35:27	98n72
39:17	53n35
41:45	25

EXODUS

2:16–21	25
2:22	98n72

SCRIPTURE INDEX

EXODUS *(continued)*

2:24	49
4:22	118
4:24	118
4:24–26	118
4:26	118
6:4–5	49
12:38	25
12:48	97n72
12:49	97n72
15:13	79
16:35	131n87
18:12	54n41
19:1	49n21
19:1–2	49
19:4–5	50
19:6	41
19:7	50n22
19:8	50n22, 51
20:1–17	121
20:2–17	50
20:10	97n71
20:18–19	50
20:21–22	50
20:22—23:33	121
20:23—23:33	50
20:24	52
21:12	53
21:14	53
21:15	53
21:16	53
21:17	53
21:23	53
21:29	53
22:19	53
22:20	53
22:24	53
23:9	97n72
24	53n36, 54, 69, 86n50, 88n56, 115, 121
24:1–11	51
24:3	51
24:4	51
24:6	51
24:7	50, 51
24:8	44n5, 51, 58, 58n54, 59, 60, 115, 116
24:10	50n28
24:11	52
24:12	50, 51n28
25	82
25:1—31:18	52
25:8	52
25:8—27:21	83
25:9	52
25:16	51, 52
26:5	132n88
26:26	132n88
26:35	132n88
27:1–9	52
28:1	52
28:2	79
28:3	52
28:4	52
28:35	53
28:40	79
28:41	52
28:43	53
29:1	52
29:10–21	52
29:14	52
29:36	52, 78
29:43	78
29:44	52
30:10	52, 78
30:20	52, 53
30:21	53
30:28	52
30:33	27
30:38	27
31:9	52
31:10	79
31:14	27
31:18	50, 51
32	115, 121
32:1–35	53
32:7	53
32:10	53
32:16	51
32:19	53
32:27	53
32:28	53
32:32–34	56n50
32:33	53
32:34–35	53

SCRIPTURE INDEX

33–34	46n10	16:2	84
33:1	53	16:29	96, 97n72
33:5	53, 79	16:30	117
34	53, 54, 69, 115, 121	17	11, 96, 97
34:1	51n28	17–18	97n71
34:6	53	17:1–9	96, 96n67
34:7	53	17:2–9	17
34:10	53, 69, 105n9, 106	17:7	96n67
34:15–16	53	17:8	97
34:29–35	54	17:10	17, 97
39:12	79	17:10–14	96
39:16	90	17:11	45, 105
40:34	78	17:12	97
40:35	78	17:13	97
		17:15	17, 97
		17:15–16	97
		18	11, 96, 97
		18:1–30	97

LEVITICUS

1–3	54	18:7–8	10n29
1–7	128	18:8	10, 14
1:1—7:38	54	18:24–25	11
2:13	44n5	18:26	97
4:2	54	18:29	10, 11
4:3	54	19:33	97n72
4:13	54	19:34	98n72
4:27	54	20:2	97n71
5:1	54	24:16	97n71
5:15	54	25:6	97n71, 97n72
5:17	54	25:47	97n72
6:2	54, 90, 123n47	27:28	110
6:7	123n47		
6:18	123		
7:1	123, 123n47		

NUMBERS

7:7	123	3:7	114
7:11	123n47	3:26	114
7:20	27	3:31	114
7:21	27	4:3	114
7:23	17	4:12	79
7:25	27	4:16	114
7:27	27	4:23	114
7:37	123	4:26	79
9:6	78	4:30	114
9:23	78	5:15	60n61
10:8–10	136n100	6:2–10	93
10:9	136	6:13	123n47
14:32	78	6:21	123n47
15:3	123	7:5	79
15:13	78		

157

Scripture Index

NUMBERS (continued)

9:12	123n47
9:14	97n72, 123n47
10:11–12	49n21
10:29–30	25
11:1	131n87
14:10	78
15:1–21	136
15:25	97n72
15:29–30	97n72
15:30	97n71
18:8–14	110
18:14	110
19:10	97n72
19:13	27n18
20:16	132n88
21:3	110n19
22:36	132n88
22:41	131n87
23:9	18
24:6	81n30
25	53n35
28	54n42, 134n94
28:1–8	134n94
28:1—29:40	133, 134, 136
28:9–10	134n94
28:11–15	134n94
28:16–25	134n94
28:26–31	134n94
29	54n42, 134n94
29:1–6	134n94
29:7–11	134n94
29:12–40	134n94
32:12	25
33:6	131n87
34:3	132n88

DEUTERONOMY

7:2	91
7:2–4	53n35
7:26	110n19
10:1–2	51
10:18	98n72
10:19	98n72
11:1	49n19
13:16	110n19
13:18	110n19
17:15	26n10
20:17	110n19
23:3	27
23:7	98n72
24:17	97n72
27:19	97n72
31:16–29	56n50
31:24	50
31:26	51
32:33	136n100
32:46	56

JOSHUA

2:1	25
2:18	131n87
3:8	132n88
3:15	131n87
3:16	44n4, 132n88
6:17	110
6:18	110n19
6:21	110n19
7:1	110n19
7:11	110n19
7:12	110n19
7:13	110n19
8:33	98n72
12:2	131n87
13:27	132n88
15:2	132n88
15:5	132n88
15:8	132n88
18:1	72n3
18:15	132n88
18:16	132n88
18:19	131n87
18:20	132n88
19:51	72n3
20:9	97n72
22:5	56
22:20	110n19
22:22	27

Scripture Index

JUDGES

1:17	110n19
7:11	131n87
7:19	131
21:11	110n19

RUTH

1:4	25
4:17	25

1 SAMUEL

9:27	132n87
15:3	110n19
23:26	132n88

2 SAMUEL

11:3	25
13:34	132n88
23:5	66n74

1 KINGS

2:3	49n19
6:24	132n87, 132n88
8:41–43	37n39
12:31	132n87
13:33	132n88
13:34	91
17:18	60n61

2 KINGS

1:3–4	11n31
2:13–25	11n31
7:5	132n87
7:8	132n88
10:31	56
19:11	110n19

1 CHRONICLES

2:7	110n19
4:41	110n19
16:39	72n3
18:17	25
22:2	25, 97n72
23:28	78
23:31	133, 134

2 CHRONICLES

2:4	133, 134
2:17	25
8:12–13	133, 134
13:11	90
24:14	79
29:19	27
30:25	25
31:3	133, 134
31:21	56
36:7	132n87

EZRA

7:24	79
7:25	25
10:8	110
10:39	79

NEHEMIAH

7:70	132n88
10:32–33	134
10:33	133, 136
12:45	78

ESTHER

8:17	25
9:27	25

Scripture Index

JOB

7:21	78

PSALMS

37:31	56, 87
39:12	98n72
40:8	56, 87
49:5	44n5
104	79
104:4	85
106:23	53n38
119:34	56

PROVERBS

23:32	136n100
24:16	89n58
31:4	136n99

ISAIAH

1:26	89n58
7:18	132n88
18:7	131
37:24	132n88
40:16	90
42:6	55n45
49:8	55n45
49:18	44n3
51:7	56, 87
54:1	10n28
55:31	55n44
56:4–7	44n5
56:7	27, 28, 28n21, 37
59:2	45
59:20	33
60:10	89n58
61:6	79
61:8	55n44
61:10	44n3
62:5	44n3

JEREMIAH

2:32	44n3
3:12–14	89n58
7:6	97n72
7:34	44n3
11:16	28
11:16–23	28
11:17	28
11:19	28
15:19	89n58
16:9	44n3
17:1	56n49
25:10	44n3
31:31	56, 61
31:31–34	55, 60, 61, 66n74
31:32	56, 57
31:33	56, 56n48, 61
31:33–34	143
31:34	56
32:31	132n87
32:33	132n87, 132n88
32:36–41	55n44
33:10–16	89n58
33:11	44n3
34:18	46n8
35:1–19	25

EZEKIEL

8:6	100n77
8:12	100n77
9:3	100n77
9:9	100n77
11:19	55n44
11:23	100n77
11:28	55n44
16:6	118
20:44	89n58
26:6	117
33:13–16	60n61
36:26	55n44
36:27	55n44
37:19–28	55n44
45:17	133, 135, 136
47:20	132n87
47:22–23	97n72

SCRIPTURE INDEX

48:1	132n87	14:11	110n19

DANIEL

1:2	132n87		

MALACHI

1:11	37n39
2:4–5	44n5
3:5	97n72

2:33	132n87
2:41	132n87
2:42	132n87
5:7	132n88
5:16	132n88
5:29	132n88
9:24	83
9:24–27	44n5

MATTHEW

1:21	65n69
2:2	40
3:7–9	39
3:10	39
3:12	39
5:9	99n74

HOSEA

2:11	133, 134, 135
2:13	135
2:14–20	89n58
2:23	89n58
3:3	10n26
3:4	135
6:7	44, 44n4
11:8	89n58

5:32	10n26
5:45	99n74
8:8	17n46, 96
8:11–12	39
9:15	99n74
10:37	111
13:17	65
13:38	99n74
15:19	10n26
17:24–27	98–99
18:21–22	142
19:9	10, 10n26,
19:28	40
21:13	37n38
23:15	26,
23:38	37n38, 100
24:2	100n77
24:15	100n77
24:51	46n8
26:28	44n5, 58, 59, 88n56, 104,
26:60	100
26:61	100
27:11	40
27:37	40
27:40	100
27:51	99
28:1	129n74

JOEL

2:16	44n3

MICAH

1:7	91

HABAKKUK

1:1–4	106
1:5	105, 105n9, 106
1:6–11	106

ZECHARIAH

7:10	97n72
9:11	44n5, 117

Scripture Index

MARK

1:4	104
1:44	78
2:19	99n74
3:29	104
7:1–4	17
7:21	10n26
7:26–30	17n46
11:17	37n38
14:24	44n5, 58, 59, 88n56
14:58	100
14:59	100
15:2	40
15:26	40
15:29	100
15:38	99
16:2	129n74
16:8	65n69

LUKE

1:9	92
1:68–69	65
1:72–73	65
1:77	65n69, 104
2:8	92
2:9	92
2:22	78
2:49	100
3:3	104
3:7–8	39
4:18	104
6:35	99n74
7:2–10	17n46
7:6	96
7:47	122
13:16	29n22
13:28–29	39
13:35	37n38, 100
15:12	132n87
16:8	99n74
18:12	129n74
19:9	29n22
19:46	37n38
20;36	99n74
22:13	40
22:20	44n5, 58, 59, 88n56
23:3	40
23:38	40
23:45	99
24:1	129n74
24:21	65n68
24:42	132n87
24:47	104

JOHN

1:16	88
1:29	28, 28n21, 40, 74, 100
1:36	28, 28n21, 74, 100
2:6	78
2:16	100
2:18–19	100
3:17	65n69
3:29	44n3
4:9	96
4:17–18	10n28
6:55	136n102
8:39	39
8:56	65
10:16	39
12:20	26
12:36	99n74
12:47	65n69
18:28	17n46, 18n46
19:19	40
19:21	40
20:1	129n74
20:19	129n74

ACTS

1:1—12:26	22
2:9–11	26
3:21	83n43
4:12	65n69
5:1	13n36
5:34–42	22
6:13–14	92, 100
6:14	100n77
7:6	97n72
7:8	44n5

Scripture Index

7:29	97n72
7:35	65n68
7:38	28
8:32	28, 74
10:28	17n46, 96
13:11	13n36
13:15	26
13:26	26
13:32–41	102, 103–6, 112, 138
13:38	109
13:38–39	102, 106
13:40	106
13:41	106
15	11, 141
15:1	75, 94, 95, 96, 119
15:1–31	94–98
15:5	75, 94–95, 96, 119
15:20	75, 95, 97
15:29	75, 95, 97
16:14	26
17:16	72
17:17	26
17:22–23	72
18:15	22
19:23	22
20:7	129n74
20:24	108n11
21	139, 141
21:18–26	91–94, 101
21:20	91
21:21	75, 92, 119
21:22	92
21:23–24	92–93
21:24	93
21:25	75, 93, 94, 95, 97
21:26	93, 94
21:27–36	93n64
21:28–30	120
22:4	22
23:9	132n88
24:14	22
24:22	22
26:24	vii
28:17–27	22

ROMANS

1:1	108n11
1:9	108n11
1:16	65n69, 108n11
1:17	vii
2:1–16	16
3:20	107, 113n24
3:27	107
3:28	107, 112n21, 113n24
3:30	7, 120
3:31	2, 7, 8, 8n19
4:2	107
4:6	107
4:7	15
4:11	118
4:12	119, 120
4:13–21	68
5:9–10	65n69
6:6	6
6:19	15
6:20	127
7:4	6
7:5	5
7:6	2, 6n5
7:7	7
7:12	2, 113n24
7:14	3
7:22	3
8:1–5	62
8:14	99n74
8:15	67
8:23	67
9	28
9:1—11:36	66
9:2	28
9:3	111
9:4	49, 58, 66–68, 69
9:6	28, 67
9:7–9	68
9:12	107
9:25	89n58
9:26	99n74
9:27	29, 67
9:32	107
10:9	65n69
10:13	65n69
11	35

ROMANS (continued)

11:1–5	29
11:3–4	67
11:6	107
11:12	29
11:13	30
11:14	29, 30
11:15	30
11:15–24	28
11:16	29
11:16–23	67
11:17	29, 30
11:17–18	29
11:18	30
11:20	30
11:21	30
11:23	30
11:24	29
11:25	32
11:25–26	32
11:26	ix, 32, 33
11:26–27	66n74
11:27	44n5, 56, 63
13:9	3
14:10–12	16
14:17	136n102
15:8	68

1 CORINTHIANS

3:13	13n35
3:16–17	74, 80n29
3:17	62
4:9–13	125
4:15	125
5:1	10, 11, 14
5:1–2	13n37
5:1–13	9–14
5:2	9, 12, 14
5:5	12, 13n35
5:6	14
5:6–7	9
5:7	12
5:9	12n32
5:10	20
5:11	9, 12, 20
5:12	9
5:13	12
6:9	20
6:9–10	12n32
6:12–20	12n32
6:19	74, 80n29
7:2	10, 10n28, 12n32
7:12	10, 10n28
7:13	10, 10n28
7:18	15
7:19	3, 120
7:29	10, 10n28
9:12	108n11
9:20	93n64
9:21	15
9:27	111
10:7	20
10:8	12n32
11:25	44n5, 58–61
11:30	13n36
12:2	12
12:3	111
12:13	12
15:33	9n25
16:2	129n74
16:22	111

2 CORINTHIANS

2:15	65n69
3:1	61n62
3:1–18	56, 58, 61–64, 69, 70
3:2	61, 62
3:3	61, 61n62, 62, 87
3:4	63
3:6	61, 62, 63
3:7	62, 63
3:7–8	2
3:8	62, 63
3:9	63
3:10	63, 130, 131
3:11	63
3:12	63
3:14	63
3:17	62
3:18	62, 63
5:10	16

6:14	15	3:29	68
6:16	74, 80n29	4:1f	6
9:3	130, 131	4:4	6
12:21	12n32	4:5	67
		4:6	99n74
		4:11	119
GALATIANS		4:19	6
		4:21–31	63, 107
1:6	108	4:22	34
1:6–7	108	4:22–31	33–35, 37, 58, 127, 128
1:7	108n11, 109	4:23	6, 34, 68
1:9	109, 111	4:24	6
2:1–14	17, 18	4:24–25	63
2:3	75	4:25	6, 63
2:11–14	96	4:24–26	34
2:16	76, 107, 112, 112n21, 113	4:26	34, 63, 128
2:17	112	4:27	10n28
2:19	107	4:28	68, 128
3:1–2	107, 120	4:29	128
3:2	107, 113, 113n24	5:1	127
3:2–3	2	5:2–3	75
3:5	107, 113, 113n24	5:4	112
3:5–7	35	5:6	120
3:6	120	5:9	9n25
3:6–13	120	5:14	113n24
3:7	120	5:22–23	62
3:8	64, 112	6:12	115
3:9	68n77	6:12–13	75
3:10	2, 107, 113, 113n24, 120	6:15	120
3:11	112	6:16	98n73
3:12	107		
3:13–17	58	**EPHESIANS**	
3:13–18	64–66, 69		
3:15	121	1:5	67
3:16	35, 124	1:7	104
3:16–22	68	1:13	65n69
3:17	121, 123	2:8	142
3:19	121, 122, 123, 124	2:9	107
3:21	107, 127	2:14–15	2
3:23	107, 126, 127	2:11,12	12n34
3:23–24	107	2:11–12	36
3:23–25	2, 5	2:11–13	49, 58, 68–69
3:24	112	2:11–22	36–38, 68
3:24–25	124	2:12	40, 98n73
3:26	99n74	2:13	36, 98n73
3:26–29	35–36	2:18	38
3:28	12	2:19	98n73
3:28–29	35		

Scripture Index

EPHESIANS (continued)

2:19–21	37
2:21	74, 80n29
3:1	122
3:14	122
5:5	20
6:2	3

PHILIPPIANS

1:28	65n69
4:7	127

COLOSSIANS

1:14	104
1:22	133
2:8	138
2:9	133
2:11	75, 138
2:11–12	119
2:12	133
2:13	138
2:13–14	2
2:14	138
2:15	138
2:16	xii, 130n75, 131, 134, 134n93, 135, 135n96, 136, 136n103
2:16–17	xi, xii, xii, 103, 129–39, 141
2:17	86n51, 132, 133
2:18	138
2:20	136n103
2:21	136n103
2:22	136n103

1 THESSALONIANS

5:3	13
5:5	99n74

2 THESSALONIANS

1:9	13
2:3	15
2:4	80n29
2:7	15
2:8	15

1 TIMOTHY

1:9	15
1:20	12n34
2:13	124n50
6:9	13

2 TIMOTHY

2:10	65n69
3:15	65n69

TITUS

1:5	122
1:11	122
2:12	82
2:13–14	15
2:14	15, 65n68

HEBREWS

1:3	78
1:7	79
1:14	79
2:3	101n79
2:10	65n69
2:17	74, 84
3:1	74
3:6	74
4:11	82
4:14–15	74
4:15	84
5:1	86
5:1–10	57
5:1–14	89
5:2	84
5:3	84, 86
5:4	83
5:5	84
5:5–10	74

Scripture Index

5:6	84, 85	8:7–12	55
5:9	89	8:8	38, 57
5:10	84, 85	8:8–9	88
5:12	101n79	8:10	38, 57, 87
6	90	8:10–11	86n51
6:1	89	8:12	88
6:1–5	89	8:13	38, 83n43, 91
6:4	89	9	80, 86n51
6:4–5	89n59	9:1	81
6:4–8	90	9:1–5	88n55
6:5	89	9:6	84
6:6	89, 90	9:7	57, 87n55
6:8	89	9:9	81, 86n52, 89
6:12	90	9:9–10	83n43, 136n102
6:12–20	90	9:10	83
6:13–20	65	9:11	57, 74, 81, 89
6:16	90	9:11–12	80
6:19	65	9:12	65n68, 83n43, 86
6:20	74, 84, 85	9:12–25	57
7	84n45	9:15	16, 57, 88
7:2	85	9:15–22	44n5
7:3	84, 85	9:18–21	87n55
7:5	83	9:20	58, 59, 60
7:8	85	9:22	45, 86, 104
7:9	83	9:23	87n55
7:9–10	84	9:24	81
7:11	83, 84, 85	9:28	65n69, 74
7:11–28	88n55	10	xi
7:12	87	10:1	86, 86n52, 89, 109, 137
7:15	84, 85	10:1–3	86
7:17	84, 85	10:1–10	137
7:19	89	10:3	87n55, 137
7:20	85	10:4	57, 86, 88, 105, 109, 127
7:21	85	10:8	137
7:23	85	10:9	137, 137n109
7:24	85	10:10	137
7:26	84	10:11	57, 78n20, 86, 88, 105, 109
7:26–28	74	10:14	86, 89
7:27	86	10:16	57
7:28	85, 89	10:16–17	44n5, 55
8	80	10:16–18	60
8:1	74, 84	10:17	86, 88
8:1–2	77, 80	10:18	104
8:2	57, 74, 80n28, 81	10:19	79
8:5	57, 74, 80n28, 81, 82, 82n33, 137	10:20	79
		10:21	79
8:6–13	44n5	10:29	44n5, 57, 58, 59
8:7	88	11:9–10	34

Scripture Index

HEBREWS *(continued)*

11:10	79
11:13	98n73
11:16	79
11:40	89
12:18–21	79
12:22	80
12:23	80, 89
12:24	80
12:22–24	79
12:24	44n5, 56
13:20	44n5, 58, 59
13:10	90

1 PETER

1:1	98n73
1:10	65n69
1:18–19	65n68
1:19	28
2:5	37n38, 74
2:9–10	40, 41
2:11	98n73
4:17	74

1 JOHN

2:1	142

REVELATION

1:12–20	74
3:12	80n29
4–5	80n29
5:6	28, 74
5:8	74
5:9	28
5:12	28, 74
5:13	74
6:1	74
6:16	74
7:9	74
7:10	65n69, 74
7:14	74
7:15	74
7:17	74
11:19	57, 58n53, 74
12:11	74
13:8	28, 74
14:1	74
14:4	74
14:10	74
14:15	74
15:3	74
15:5–8	74
16:1	74
16:17	74
17:14	74
18:23	44n3
19:2	10n26
19:7	74
19:9	74
21:2	44n3
21:9	44n3, 74
21:14	74
21:22	74
21:23	74
21:27	74
22:1	74
22:3	74
22:17	44n3

www.ingramcontent.com/pod-product-compliance
Lightning Source LLC
Chambersburg PA
CBHW050809160426
43192CB00010B/1702